Wildflowers of Houston
and Southeast Texas

WILDFLOWERS OF HOUSTON AND SOUTHEAST TEXAS

by John and Gloria Tveten

Photographs by the authors

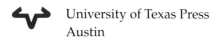

University of Texas Press
Austin

Requests for permission to reproduce material from this
work should be sent to Permissions, University of Texas
Press, P.O. Box 7819, Austin, TX 78713-7819.

⊛ The paper used in this publication meets the
minimum requirements of American National Standard
for Information Sciences—Permanence of Paper for
Printed Library Materials, ANSI Z39.48-1984.

Library of Congress Cataloging-in-Publication Data

Tveten, John L.
    [Wild flowers of Houston]
    Wildflowers of Houston and Southeast Texas / John &
    Gloria Tveten ; photographs by the authors. — 1st
    University of Texas Press ed.
        p.   cm.
    Originally published: Wild flowers of Houston. Houston,
    Tex. : Rice University Press, © 1993.
    Includes bibliographical references (p.   ) and index.
    ISBN 0-292-78151-2 (pbk. : alk. paper)
    1. Wild flowers—Texas—Houston Region—
    Identification.   2. Wild flowers—Texas—Houston
    Region—Pictorial works.   I. Tveten, Gloria A., 1938–
    II. Title.
    [QK155.T84   1977]
    582.13′09764′1411—dc21   97-3255

We dedicate this book to

Tuko Darwin Tveten

and to the memory of

Pearl Olsgard Tveten

who taught their children to

enjoy the natural world

and to

Randell A. Beavers

Larry E. Brown

Charles D. Peterson

and the staff of the

Robert A. Vines Environmental Science Center

who helped us in this project and who open the

doors to the world of nature to schoolchildren

and adults in our community

CONTENTS

ACKNOWLEDGMENTS

We have received the assistance of many individuals and organizations during the preparation of this book. We are particularly indebted to the Robert A. Vines Environmental Science Center and Director Randell Beavers for the use of the Center's herbarium and reference material. Botanists Charles Peterson and Larry Brown aided greatly in identifying numerous specimens collected during the course of our field work.

Many wildflowers were observed and photographed on the grounds of the Houston Arboretum and Nature Center, the Mercer Arboretum and Botanic Gardens, the Armand Bayou Nature Center, and the Houston Audubon Society's Edith L. Moore Nature Sanctuary. We thank them for their help in this project and for their continuing efforts in nature education and conservation so vital to the preservation of our native plants and animals.

Gary Freeborg, Doug Williams, and Bob Honig provided valuable information on local plants and aided us in finding several species, while Martha Henschen and Jim Powell of The Chickadee Nature Store have been a constant source of information on botanical and wildflower literature.

We offer special thanks to editors Susan Fernandez and Susan Bielstein and the staff of Rice University Press, who believed in this book and worked so patiently with us.

Finally, we are indebted to the Houston Museum of Natural Science for the financial backing necessary to include color photographs of so large a selection of Houston's beautiful and fascinating wildflowers.

INTRODUCTION

This guide is intended for a broad audience without botanical training. We have kept the use of technical terms to a minimum, defining those that have no common counterpart in everyday language. We believe that the brief descriptions, along with the color photographs, will enable the interested observer to identify most of the wildflowers that occur in the immediate Houston area.

No book of this scope, of course, can treat all the flowers that might be encountered, but this one has the advantage of focusing on a limited area. Most of the available wildflower books treat the entire state or a large region of it, and the options are even more numerous. The 210 species included here were selected as representative of Houston flora and the various families found along area roadsides, in vacant lots, and even as "weeds" in urban lawns and gardens. Where several similar species occur, one may need to consult more technical manuals. However, most readers will be content to identify such confusing plants to the genus level. In those cases, the most abundant of the closely related species have been selected for inclusion in this book.

Species accounts are arranged by color: white, yellow, red/pink, blue/violet, and green/brown. It is not always possible to draw distinct boundaries between these color groups, particularly in the case of the purplish flowers. For them, the reader will want to compare a plant with the pictures and descriptions in both the red/pink and blue/violet sections. Individual flowers may also vary in color within a species. For example, some plants have blossoms ranging from white to pale pink or blue. In spite of the problems in classifying flowers by color, most beginning enthusiasts will find the system easier to use than a classification by family.

We have kept botanical descriptions to a minimum within the accounts and have included other information on such topics as folklore, the edibility or poisonous properties of the plants, medicinal uses, and the sources of their common and scientific names. The reader may also wish to consult the preliminary summaries of the various plant families in order to place species in a broader context.

All photographs were taken in their natural settings by the authors. However, we frequently used an electronic flash in order to obtain the sharpness and depth of field necessary to portray the flowers in detail. Too often, dim light and brisk winds make photography by natural light all but impossible, and we have placed a premium on photos useful for identification.

NOMENCLATURE

Both the common and scientific names are given for each species, as well as the common and scientific names of its family. While the Latinized names may at first seem intimidating, they provide the only means for positive identification. We have attempted to select the common name most frequently used, consistent with good nomenclatural procedure; however, many of our wildflowers travel under a host of colloquial names. These are listed as alternate names for each species and are included in the index to aid in finding a particular flower.

Various references differ in the use of hyphens in common names. One book, for example, may call our common pink spring flower an "evening primrose," while another hyphenates the name to "evening-primrose." We prefer the latter form, because flowers of this family are not true primroses; they belong, instead, to a distinct family of the evening-primroses. Usually we have employed the hyphenated names, which are the bane of editors but which help to refine an inexact nomenclature.

In scientific usage, the name of each plant is written as a binomial: *Oenothera speciosa*, for example, to designate our showy evening-primrose. Such names are italicized, and the first part, the genus, is capitalized. Plants in the same genus are more closely related to each other than to those in other genera within the same family. Subspecies or varieties within a single species are accorded an additional term.

Although each scientific name should be unique to a particular species, taxonomy changes continually as botanists clarify relationships among our myriad plants. Thus, books and checklists may use different names in reference to the same plant, depending on the time of their publication and the authority they chose to follow. Even scientists disagree at times.

In general, we have chosen to follow the classification and nomenclature of the 1990 *Checklist of the Vascular Plants of Texas* by Stephan Hatch, Kancheepuram Gandhi, and Larry Brown. With a few exceptions, that list is in agreement with Marshall Johnston's 1988 *The Vascular Plants of Texas*, which updates the earlier *Manual of the Vascular Plants of Texas* by Johnston and Donovan Correll.

FINDING HOUSTON WILDFLOWERS

Wildflowers occur everywhere in Houston, from downtown vacant lots to woodland edges and roadside ditches on the perimeter of the city. When we stopped for a quick lunch at a fast-food restaurant within the 610 Loop, we discovered a host of flowers along a drainage ditch nearby and spent the remainder of the day photographing them. Periodic walks along Braes Bayou near Hermann Park and White Oak Bayou on the north side of the city produced numerous other species. A vacant lot on the west side proved to be a treasure trove of winecups, herbertias, and other showy plants.

Houston's location offers a variety of habitats, each harboring different flowers. Fields on the west side of the city contain flowers typical of the Katy prairies, while woodlands on the north contain species that might be found in the Big Thicket of East Texas. Eastward along the upper reaches of Galveston Bay one finds wildflowers of the brackish and saline coastal marshes.

The species in bloom change with the seasons, and we surveyed the city and the surrounding area every week or two during a two-year period. Each excursion produced new and delightful discoveries. In addition, plants that normally bloom in the spring may put on new growth and bloom again after heavy late-summer rains. Except after a hard freeze, wildflowers can be found virtually throughout the year.

WILDFLOWER GARDENING

The trend toward gardening and landscaping with native trees, shrubs, and wildflowers should be encouraged. Many of our native species are as attractive as the cultivated hybrids, and they are adapted for our soils and climate, requiring a minimum of care. Even the smaller, less dramatic flowers have a unique and delicate beauty that makes them worthy of consideration. A little planning can provide a garden attractive to birds, butterflies, and other wildlife—a backyard sanctuary that helps to counteract the serious loss of habitat occurring throughout the area.

Occasionally wildflowers can be transplanted from sites threatened by construction; however, plants should never be taken from the wild indiscriminately. Wildflower seeds and plants are readily available from nurseries and at native-plant sales. Whether you grow them in your garden or simply observe them along the roadsides, Houston wildflowers can provide countless hours of enjoyment throughout the year.

FAMILIES OF FLOWERING PLANTS

ACANTHACEAE – *Acanthus Family*

A large family named for the genus *Acanthus,* which does not occur in our area, the Acanthaceae contains some 250 genera and 2,500 species of herbs, shrubs, and vines in tropical and temperate regions of the world. The name comes from the Greek *akantha,* "thorn," referring to the spiny leaf-margins of some species. Leaves are opposite and simple; the corolla is usually two-lipped, with four or five lobes. The ruellias are the most common family members in the Houston area.

AIZOACEAE – *Carpetweed Family*

A large family centered in South Africa, the carpetweed family takes its name from the African genus *Aizoon.* Opposite leaves are often fleshy and succulent. Family members lack petals and have four or five sepals. Sea purslane is common along the Texas coast.

ALISMATACEAE – *Water-plantain Family*

Represented in our area by the arrowheads and burheads, the family takes its name from an ancient Greek name for the European water-plantain. Long-stalked leaves grow in clumps in the water or in the muddy soils of ditches, marshes, and swamps. Flowers have three white petals and three sepals; the stamens and pistils may be in separate flowers.

AMARANTHACEAE – *Amaranth Family*

Most members of this large, widespread, mainly tropical family are unattractive plants with clusters of inconspicuous flowers. The flowers have no petals, and the five sepals are subtended by bracts. We include alligator-weed, which is common in Houston and is more showy than most amaranths. Several species in our area are called "pigweeds," while another representative is the introduced *Salsola kali,* the Russian-thistle, or "tumbleweed." The name comes from the Greek *amarantos,* "unfading," for the persistent dry calyx and bracts.

AMARYLLIDACEAE – *Amaryllis Family*

A large family of mainly tropical distribution, the Amaryllidaceae resembles the Liliaceae. Indeed, most of our species are erroneously called "lily." Both families have six tepals, the combined petals and petallike sepals, and six stamens. In the Amaryllidaceae, however, those parts join above the ovary. Long, slender leaves arise from a perennial bulb, and flowers appear on a long, leafless stalk. Hybrid amaryllis and daffodils are widely cultivated.

APIACEAE – *Parsley Family*

This family has long appeared under the old Linnaean name Umbelliferae; however, that does not contain the prescribed *-aceae* ending adopted for uniformity. Most botanists now classify this worldwide family of about two hundred genera and three thousand species as the Apiaceae. Members can be recognized by their small, five-petalled flowers arranged in clusters called umbels, from the Latin word for a parasol or umbrella. The slender flower stalks, known as pedicels, arise from a common point on the stem, like ribs of an umbrella. Those clusters combine further into larger compound umbels.

Aromatic leaves of the Apiaceae are usually finely divided, and the fruits may aid in identification. The family contains such familiar vegetables and seasoning plants as celery, parsley, carrot, dill, parsnip, caraway, coriander, and anise. However, it also includes the deadly water hemlock and poison hemlock.

ARACEAE – *Arum Family*

This large, mostly tropical family contains more than a hundred genera and two thousand species. The tiny flowers lack petals and are crowded together on a fleshy spike called a spadix, which is then surrounded by a large specialized bract, the spathe. The cultivated calla lily and various philodendrons belong to the Araceae, as do the plants that provide such staples of the tropical diet as taro and dasheen. Jack-in-the-pulpit is the best known of the native species, but green dragon occurs more frequently in the wooded areas near Houston.

ASCLEPIADACEAE – *Milkweed Family*

The Asclepiadaceae, named for the Greek god of medicine, contains a milky latex sap. Several milkweeds of the genus *Asclepias* occur in our area and are most easily recognized by their unique, complex blooms. Above the normal sepals and petals of the flower is a corona of five cuplike nectar receptacles, or hoods. A curved horn arises from the base of each hood. Favored nectar plants for many insects, the milkweeds also serve as larval food plants for the well-known monarch and queen butterflies. The large pods split open to set adrift flattened seeds with tufts of silky hairs.

ASTERACEAE – *Sunflower Family*

The large and complex sunflower family contains many Houston species. Until recently it was called the Compositae by most botanists. A majority of the flowers are yellow; however, some are white or various shades of purple. So numerous and confusing are the species that professionals and amateurs alike refer to them as DYCs, "damn yellow composites." As many as a thousand genera and twenty thousand species occur worldwide.

The flowers are more complicated than they first appear. What seem to be the petals of a sunflower are actually small complete flowers called "ray flowers." The central disk of the flower head comprises many other small tubular flowers called "disk flowers." In effect, what at first seems to be a single flower is really a large cluster of tiny flowers working together to attract a pollinator; hence, the name composite.

Included in the Asteraceae are such garden cultivars as the asters, zinnias, and chrysanthemums; edibles, including lettuce and artichokes; and abundant "weeds" like dandelions, thistles, and ragweeds. Most family members have both types of flowers; however, some, like the dandelion, have only ray flowers. Others, including the thistles, have only disk flowers. Many local species can be identified by comparison with the plates; others may require scientific keys and microscopic examination.

BIGNONIACEAE – *Trumpet-creeper Family*

Primarily a family of the tropics, the Bignoniaceae comprises more than one hundred genera and seven hundred to eight hundred species of trees, shrubs, and woody vines. The large, showy, tubular or trumpet-shaped flowers are generally two-lipped and five-lobed. Leaves may be either simple or compound. Both trumpet-creeper and cross-vine occur frequently in Houston, as does the catalpa tree.

BORAGINACEAE – *Forget-me-not Family*

About one hundred genera and two thousand species compose the family Boraginaceae. They differ widely in appearance, but most have their flowers in one-sided, tightly coiled inflorescences that gradually uncoil as the flowers and fruits develop. Individual flowers are funnel-shaped and five-lobed, and the stems and leaves are often densely hairy. According to Bare, the family is named for the genus *Borago*, a name dating back to thirteenth-century herbals. It was apparently derived from the Spanish and medieval Latin *borra* or *burra*, meaning "stiff hair." Cultivated forget-me-nots, heliotropes, and comfrey are often grown in gardens. Seaside heliotrope and fringed puccoon represent the family in Houston.

BRASSICACEAE – *Mustard Family*

Now usually called the Brassicaceae to conform to botanical rules of nomenclature, the mustard family was formerly known as the Cruciferae. That name reflected the crosslike arrangement of the four petals. *Brassica* is the Latin word for "cabbage." Small flowers occur in terminal clusters and give way to elongated or flattened pods, the shape of which is often helpful in identifying the pungent mustards. The large family contains more than three thousand species that are particularly abundant and diverse in the cooler regions of the Northern Hemisphere. Cabbage, cauliflower, broccoli, turnip, radish, rutabaga, and watercress are all Brassicaceae. Typical of the native mustards is Virginia peppergrass, an abundant plant throughout Houston.

BROMELIACEAE – *Bromeliad Family*
This large and diverse family of some sixty genera and nearly two thousand species is indigenous to the New World and resides primarily in tropical America. Its best-known member is probably the pineapple, but many of the bromeliads are also cultivated as ornamentals. Most have long, narrow leaves and three-petalled flowers. Texas hosts two genera of bromeliads: the spiny-leaved, terrestrial *Hechtia* of the West and three epiphytic "air plants" in the genus *Tillandsia*. One of the latter, the familiar Spanish-moss, grows abundantly on tree limbs throughout Houston.

CAMPANULACEAE – *Bluebell Family*
The name "bluebell" is widely applied to plants with blue, bell-shaped flowers; however, botanists use it specifically for members of the Campanulaceae. The family takes its name from the Latin *campana*, meaning "bell." Most species have blue flowers with five flaring lobes. Current usage also places the lobelias in this family, although some authors accord them their own family, the Lobeliaceae. The latter have distinctly two-lipped flowers, with two small lobes above and three larger lobes below.

CAPRIFOLIACEAE – *Honeysuckle Family*
Consisting mainly of shrubs and woody vines, this family of the Northern Hemisphere takes its name from the Latin *caper*, "billy goat," or *capra*, "nanny goat," and the word *folium*, "leaf." One early botanical handbook noted that the plants seem to caper about in the trees and shrubs like goats. Most of the fifteen genera and four hundred species have five petals united in either trumpet-shaped or distinctly two-lipped flowers. Our honeysuckles and elderberry are included here.

CARYOPHYLLACEAE – *Pink Family*
A family of about two thousand species centered in the Mediterranean region, the Caryophyllaceae takes its name from the Greek *karyophyllon*, the clove tree, because many flowers have the odor of cloves. Mostly annual or perennial herbs, the plants have simple opposite or whirled leaves and stems that are swollen at the nodes. Flower parts are in fours or fives. Best known of the cul-

tivated species are the carnations and the pinks, while the common chickweed treated in this book is an abundant winter weed in Houston lawns.

COMMELINACEAE – *Spiderwort Family*

This largely tropical and subtropical family contains the spiderworts of the genus *Tradescantia* and the dayflowers, *Commelina*. The latter genus and the family take their names from the Commelin brothers, who were Dutch botanists. Leaves are narrow and parallel-veined, their bases sheathing the succulent stem. Three-petalled flowers are usually blue or purple. Spiderworts have three equal petals; dayflowers have a smaller lower petal.

CONVOLVULACEAE – *Morning-glory Family*

Most of these plants with trailing, climbing stems and showy, funnel-shaped flowers need little introduction. Morning glories are widely planted as ornamentals, and the sweet potato belongs to the same genus, *Ipomoea*. The family name comes from the Latin *convolvere*, "to entwine," referring to the growth habit that has earned the name "bindweed" for many of our native species. Dichondra, or pony-foot, an abundant lawn weed, also is included in the family.

CUCURBITACEAE – *Gourd Family*

Most people encounter this important family through the pumpkins, squash, watermelons, cucumbers, cantaloupes and honeydew melons, or the ornamental and utilitarian gourds. Our smaller native species are less widely known but easily recognized by their growth habits and fruits. The annual or perennial vines sprawl on the ground or climb by means of coiling tendrils. Male and female reproductive parts are contained in separate five-lobed flowers.

CUSCUTACEAE – *Dodder Family*

The dodders are parasitic, twining vines with threadlike yellowish stems and tiny white flowers. The small roots quickly degenerate, and dodder penetrates other plants to take sustenance from the unwitting hosts. Several species occur in Texas and in the Houston area, and they are extremely difficult to distinguish. The family name comes from the Arabic *kuskut*, meaning a tangled twist of hair. Dodders were formerly included in the Convolvulaceae with the morning glories.

CYPERACEAE – *Sedge Family*

Members of this large and diverse family look much like the grasses, but their stems are often triangular in cross section, and the narrow leaf bases form closed sheaths around the stem. The flowers are inconspicuous, and the family is beyond the scope of most wildflower books. However, the common white-topped sedge, *Rhynchospora colorata*, is included here because its white bracts attract attention along area roadsides. The name comes from the Greek *kyperos*, an ancient epithet for the plants. Most are troublesome weeds; however, the Egyptians made their papyrus from a sedge.

EUPHORBIACEAE – *Spurge Family*

Members of this enormous and widespread family exude a bitterly pungent, often poisonous, milky sap. Flowers typically lack petals, and the sexes are separate. The euphorbias, however, are of great economic value, since they include the rubber tree, castor- and tung-oil plants, and the *Manihot* species. The latter is a staple starchy crop of South America from which cassava, manioc, and tapioca are prepared. Ornamental euphorbias include the poinsettia and crown-of-thorns. The Chinese tallow tree now so abundant in Houston is also a euphorbia. The family name honors Euphorbos, a physician of ancient Greece. The name "spurge" comes from Latin through Old French and means "to purge or cleanse," referring to the purgative effects of the oils.

FABACEAE – *Pea Family*

A wide variety of trees, shrubs, vines, and herbs compose the Fabaceae, formerly called the Leguminosae. Some authors list as many as eighteen thousand legumes, including such important food crops as the various peas and beans and fodder crops like clover and alfalfa. Most legumes also have root nodules that harbor nitrogen-fixing bacteria, which enrich the soil. Atmospheric nitrogen cannot be utilized by plants, and the bacteria convert nitrogen from the air into soluble compounds necessary for plant growth and for the synthesis of proteins.

Three distinct flower types are represented in the Fabaceae. Some flowers have the typical pea shape, with an upright banner petal, two side petals called wings, and two lower petals united into a keel. The senna group has flowers that lack a distinct banner and keel. The third group, sometimes accorded its own family, contains the mimosa-like flowers, tiny symmetrical florets with extended stamens that form a fluffy cluster.

The Fabaceae include peas and beans, indigos, clovers, vetches, acacias, mesquites, and the famous Texas bluebonnet and other lupines. Most species in our area have compound leaves, and the arrangement of the leaflets is critical to identification.

FUMARIACEAE – *Fumitory Family*

Sometimes termed the bleeding-heart family, the Fumariaceae includes such attractive and oddly shaped flowers as the bleeding-heart and Dutchman's-breeches. The yellow corydalis occurs in the Houston area. Leaves are alternate and strongly dissected into narrow segments, and the flowers have four petals of different sizes and shapes. The family name comes from the Latin *fumus*, meaning "smoke." According to Pliny, juice of a European species causes the eyes to water as if exposed to smoke. These unusual plants are classified by some authors as a subfamily of the Papaveraceae, the poppy family.

GENTIANACEAE – *Gentian Family*

The gentians are smooth, hairless plants with opposite leaves and attractive flowers. The four or five petals (occasionally more) fuse at their bases into a short tube to produce a bell-shaped or trumpet-shaped blossom with flaring lobes. Meadow pink and the two prairie-gentians are common species that add color to Houston-area fields in spring and summer. The name reportedly comes from Gentius, an Illyrian king of the second century before Christ, who recommended a European plant of the family as a cure for bubonic plague.

GERANIACEAE – *Geranium Family*

Geraniums take their name from *geranos*, the Greek word for "crane." The unusual fruit has a long beak, resulting in such common names as crane's-bill and stork's-bill. Most family members have showy white, pink, or purple flowers and long-stalked leaves that are deeply lobed or dissected. The popular cultivated geraniums originated in Africa and occupy a different genus than our native species.

HYDROPHYLLACEAE – *Waterleaf Family*

This small family of about twenty genera and fewer than three hundred species occurs on most continents but is centered in western North America. Only a few species are grown as ornamentals, and the family is little known and of little economic importance. The five petals unite at the base to produce funnel-shaped, bell-like, or tubular flowers, which are usually blue or purple. Western Texas has several species in the genera *Phacelia* and *Nama*. The most common family member in Houston appears to be blue waterleaf, *Hydrolea ovata*, treated here.

IRIDACEAE – *Iris Family*

The Iridaceae contains such popular garden flowers as the iris, gladiolus, crocus, and freesia. Most abundant in Houston are the little blue-eyed grasses that line area fields and roadsides in the spring. Long, slender leaves fold lengthwise to overlap each other at the base and embrace the stem. Flowers have three petals and three colorful, petallike sepals. They differ from the lily and amaryllis families by having only three stamens instead of six. The fruit is a three-lobed capsule.

Iris of Greek mythology was the goddess of the rainbow and the messenger of the gods. The iris also serves as the "fleur-de-lis" of French royalty.

LAMIACEAE – *Mint Family*

Formerly called the Labiatae, the mint family is a large and cosmopolitan group of approximately 180 genera and 3,500 species. Most can be recognized by their square stems and paired leaves, although members of a few other families share those characteristics. Flowers borne in terminal spikes or in clusters from the leaf axils usually have five petals fused into a two-lipped tube. Minute glands on the foliage produce aromatic oils, and the Lamiaceae contains such culinary herbs as basil, oregano, thyme, sage, savory, and rosemary. Important honey plants, the native mints also prove popular with hummingbirds and butterflies.

LILIACEAE – *Lily Family*

Herbaceous perennials from bulbs, corms, or rhizomes, the lilies have narrow, parallel-veined leaves and flowers with six petaloid segments and six stamens. The flower segments, called tepals, consist of three petals and three petallike sepals attached in two ranks below the ovary. The similar flower parts of the amaryllis family attach above the ovary. Most land areas of the world host a variety of the more than two hundred genera and four thousand lily species. The Liliaceae contains the onion, garlic, and asparagus as well as such favorite horticultural plants as tulips, hyacinths, and ornamental lilies.

LINACEAE – *Flax Family*

The Linaceae contains ten to twelve genera and about two hundred species scattered through the temperate regions of the world. Only one genus, *Linum*, occurs in Texas. The flax species are slender plants with small, narrow leaves and delicate five-petalled flowers. A cultivated form produces linen fiber and linseed oil. *Linum* was the ancient name for this valuable plant that has been grown for thousands of years.

LOGANIACEAE – *Logania Family*

The logania family is primarily tropical, but a few species occur in the southern states. Best known is Carolina jessamine, *Gelsemium sempervirens,* the species treated here. Family members have simple, paired leaves connected by a ridge around the stem. Four or five petals join to form tubular flowers containing an equal number of stamens.

LYTHRACEAE – *Loosestrife Family*

The Lythraceae occur primarily in tropical America and vary so greatly that the family is hard to characterize. Most have simple, opposite leaves and from four to six petals that often seem strangely crumpled, like crepe paper. The genera *Lythrum* and *Ammannia* occur in Houston and are represented here, but Houstonians will be most familiar with a larger member of the loosestrife family, the popular and colorful crepe-myrtle tree.

MALVACEAE – *Mallow Family*
The mallow family contains such familiar plants as cotton, okra, rose-of-sharon, and the cultivated varieties of hibiscus and hollyhocks. It also contains some of the largest and showiest of our native wildflowers. A worldwide family of more than a thousand species, it is particularly abundant in the American tropics. Leaves are alternate, simple, and stalked and frequently are densely covered with branching or glandular hairs. The unifying feature that makes any of the Malvaceae immediately recognizable is the presence of numerous stamens that unite to form a protruding tube around the pistil. The family name comes from *malva*, the old Latin name for mallows.

ONAGRACEAE – *Evening-primrose Family*
Two genera of the family Onagraceae are particularly common in Houston: *Oenothera*, usually called evening-primrose, and *Gaura*. Both have flowers with four petals, but the petals of the former are evenly spaced, while the petals of the gauras are typically borne together on the upper side of the flower. Another common genus, *Ludwigia*, occurs in marshy areas and wet ditches. Called the water-primroses, the latter species may have more than the four petals typical of the Onagraceae.

Most of these flowers open in the evening or early morning and close by midday. The genera are relatively easy to recognize, but individual species often prove extremely difficult. The evening-primroses are not related to the true primroses, the Primulaceae, and Rickett comments that "it is unfortunate that such an assemblage of species, many of them handsome, should have acquired no English names of their own."

ORCHIDACEAE – *Orchid Family*
One of the largest plant families in the world, the Orchidaceae contains an estimated twenty thousand to thirty thousand species. Most occur in tropical climates, but some inhabit temperate regions as well. Texas hosts several wild orchids, from the bogs of the Big Thicket to the rocky canyons of Big Bend. Only the white, spiral spikes of ladies'-tresses, genus *Spiranthes*, are likely to be found in Houston.

Orchids have three petals and three petallike sepals. One petal is usually larger than the others and modified into a broad lip. The reproductive parts are fused into a column above the ovary. Various orchid species have evolved specialized relationships with pollinating insects, and their roots require the association with certain fungi. The name comes from the Greek *orkhis*, meaning "testicle," referring to the shape of the tubers of some species. Enormously popular in cultivation, the orchids have been called the royal family of flowering plants. Native species, however, should never be picked or transplanted from their natural environment.

OXALIDACEAE – *Wood-sorrel Family*

The Oxalidaceae contains about eight genera and nearly one thousand species that are widespread throughout the tropical and subtropical regions of the world. However, only one genus, *Oxalis,* is represented in Texas. Our species have cloverlike leaves with three heart-shaped leaflets that fold at night. Oxalic acid takes its name from the botanical name of these plants and imparts the sour taste to the foliage. Several of the Oxalidaceae are planted as ornamentals, while the tropical carambola produces an edible fruit.

PAPAVERACEAE – *Poppy Family*

About two hundred species in twenty-six genera compose the poppy family, which is found throughout the subtropical and temperate regions of the Northern Hemisphere. Most are annual or perennial herbs, although a few shrubs and trees also occur. Leaves are alternate and usually deeply lobed or divided; flowers have twice as many petals as sepals. Family members produce an acrid, colored or milky sap. Horticulturists grow several ornamental poppies, while one Old World species, *Papaver somniferum,* yields opium. Seeds of the latter, however, can be used in baking and for oil.

PASSIFLORACEAE – *Passion-flower Family*

Often cultivated for their unusual and colorful flowers and for their edible fruits, members of the Passifloraceae inhabit the American tropics. Two native species occur in Houston, and both are treated here. The herbaceous vines climb by means of tendrils, and the flowers have distinctive coronas of threadlike filaments. The family takes its name from the blossoms in which early Spanish explorers found signs of the passion of Christ. Although several species in the genus *Passiflora* produce edible fruits, other tropical genera may be toxic. Some are used to stupefy fish or to tip poison darts. Botanists identify about six hundred species in a dozen genera of the passion-flower family.

PHYTOLACCACEAE – *Pokeweed Family*

A family that includes seventeen genera and slightly more than one hundred species of herbs, shrubs, trees, and vines, the Phytolaccaceae occurs mainly in the American tropics and subtropics. Flowers have four or five colored sepals and no petals. Only a single species in each of four genera inhabits Texas. Most abundant are pokeweed, *Phytolacca americana,* and rouge-plant or pigeon-berry, *Rivina humilis.* The former is described here.

POLEMONIACEAE – *Phlox Family*

The phlox family includes approximately three hundred plant species in fifteen genera, most of them in the western United States. The family takes the name Polemoniaceae from the genus *Polemonium*, the ancient name for Greek valerian. Also included in the family are numerous species of *Phlox* and *Gilia*. Both of those genera are popular in cultivation. Tubular or bell-shaped flowers have five lobes, and the five stamens arise from the corolla tube.

POLYGONACEAE – *Buckwheat Family*

Some eight hundred species in thirty-five to forty genera compose the Polygonaceae, and most occur in the temperate regions of the Northern Hemisphere. The name comes from the Greek *poly,* "many," and *gonu,* "knee" or "joint," referring to the jointed stems with swollen nodes. Flowers are usually small and clustered in spikes or heads. They lack petals but often have brightly colored sepals. Rhubarb and buckwheat are cultivated as foods, while numerous wild buckwheat, smartweed, knotweed, and dock species occur as common "weeds." Swamp smartweed and curly dock represent the genera *Polygonum* and *Rumex,* which occur abundantly in the Houston area.

PONTEDERIACEAE – *Pickerel-weed Family*

These perennial aquatic or marsh plants float on the surface or rise from creeping roots in the mud of wet ditches and pond edges. The family of about thirty species in six genera inhabits fresh water in the warm regions of the world. Flowers may be either single or in crowded spikes. Six-lobed, they have three sepals and three petals, all of which look much alike and are called "tepals." Best known, perhaps, is the water-hyacinth, but pickerel-weed and blue mud-plantain also occur in Houston. All three are illustrated here.

PORTULACACEAE – *Purslane Family*

The cultivated moss-rose, *Portulaca grandiflora,* is undoubtedly the most familiar of some five hundred members of the purslane family. However, smaller native *Portulaca* species occur in Houston and deserve attention for their charming and colorful little flowers. Although a cosmopolitan family, the Portulacaceae is best represented in the western states and in the Andes of South America. Most are annual or perennial herbs with thickened, succulent stems and leaves. Flowers generally have two sepals and four or five petals.

PRIMULACEAE – *Primrose Family*

The true primroses should not be confused with the evening-primroses of the family Onagraceae. The Primulaceae takes its name from the European species *Primula veris,* which served as the type species for the genus. *Primulus* is the diminutive of the Latin *primus,* "the first," while *veris* means "of spring." No member of that genus occurs naturally in Texas, but we claim several genera and species belonging to the family. Domestic varieties are also widely cultivated, including species of *Primula* and *Cyclamen*. From twenty to thirty genera and about one thousand species inhabit the north temperate regions of the globe. Most have flowers with five petals that either join to form a distinct tube with flaring lobes or join only at the base. The five stamens are inserted opposite the bases of the petals, rather than in the gaps between them, as is true of flowers in most other families. Scarlet pimpernel represents the Primulaceae in Houston.

RANUNCULACEAE – *Buttercup Family*

Also called the crowfoot family, the Ranunculaceae contains between fifteen hundred and two thousand species in forty to fifty genera, depending on the classification followed. Although widespread, the various species occur most abundantly in northern temperate regions. Many have bright, showy blossoms and prove popular both as wildflowers and in cultivation. Houston natives include the anemones, clematis, delphiniums, and buttercups, while gardeners across the country grow columbines and peonies. Some species lack petals but have colored, petallike sepals, and the leaf blades are often deeply lobed or divided into slender segments. Many species have several pistils, which combine with numerous stamens to form a bushy cluster of reproductive parts in the center of each flower.

ROSACEAE – *Rose Family*

This large family of some one hundred genera and three thousand species of trees, shrubs, and herbs plays an enormous role in our daily lives. It includes such familiar foods as the apple, pear, cherry, plum, peach, apricot, quince, loquat, almond, strawberry, and raspberry. In our gardens and in the wild we find spirea, the hawthorns, and numerous species and horticultural varieties of roses. Most of the Rosaceae have five sepals and five petals, with numerous stamens and one or more pistils. The base of the flower forms a cup with the petals and stamens attached along the margin. The pistils are usually mounted on a dome in the center of the flower.

RUBIACEAE – *Madder Family*

A very large family of five hundred genera and six thousand species, the Rubiaceae takes its name from the Eurasian genus *Rubia*. It stems from the Latin *ruber*, "red," referring to the red dyestuff madder that was obtained from the roots. To most people, however, the family is better known for an essential element in their daily lives—coffee. Quinine is also obtained from a member of this largely tropical group, while the cultivated gardenias come from milder climates.

Our members of the madder family are mostly small "weeds" that are easily dismissed, yet they have charming flowers when examined closely. Leaves are paired or in whorls around the stem, and most flowers have four petals, sepals, and stamens, although a few species have flower parts in threes or fives. Species covered in this book include buttonweed, bedstraw, partridge-berry, and the bluets.

SAPINDACEAE – *Soapberry Family*

The Sapindaceae contains approximately two thousand species of trees, shrubs, and vines in 150 genera. Most occur in tropical regions of Asia and America, but a few extend their range into temperate zones. Best known in Texas are the soapberry tree and Mexican buckeye; however, the common balloon-vine occurs throughout the Houston area and is pictured in this volume. The family name reflects the soapberry genus *Sapindus* and stems from the Latin *sapo*, "soap," and *indicus*, "Indian." Both scientific and common names refer to the abundant lather produced by the saponin in the fruit pulp, which was widely used as a substitute for soap.

SAURURACEAE – *Lizard's-tail Family*

This small family contains only seven species in five genera and inhabits wet areas in North America and Asia. Flowers lack both sepals and petals and grow in crowded spikes. A single species, the lizard's-tail, *Saururus cernuus*, occurs in eastern Texas. Both the scientific and common names derive from the appearance of the flower spike.

SCROPHULARIACEAE – *Snapdragon Family*

This large and complex, worldwide family contains at least three thousand species in about 220 genera. Also called the foxglove or figwort family, it includes such well-known wildflowers and garden cultivars as Indian paint-brushes, snapdragons, penstemons, monkey-flowers, and foxgloves. The latter are the source of the drug digitalis. Flowers typically have five petals joined to form a two-lipped tube, but some species show little difference between the petals of the upper and lower lips. While many of the Scrophulariaceae are large and colorful, others have small blossoms and are easily overlooked.

SOLANACEAE – *Nightshade Family*

Sometimes called the potato or tomato family, the Solanaceae contains not only those prominent food plants but other edibles such as the green and red peppers, eggplant, and ground-cherry. Tobacco and cultivated petunias also belong to the nightshade family. While many species produce edible fruits or tubers, others are extremely toxic and contain such poisonous alkaloids as atropine, scopolamine, and nicotine. More than two thousand species in about ninety genera are widely distributed, particularly in the Western Hemisphere. Several nightshades and horse-nettles of the genus *Solanum* and the ground-cherries, *Physalis*, occur frequently in Houston. Their five petals unite to form star-shaped or wheel-shaped flowers with five stamens at the center.

TYPHACEAE – *Cattail Family*

While virtually everyone is familiar with the tall, strap-leaved cattails that grow in freshwater marshes and along streams and water-filled ditches, we do not often think of them as wildflowers. The brown "cat's tail," however, contains thousands of tiny flowers, each consisting of little more than a single pistil. Above these female flowers is a more slender spike of staminate flowers, which drop off after shedding their pollen. Fertilized pistils then become small fruits with long hairs, bursting from the spike to drift with the wind. The Typhaceae contains but a single genus, *Typha*.

VALERIANACEAE – *Valerian Family*

The four hundred species contained in thirteen genera of the valerian family occur primarily in the Northern Hemisphere but are also found in the Andes of South America. Most are annual or perennial herbs. Our few species of the genus *Valerianella*, called corn-salad, have opposite leaves and small flowers clustered at the tips of the stems and branches. Their corolla tubes are five-lobed.

VERBENACEAE – *Vervain Family*

Also called the verbena family, the Verbenaceae contains a vast array of both woody and herbaceous plants that inhabit all but the Arctic and Antarctic. Botanists list more than three thousand species and subspecies in at least seventy-six genera. Many have paired leaves on a stem that is square in cross section. Flowers typically have tubular corollas with five slightly unequal lobes. *Verbena* is Texas' largest genus and includes many native and cultivated species with bluish or purple flowers. *Lantana* and *Phyla* are also prominent in Houston and are included here.

VIOLACEAE – *Violet Family*

The familiar violets and pansies of the genus *Viola* constitute half of the eight hundred Violaceae species; however, some tropical genera contain vines, shrubs, and even small trees. Only the violets and the green-violets, *Hybanthus*, occur in Texas. The typical violets are easily recognized by their irregular, five-petalled flowers, the lower petal of which is spurred. Identification of the many species, which frequently hybridize, is far more difficult. Two species representative of the Houston area are treated in the text.

BEAKED BURHEAD

Echinodorus rostratus

ALISMATACEAE Water-plantain Family

SIZE
Plant: 16–30 inches.
  Flower stalk erect,
  often branched.
Flower: ½–1 inch,
  3-petalled, perfect.

LEAVES
Broad, rounded blade
  on long stalk.

BLOOMS
May – October

Burheads grow in the mud or shallow water of ponds and wet ditches, much like the more common arrowheads, *Sagittaria*. While the arrowheads have separate male and female flowers, however, burheads have perfect three-petalled flowers containing both pistils and stamens. Their tiny fruits, or achenes, form round, spiny, burlike heads, each head arising from the many pistils in a single flower. The genus *Echinodorus* takes its name from the Greek *echinos*, "hedgehog," and *doros*, a "leather sack," the latter referring to the outer wall of the achene. Sharp beaks on the achenes give this species the name *rostratus*, which means "beaked."

We found burhead north and east of Houston in the Humble and Crosby areas, but it presumably ranges more widely around the city. Erect flower stalks may be simple or branched and up to thirty inches tall, while leaves have broadly rounded blades on long stalks. Plants are sometimes sold for water gardens and tropical-fish aquaria under the name "poor man's lace plant."

WAPATO

Sagittaria latifolia

Common arrowhead, Duck-potato

ALISMATACEAE Water-plantain Family

SIZE
Plant: 1–4 feet.
Flower: 1–1½ inches,
* 3 petals. Upper*
* whorls male, lower*
* whorls female.*

LEAVES
Long-lobed, arrowhead
* shape, long-stalked.*

BLOOMS
May – August

Wapato, or common arrowhead, ranks as the most widespread and abundant of its genus across North America. However, it occurs less frequently in the Houston area than does delta arrowhead, *Sagittaria platyphylla*. Found occasionally in wet ditches and shallow ponds, wapato has the long-lobed, arrowhead-shaped leaves from which the genus takes its name. *Latifolia* means "broad-leaved," but not all plants have leaves as broad as those pictured.

As with other arrowhead species, flowers are borne in whorls of three around the stem, with male flowers on the upper portion of the stem, female flowers on the lower portion. The three fragile white petals drop early in the blooming cycle.

The name "wapato" comes from the northwestern Indians, who made the tubers of this arrowhead a mainstay of their diet. The diaries of the Lewis and Clark Expedition note that on November 5, 1805, members were invited into an

Indian lodge near the Columbia River, where they were fed arrowhead tubers roasted in embers until soft. They pronounced them agreeable in taste and a fine substitute for bread. Indian women, the diaries said, obtained the small tubers formed on the fibrous roots by wading in the water and digging with their toes.

Plains tribes such as the Dakota, Pawnee, and Omaha, as well as the Algonquin, also ate boiled or roasted arrowhead tubers. Tea made from the tubers was used for indigestion, and poultices were applied to wounds and sores, although the milky sap is known to cause dermatitis. Leaf tea was believed to ease rheumatism. Replaced by potatoes and other starches in the modern diet, wapato tubers still feed ducks, muskrats, and other wildlife, while waterfowl consume the seeds.

DELTA ARROWHEAD

Sagittaria platyphylla

ALISMATACEAE Water-plantain Family

SIZE
Plant: 1–3 feet,
  forming dense
  colonies.
Flower: 1 inch,
  3 petals. Upper
  whorls male, lower
  whorls female.

LEAVES
Lancelike blade on long
  stalk.

BLOOMS
April – October

Delta arrowhead grows in abundance in the shallow water and mud of Houston bayous and ditches and in surrounding freshwater marshes and ponds, often forming dense colonies. The genus name comes from the Latin *sagitta,* meaning "arrow," but this species does not have the lobed, arrow-shaped leaves of *Sagittaria latifolia. Platyphylla* means "broad-leaved" and refers to the broad lance-shaped or oval leaf blades borne on long stalks. About ten species and several varieties of arrowheads occur in Texas, and individual leaf shapes vary enormously and intergrade among those species. Exact identification rests on careful examination of the flowers and fruits, but most of the plants found in central Houston appear to be this species.

The one-inch flowers have three fragile white petals that drop quickly. Lower three-flowered whorls contain pistillate, or female, flowers; upper whorls contain staminate, or male, flowers at the nodes of the leafless stalk.

ALLIGATOR-WEED

Alternanthera philoxeroides

Chaff flower

AMARANTHACEAE Amaranth Family

SIZE
Plant: 1–2 feet, rooting
at nodes.
Flower: Minute,
combined in 1-inch
heads.

LEAVES
Opposite, thick and
succulent, smooth.

BLOOMS
March – August

Originally native to South America, alligator-weed has become a problem in some of the waterways along the Gulf Coast. The aquatic or semi-terrestrial plant roots at the nodes of the fleshy stems to form large mats in shallow water. In 1976 the Texas Legislature, on recommendation of the Texas Parks and Wildlife Department, passed legislation prohibiting the import, transport, sale, or release of alligator-weed, water-hyacinth, water fern, elodea, and several other troublesome species. The Department also introduced flea beetles along Oyster Creek in Fort Bend County to feed on the noxious weed. Before that introduction the Brazos River Authority spent thousands of dollars each year on chemical control, and concentrations were so high that water backed up behind the mats to flood bridges and erode their pilings.

"Flea beetles eat only alligator weed and in four years the insects have all but eliminated such vegetation," noted a TP&W release. "The beetles starve when they run out of alligator weed." Eradication was not complete, however, and colonies of alligator-weed now occur along many of the bayous and drainage ditches in Houston and the immediate area.

Tiny flowers, enclosed by stiff bracts, appear from March through August. Numerous flowers and bracts combine in a single headlike spike at the tip of the stem or in the leaf axils, appearing at first glance to be a single blossom.

DRUMMOND RAIN-LILY

Cooperia drummondii

Evening-star rain-lily, Cebolleta

AMARYLLIDACEAE Amaryllis Family

SIZE
Plant: 8–12 inches.
Flower: 1 inch across;
  tube 3–7 inches long.

LEAVES
Slender, grasslike.
  Often appear after
  blooming.

BLOOMS
May – September

Rain-lilies spring up quickly from large, deeply set bulbs in lawns and vacant lots and along Houston roadways after heavy rains. Although they sometimes bloom in spring, the delicate trumpets appear more frequently in late summer and early fall. Flowers open in the evening and last up to three or four days before wilting. The six flaring, petallike segments are white with a pinkish tinge on the outer surfaces.

The most widely distributed of several *Cooperia* species, *drummondii* is not a lily at all, but rather a member of the amaryllis family. Earlier authors placed it in the genus *Zephyranthes*, a closely related genus whose members are also called rain-lilies. The bane of editors and grammarians, the name "rain-lily" is frequently written as a single, unhyphenated word (rainlily) or as two separate words (rain lily). We prefer the hyphenated form, because the plant is not a true lily; however, that style seems to be slowly disappearing from the literature.

SOUTHERN SWAMP-LILY

Crinum americanum

Florida crinum, String-lily

AMARYLLIDACEAE Amaryllis Family

SIZE
Plant: 2–4 feet. From
  submerged bulb.
Flower: To 4 inches,
  6 "tepals" unite in
  long tube below
  narrow lobes.
  6 stamens
  protruding.

LEAVES
Long, straplike,
  succulent.

BLOOMS
May – November

The swamp-lily is one of our area's most attractive wetland plants. Widespread in the coastal plain from Florida to Texas, it prefers freshwater marshes and swamps, where it grows along wooded banks and in shallow water. It occurs particularly in the San Jacinto and Trinity river drainages east of Houston and blooms throughout the summer and fall.

Straplike leaves from two to four feet long arise directly from a large, long-necked bulb and often persist throughout the year. Two to six showy white blossoms, sometimes tinged with pink, top the tall, erect flower stalk. Six "tepals," the combined petals and sepals, form a slender tube up to four inches long but separate into long, narrow lobes that bend backward. The six long, purple stamens extend conspicuously from the mouth of the flower.

Despite its common names and the fact that *crinum* is the Greek word for "lily," southern rain-lily belongs to the amaryllis rather than the lily family. This technical distinction is based on the fact that the floral parts attach above the ovary rather than below as in the lilies.

SPIDER-LILY

Hymenocallis liriosme

Western spider-lily

AMARYLLIDACEAE Amaryllis Family

SIZE
Plant: 1–3 feet. From large bulb.
Flower: To 7 inches. Stamens connected by a delicate membrane.

LEAVES
To 30 inches, shiny, straplike.

BLOOMS
March – May

Spider-lilies bloom profusely in freshwater marshes and wet ditches, particularly east of Houston toward the coast and northward toward the Big Thicket. Flowers up to seven inches across occur in clusters of three to seven at the top of a leafless, sharply two-edged stalk. They usually open sequentially, so that the plant remains in bloom for many days. Shiny, straplike leaves measuring up to thirty inches long appear with the flower stalk from a large bulb.

Three narrow petals and three sepals look alike and are collectively called "tepals." They unite at the base to form a long tube tinged with yellow in the throat. The six stamens are joined in their lower portions by a thin membrane to form a delicate, spreading cup that readily distinguishes the spider-lily from the southern swamp-lily.

The genus name for the spider-lilies stems from the Greek *kallos*, "beautiful," and *hymen*, "membrane," referring to the characteristic webbing between the stamens. *Liriosme* means "fragrant lily." In spite of these names, spider-lilies are members of the amaryllis family. Like most of that group, their bulbs contain poisonous alkaloids.

Hymenocallis liriosme has been called *H. occidentalis* by some authors. Two other similar species occur in eastern Texas. *H. eulae* blooms in deep East Texas in late summer, after its leaves have begun to wither. *H. caroliniana* inhabits much the same range as *liriosme* and blooms with it in the spring. *H. caroliniana* is a larger plant, with wider leaves and tepals, and its stamens extend farther beyond the edge of the connecting membrane. The differences are not immediately obvious, and most observers will be content to call all of the plants "spider-lilies."

BISHOP'S-WEED

Ammi majus

Greater ammi

APIACEAE Parsley Family

SIZE
Plant: To 3–4 feet, branching.
Flower: Small. In large, rounded clusters.

LEAVES
To 8 inches. Pinnately divided into narrow, toothed leaflets.

BLOOMS
April – June

A Eurasian species, bishop's-weed has been widely introduced in the Americas and occurs in scattered locations around Houston. We found it particularly abundant in eastern Harris County along the upper reaches of Galveston Bay, blooming from April until June. Bishop's-weed, like many other plants in its family, contains toxic compounds and has been suspected in livestock poisonings. It may also cause photodermatitis, or skin burns, in sensitive skin exposed to sunlight. Jones, in *Flora of the Texas Coastal Bend*, calls the plant "Queen Anne's lace," but that name is usually reserved for another of the Apiaceae, *Daucus carota*, that does not normally occur in our area.

Bishop's-weed grows as an erect, branching annual three to four feet tall. Leaves are pinnately divided into extremely narrow lance-shaped leaflets with toothed margins. Tiny white flowers appear in complex umbels, forming broadly rounded, showy clusters.

CHERVIL

Chaerophyllum tainturieri

Tainturier chervil

APIACEAE Parsley Family

SIZE
*Plant: 6–30 inches,
   erect annual,
   branched, covered
   with downy hairs.
Flower: Tiny, in small
   umbels.*

LEAVES
*Triangular, finely
   divided.*

BLOOMS
March – May

Chervil ranks as one of the Houston area's most abundant spring wildflowers, for it lines roadways and covers vacant lots from March through May. The tiny white flowers would scarcely be noticeable alone, but they form small umbels, or flat-topped clusters, atop the six- to thirty-inch plants, combining like snow flakes into scattered white drifts. Fernlike leaves are equally attractive. Roughly triangular in shape, they are "ternate-pinnately dissected." Most divide into three parts, each of which is further divided, and those segments are again divided or deeply lobed. The resulting leaf, hardly recognizable as a single unit, resembles delicate lace. Conspicuous leafy bracts surround the small flower clusters and the resulting spindle-shaped, ribbed, quarter-inch fruits.

   The imposing scientific name was the Greek name for chervil, a different Old World species now placed in another genus. It simply means "delightful leaf." This American species was named after L.F. Tainturier des Essarts, who sent plants of Louisiana to English botanist Sir William Hooker during the 1820s and 1830s. Author and editor of many noted botanical works, Hooker later served as director of the Royal Botanic Gardens at Kew.

BUTTON SNAKEROOT

Eryngium yuccifolium

Rattlesnake master, Yuccaleaf snakeroot

APIACEAE Parsley Family

SIZE
*Plant: 2–4 feet, upper
    stem branching.
Flower: Tiny, compact
    in round 1-inch
    heads.*

LEAVES
*To 3 feet, narrow, stiff,
    edges bristly.*

BLOOMS
May – August

Button snakeroot looks like no other plant within our area. The slender, solitary stems reach two to four feet and bear stiff, narrow, parallel-veined leaves with sharp bristles along the margins. Most of the long leaves cluster at the base, while smaller leaves clasp the stem. Round, buttonlike terminal heads contain numerous small, greenish white flowers packed closely together and surrounded by sharp-pointed leaflike bracts. Other sharp bracts subtend the flower heads.

The genus name comes from the Greek *eryngion*, a historic name used by Hippocrates for a medicinal plant. *Yuccifolium* refers to the long, bristly leaves resembling those of the unrelated yuccas. Such common names as "snakeroot" and "rattlesnake master" owe their origins to the use by Native Americans and early settlers of poultices of the root for treatment of snakebite. Countless other medicinal uses, from prevention of whooping cough to a cure for impotency, have been claimed for button snakeroot.

An inhabitant of open, sunny terrain, this unusual member of the parsley family occurs sparingly in fields and along roadsides throughout the Houston area. It blooms during the summer.

VENUS'-COMB

Scandix pecten-veneris

Crow-needles, Shepherd's-needle

APIACEAE Parsley Family

SIZE
Plant: 6–12 inches,
* branching near base.*
Flower: Tiny, in small
* umbels.*

LEAVES
Twice- or thrice-
* divided into fine*
* leaflets.*

BLOOMS
March – April

About a dozen members of the genus *Scandix* occur throughout the Mediterranean region, but only one has naturalized in North America. Venus'-comb
ranges across much of the U.S. and inhabits coastal and blackland prairies in
Texas. In Houston it occurs sparingly in disturbed soils along roadways and
bayou banks. We found it particularly along Braes Bayou near Highway 288.
The species' scientific name translates as "comb of Venus."

Those "combs" of long, slender fruits most easily characterize the low-
growing annual plant, which sends up branching stems from a slender taproot.
Tiny white flowers occur in March and April and are soon followed by the two-
to three-inch fruits. The leaves are delicately lacy and fernlike, each leaf divided
two or three times into fine, narrow leaflets. Venus'-comb resembles the more
abundant chervil, but the elongated fruits are distinctive.

SHORE MILKWEED

Asclepias perennis

Marsh milkweed

ASCLEPIADACEAE Milkweed Family

SIZE
*Plant: 12–18 inches,
    slender stems
    usually unbranched.
Flower: Small, in loose
    clusters.*

LEAVES
*2–5 inches long,
    narrow, opposite.*

BLOOMS
April – September

This slender perennial milkweed grows mainly in marshy areas, often partially concealed by tall grasses and sedges. A southeastern species, it occurs most frequently along the upper reaches of Galveston Bay near Baytown and La Porte and along the San Jacinto and Trinity river drainages east and north of Houston. The small white flowers are tinged with pink and grow in loose clusters at the tips of the erect stems. The seed pods hang downward. While most milkweeds are tough, vigorous plants, *perennis* seems unusually delicate, with its slender stems that branch only at the base and its narrow, thin leaves.

Although shore milkweed blooms from spring through fall, it is most abundant in early September. It serves as a common late-summer host for monarch and queen butterflies, probably because its tender leaves are more palatable for small caterpillars than the tougher foliage of the widespread green milkweed.

BUSHY ASTER

Aster dumosus

ASTERACEAE Sunflower Family

SIZE
Plant: To 3 feet, stems
  much-branched.
Flower head: About
  ¼ inch, whitish.

LEAVES
To 1 inch, very
  narrow. Shed in
  early fall.

BLOOMS
September –
  November

An eastern species that ranges from Maine to Michigan and southward to Florida and Texas, bushy aster occurs in our state only in East Texas and along the coast. However, it appears to be fairly common in Houston, where it grows in vacant lots and open fields. A perennial, it has arching, much-branched stems up to three feet long, and it spreads from slender rhizomes to form thick clumps. The local variety of *Aster dumosus* looks much like heath aster, *A. ericoides,* and separation requires careful study.

While most references list bushy aster as having blue or pale lavender ray flowers, those examined in Houston had very short, white rays and pale yellow or whitish disk flowers. Although spanning no more than a quarter of an inch, the abundant, short-stalked flowers mass together to make an attractive display. The leaves are small and very slender, usually no wider than a sixteenth of an inch.

Approximately twenty aster species occur in Texas, and some have several varietal forms. It is a baffling genus, and the beginner will do well to identify most forms simply as asters. The genus offers challenges even for the professional botanist.

SHEPHERD'S NEEDLE

Bidens alba

Spanish needles, Beggar-ticks, Sticktight

ASTERACEAE Sunflower Family

SIZE
*Plant: 3–4 feet,
    occasionally taller.
Flower head: To
    1 inch. Rays white,
    disk yellow.*

LEAVES
*Midstem leaves divided
    into 3 to 7 toothed
    segments.*

BLOOMS
*Throughout the year,
    until killing frost.*

Bidens alba was formerly classified as *B. pilosa* and will be found under that name in almost all publications presently in use. It is one of the few members of its genus with white ray flowers surrounding the yellow central disk; most species have yellow rays or none at all. Shepherd's needle ranges widely in the American tropics and occurs in the United States from the Carolinas and Florida to Texas. Although Clair Brown calls it "locally abundant" in portions of Louisiana, Correll and Johnston consider it "infrequent" in Texas.

We first photographed *alba* at several locations in Houston along Old Katy Road west of Loop 610. Later, we found it growing profusely on several vacant lots near the Brown Convention Center in downtown Houston. This population blooms almost constantly throughout the year, until felled by a hard freeze. The identification was confirmed by Larry Brown, who considers the specimens to be the first documented record from Harris County. Although apparently a recent addition to Houston's flora, *Bidens alba* seems firmly entrenched within the city.

A tall, erect annual, it grows to a height of three to four feet and is reputed to reach six feet. Leaves at the base are simple, but those on the middle of the squarish stem are pinnately divided into three, five, or seven oval, toothed segments. Flower heads range up to one inch in diameter and normally contain about five white ray flowers around a compact head of yellow disk flowers.

The mature spindle-shaped fruits are tipped with two barbed spines, or awns, that give rise to the various common names of the species. The fruits do, indeed, stick tightly, and the distribution system is apparently an effective one, for shepherd's needle has spread over wide areas of the Americas. It is highly attractive to butterflies, and many different species can be found sipping nectar at the pretty flower heads.

LANCELEAF INDIAN PLANTAIN

Cacalia ovata

ASTERACEAE Sunflower Family

SIZE
Plant: 3–6 feet, erect,
unbranched except
at tip.
Flower head: ½ inch.
Disk flowers only, in
flat-topped clusters.

LEAVES
4–7 inches long, 1–2
inches wide.
Alternate on stem,
smooth, 5-veined,
entire or toothed.

BLOOMS
June – October

This tall, rather ungainly plant appears in older books as *Cacalia lanceolata*. Although not particularly attractive, it is impossible to overlook, for it stands three to six feet tall in open fields and along roadsides. Correll and Johnston list it as "infrequent" in east and southeast Texas, but it grows in abundance around Houston, particularly east of the city in the Channelview-Baytown-Clear Lake area.

The stout, tough stems stand erect and branch only at the tips. They bear alternate, long-stalked leaves from four to seven inches long and one to two inches wide. Upper leaves are smaller and clasp the stem. The flower heads contain only disk flowers, about five to a head, and are arrayed in loose, flat-topped clusters. The bracts (called phyllaries) that surround the flower heads are not wing-keeled like those of prairie Indian plantain.

Lanceleaf Indian plantain blooms from June through October, only slightly overlapping the spring blooming season of prairie Indian plantain.

PRAIRIE INDIAN PLANTAIN

Cacalia plantaginea

Prairie plantain, Groove-stem Indian plantain,
Finned Indian plantain

ASTERACEAE Sunflower Family

SIZE
Plant: 2–5 feet, erect,
*   branching only at*
*   the top.*
Flower head: ½ inch.
*   Disk flowers only, in*
*   broad clusters.*

LEAVES
4–8 inches, broad,
*   mostly basal.*

BLOOMS
April – June,
*   occasional in fall.*

Classified as *Cacalia tuberosa* by some authors, prairie Indian plantain blooms primarily in the spring. Only after extensive summer rain does this tall, coarse perennial rebloom in the fall. It ranges throughout the eastern portions of Texas and occurs sporadically in fields and roadside ditches around Houston.

The upright, grooved stem reaches two to five feet and branches only in the flowering portion. Numerous half-inch flower heads contain only disk flowers and form large, flat-topped clusters. Five bracts surrounding each flower head have winglike keels down the midrib. Leaves are four to eight inches long and are distinctly broader than the leaves of lanceleaf Indian plantain. Most cluster at the base and have long stalks, while stem leaves are smaller, stalkless, and alternate.

Cacalia plantaginea can be distinguished from *C. ovata* by its wider, mostly basal leaves and by the winged keels on the phyllaries, or flower-head bracts. Similar species were used by various Native American tribes as poultices for cuts, bruises, and tumors.

HAIRY HORSEWEED

Conyza bonariensis

ASTERACEAE Sunflower Family

SIZE
Plant: To 4 feet.
Densely hairy.
Flower head: ¼ inch,
in clusters at tips of
stems. Rays short,
white.

LEAVES
To 6 inches, some
toothed or lobed.

BLOOMS
At least June – July

Hairy horseweed is apparently a recent immigrant to Texas from tropical America. Wagner, Herbst, and Sohmer note in their *Manual of the Flowering Plants of Hawaii* that it probably originated in South America but was naturalized in Hawaii before 1871. It has also colonized the Caribbean islands and is virtually cosmopolitan in tropical regions. Correll and Johnston noted in 1979 that *Conyza bonariensis* was rare in eastern Texas, having been collected once near College Station and once near Orange. However, while working on this book, we found hairy horseweed growing abundantly in portions of downtown Houston, springing up even around parking meters and in sidewalk cracks.

The robust annual grows three to four feet tall, sometimes branching at the base and then branching again in the upper portions. Leaves are numerous on the stems, up to six inches long, and occasionally toothed or lobed. Unlike the more widespread *Conyza canadensis*, *C. bonariensis* has grayish green leaves and is covered with long gray hairs. Flower heads average larger, to one-fourth inch, and contain two or three rows of tiny white ray flowers around the central disk flowers. Because the surrounding bracts are as long as the florets, the heads do not appear to open fully. The combined flower heads form larger clusters embracing the tips of the stems. When mature, the parachuted achenes, or "seeds," drift on the breeze, undoubtedly spreading this newcomer across the city.

HORSEWEED

Conyza canadensis

Horsetail, Muletail, Horseweed fleabane, Canada fleabane

ASTERACEAE Sunflower Family

SIZE
Plant: To 6 feet,
  robust.
Flower head: ⅕ inch.
  Rays short, white.

LEAVES
1–4 inches, alternate,
  narrow.

BLOOMS
June – November

Horseweed grows abundantly in open places and along woodland edges throughout the Houston area. A tall, rank annual sometimes reaching six feet, it has small blooms and hardly qualifies as one of our more attractive wildflowers. The sturdy stems are heavily cloaked in narrow, alternate leaves from one to four inches long. Elongated clusters contain flower heads scarcely one-fifth inch across, each with a single row of short, white ray flowers surrounding a few creamy disk flowers. The phyllaries, or surrounding bracts, are nearly as long as the rays, so that the flower heads always appear half closed. Ray flowers contain only female parts; disk flowers are bisexual.

    Conyza is an ancient name for fleabane, and early manuals placed these species in the genus *Erigeron.* They have a strong, pungent smell from terpene oils secreted by numerous glands. Horseweed was used medicinally by Native Americans and early settlers for a number of ailments. Widespread throughout Texas and most of North America, horseweed has also invaded the Old World. Rickett notes that it flourished in the ruins of London after the German bombings of World War II.

YERBA DE TAJO

Eclipta prostrata

Yerba de tago, False daisy

ASTERACEAE Sunflower Family

SIZE
*Plant: To 2–3 feet,
 usually smaller.
 Upright or
 sprawling, with
 branching stems.
Flower head: ¼ inch.
 Short rays white;
 disk flowers white.*

LEAVES
*To 3 inches, opposite,
 narrow, finely
 serrated.*

BLOOMS
April – November

Yerba de tajo is one of the charming little wildflowers the casual observer seldom notices, although it ranges across most of Texas. Because of its small size, few of the popular flower books include it among their illustrations. It was formerly called *Eclipta alba,* but the newest checklists treat it as *E. prostrata.* A plant of wet ditches, low bayou banks, and the edges of freshwater marshes, it occurs throughout the Houston area. Some authors suggest it may have been introduced to the Americas, but it presently inhabits warm climates around the world.

An annual plant reaching two to three feet in height, yerba de tajo has upright or sprawling stems that sometimes root at the nodes. Short, stiff hairs cover the stem and both leaf surfaces, making them rough to the touch. The leaves are narrow and sharply pointed, with finely serrated margins.

Solitary flower heads are borne on short stalks from the leaf axils and measure one-fourth inch in diameter. Tiny white ray flowers ring the cluster of white disk flowers. The former are fertile female flowers; the latter contain both male and female parts. *Eclipta* comes from the Greek *ekleipein,* meaning "to lack," referring to the absence or minute size of the pappus. Pappus bristles or scales surround the bases of individual florets of members of the sunflower family and become the "parachutes" on the fruits of many species.

PHILADELPHIA FLEABANE

Erigeron philadelphicus

Daisy fleabane, Fleabane daisy, Philadelphia daisy

ASTERACEAE Sunflower Family

SIZE
Plant: 1–3 feet, erect.
Flower head: ½–¾
    inch. Rays white
    or pinkish, many,
    fringelike; disk
    yellow.

LEAVES
To 6 inches. Basal
    leaves long-stalked,
    toothed; upper
    leaves smaller,
    clasping.

BLOOMS
February – May

Philadelphia fleabane is one of the earliest spring wildflowers, appearing in February or March and remaining into May. It often accompanies paintbrush, bluebonnets, and evening-primroses along Houston roadways and across the fields. From one to three feet tall, the slender, upright stems tipped with whitish flower heads tower over the lower-growing plants.

Spanning about three-fourths of an inch, the flower heads contain more than 150 white or pale pink threadlike ray flowers surrounding a compact central disk of yellow disk flowers. The heads grow at the ends of slender branches and form a large, loose cluster. Basal leaves measuring up to six inches are long-stalked and toothed; smaller upper leaves clasp the hairy stem.

Philadelphia fleabane was first named from the Philadelphia area and ranges over much of the U.S. and southern Canada. It is one of the largest of a genus represented by about fifteen species in Texas. Most can be distinguished from the asters and other daisies by the enormous number of threadlike ray flowers. The name *Erigeron* is of obscure origin, and authors disagree on its derivation. "Fleabane" comes from the country belief that the plant repels fleas and other insects, and dried bunches of it often hung over cottage doors.

Aromatic teas made from fleabanes have been used through the ages for a multitude of ailments. Philadelphia fleabane was listed in the *U.S. Pharmacopoeia* from 1831 to 1882 as a stimulant and diuretic, according to Bare. It should be noted, however, that it also causes contact dermatitis on sensitive skin.

LATE-FLOWERING BONESET

Eupatorium serotinum

Late eupatorium, Late-flowering thoroughwort

ASTERACEAE Sunflower Family

SIZE
Plant: 3–6 feet, stems branched in upper portions.
Flower head: ¼ inch. Rays absent, disk flowers white.

LEAVES
2–4 inches, tapering, coarsely toothed.

BLOOMS
August – November

This rough, rank perennial stands three to six feet tall and forms colonies along bayous and woodland edges and in fields throughout the Houston area. The small, grayish white flower heads grow in clusters, and those clusters combine in larger masses across the tips of the branches to provide an attractive display from August through November. The flower heads contain ten to fifteen tiny disk flowers and lack ray flowers.

The two- to four-inch lanceolate leaves have long stalks and are broadest at the base. Leaf margins are coarsely toothed.

Various names of this tall autumn wildflower reflect its early medicinal uses. *Eupatorium* stems from King Mithradates Eupator, who used a plant of the genus for liver ailments in the first century B.C. A tea brewed from the leaves was once used to treat dengue fever, also called "break-bone fever." Hence, the name "boneset." "Thoroughwort" can be traced to the herb's reputed thoroughness in allaying fevers and chills. Durant notes that reports on the tea's palatability were mixed. Some described its "clear, clean, bitter taste," while others proclaimed it a "nauseous draught."

WHITE CAT'S-EAR

Hypochoeris microcephala var. *albiflora*

ASTERACEAE Sunflower Family

SIZE
Plant: 1–2 feet,
  slender, branching
  near top.
Flower head: ½ inch,
  white rays only.

LEAVES
Basal leaves to 8 inches
  in rosette, deeply
  lobed. Stem leaves
  smaller, narrow.

BLOOMS
April – May, perhaps
  longer.

Cat's-ear might most easily, if unscientifically, be described as a white-flowered false-dandelion whose flower heads never seem to open completely. It receives mention in very few of the common wildflower books presently in use. Ajilvsgi (1979) lists it as "uncommon and local in the Big Thicket" and notes that it blooms from May through September. Correll and Johnston call it "rare and local" in Southeast Texas, citing one record north of Orange. However, while working on this book, we found white cat's-ear to be unusually abundant in April and May along mowed bayou banks and drainage ditches throughout the western portions of Houston. Along some city streets it was the most common of all wildflowers, forming dense colonies of slender stems.

The erect perennial sends up one to three stems from a stout root, the stems branching repeatedly in their upper portions and reaching a height of one to two feet. Basal leaves are deeply lobed, sometimes with narrow segments, not unlike those of the false-dandelion genus *Pyrrhopappus*. Stem leaves are greatly reduced and very narrow. Flower heads borne at the tips of the stalks span one-half inch and contain only closely packed ray flowers. Ripened achenes, or "seeds," are spindle-shaped with a long, slender beak tipped by the feathery bristles of the pappus. With these "parachutes," the fruiting head looks much like that of a dandelion.

Hypochoeris was a Greek name used by Theophrastus for a related group of plants, and Linnaeus adopted it when naming the genus. *Microcephala* simply means "small-headed." Most of the species occur in South America, and this white-flowered variety of cat's-ear apparently originated there and advanced into Texas. It appears to be establishing a firm base in Houston, where its wind-blown seeds will continue to disperse across the countryside.

CLIMBING HEMPWEED

Mikania scandens

Climbing boneset, Hemp-vine

ASTERACEAE Sunflower Family

SIZE
*Plant: Herbaceous
   vine, stems 15 to 20
   feet.*
*Flower head: ¼ inch.
   Rays lacking. 4 disk
   flowers.*

LEAVES
*2–4 inches, opposite,
   triangular or heart-
   shaped, wavy
   margins.*

BLOOMS
June – November

A trailing, low-climbing perennial vine, climbing hempweed is the only vining member of the sunflower family common in Texas. Slender, branching stems reach fifteen feet or more and form dense tangles that cover supporting shrubs or fences in summer and early fall. Hempweed ranges throughout the Houston area but prefers wet soils in bottomlands and along the edges of streams and marshes. The genus was named for botanist J.C. Mikan, while the species name, *scandens*, means "climbing."

The paired, long-stalked leaves are broadly triangular or heart-shaped, usually with a long, tapering apex. Margins are wavy or shallowly toothed. Individual quarter-inch flower heads lack ray flowers, and each contains four disk flowers of a dirty white or pinkish color. Although not particularly attractive, they form numerous showy terminal clusters that resemble those of the bonesets in the genus *Eupatorium*. Hence, the much-used name "climbing boneset."

FALSE RAGWEED

Parthenium hysterophorus

Santa Maria, Feverfew, Ragweed parthenium, Cicutilla

ASTERACEAE Sunflower Family

SIZE
Plant: 12–40 inches.
Flower head: ³⁄₁₆ inch.
  Both ray flowers
  and disk flowers
  white.

LEAVES
To 8 inches. Deeply
  divided or lobed.

BLOOMS
August – October

An immigrant from tropical America, false ragweed has moved steadily northward to colonize the southern states. It occurs as a common annual in the disturbed soils of Houston roadsides and vacant lots, where its coarse, branching stems reach a height of twelve to forty inches. The aromatic leaves are alternate and divided or deeply lobed into many segments. A rosette of large basal leaves usually dies before flowering; upper stem leaves are smaller and less deeply divided.

Flower heads contain five very short rays, the only flowers that prove fertile. Although the numerous disk flowers appear perfect, they do not mature. Ajilvsgi notes that the small white flower heads "resemble tiny cauliflowers." They are numerous at the top of the plant, forming larger spreading clusters.

The abundance of light pollen makes false ragweed a major cause of hay fever. The *AMA Handbook of Poisonous and Injurious Plants* lists it as a source of contact dermatitis, and Tull says that it has caused an epidemic of allergic dermatitis in India, where it has recently become a common weed.

FROSTWEED

Verbesina virginica

Virginia crownbeard, White crownbeard, Ice plant,
Tickseed, Tickweed, Squaw-weed, Indian tobacco

ASTERACEAE Sunflower Family

SIZE
*Plant: 3–7 feet, coarse,
    lower stem winged.
Flower head: ½ inch,
    in broad compound
    clusters. 3–4 white
    ray flowers, disk
    flowers white.*

LEAVES
*4–8 inches, coarsely
    toothed, lower leaves
    stalked.*

BLOOMS
August – November

A coarse, sturdy perennial, frostweed stands three to seven feet tall. With the first freeze, the stem splits to expel a frothy sap that forms showy masses of ice crystals. Thus the name "frostweed." It prefers semishaded locations in open woodlands or along stream banks and produces extensive colonies in such habitats throughout the Houston area, blooming from August into October or November.

The hairy stems branch only in the flowering portion. Large lance-shaped lower leaves are coarsely toothed and taper to long-stalked bases that run down the stem, forming characteristic wings. Upper leaves are smaller and stalkless. Flower heads span up to one-half inch and contain three or four white ray flowers and several white disk flowers. Small clusters of these flower heads combine in larger flat terminal clusters, providing a showy display in the fall, when butterflies, beetles, and other insects visit them in great profusion.

The genus *Verbesina* apparently takes its name from the resemblance of the foliage to some species of *Verbena*, an unrelated group of plants. Ajilvsgi notes that the leaves of frostweed were dried and used as a tobacco substitute by American Indians and Mexicans.

Seaside Heliotrope

Heliotropium curassavicum

Salt heliotrope, Chinese-pusley, Quailplant, Cola de mico

BORAGINACEAE Forget-me-not Family

SIZE
Plant: To 18 inches,
much-branched.
Trailing to form
mats.
Flower: To ⅛ inch.
On one side of tight,
unfurling coil.

LEAVES
To 2 inches, thick,
succulent, rubbery,
waxy.

BLOOMS
March – November

A low, trailing plant with branching stems, seaside heliotrope forms sprawling mats on sandy beaches and mudflats and along roadsides. Although found most abundantly around Galveston Bay, it also occurs elsewhere across the Houston area. It prefers saline or alkaline soils and survives the parching environment of sun, salt, and sand by having succulent, rubbery foliage. The thick, blue-green leaves are covered with a whitish waxy coating, further protecting them from dehydration.

Small white or pale bluish five-lobed flowers have yellow throats and grow along one side of single or paired clusters called cymes. Up to four inches long, these cymes are tightly coiled and unfurl gradually as the numerous flowers mature from base to tip. Such coiled arrangements characterize the genus. The Spanish name *cola de mico* means "monkey's tail."

Seaside heliotrope occurs widely throughout North and South America, the West Indies, the Pacific islands, and Australia. It probably originated in tropical America, and the species name, *curassavicum*, means "of Curacao."

The genus name comes from the Greek *helios*, "sun," and *trope*, "to turn." According to legend, Apollo loved Clytie but chose instead her sister Leucothoe. Clytie then pined away, and on her death Apollo remorsefully changed her into a flower that always turned toward the sun.

VIRGINIA PEPPERGRASS

Lepidium virginicum

American peppergrass, Poor-man's pepper,
Virginia pepperweed, Penny cress, Lentejilla

BRASSICACEAE Mustard Family

SIZE
Plant: 6–24 inches,
much-branched
from leaf axils.
Flower: ¹⁄₁₀ inch,
4-petalled, in slender
racemes.

LEAVES
Basal rosette of
deeply lobed leaves
to 6 inches, usually
disappears by
flowering time.
Stem leaves much
smaller, shallowly
lobed or entire.

BLOOMS
February – May, less
frequently in fall.

Peppergrass grows abundantly along Houston roadways and in vacant lots and fields. This early spring annual or biennial begins with a basal rosette of spatulate, deeply lobed leaves up to six inches long. By the time the flowers begin to open, however, the basal leaves have withered. Stem leaves become progressively smaller and less lobed up the stalk. Tiny white flowers have four petals and usually only two stamens; they grow in slender spikes, or racemes, at the tips of the much-branched plant.

Most characteristic of all, perhaps, are the flat, rounded seedpods with notched tips. The shapes of their fruits aid greatly in separating the numerous members of the mustard family into their appropriate genera. The fruits of the peppergrasses give rise to the genus name *Lepidium*, meaning "little scale," and the common British name of "penny cress."

The small flat pods and flowering tips have a peppery taste and can be used in salads or as a seasoning in soups and stews. Native Americans used bruised leaves or leaf tea for treating poison-ivy rash and scurvy, and they placed poultices of leaves on the chest for croup. The latter use, however, can cause skin irritation and blisters from the aromatic oils present in many of the mustards.

JAPANESE HONEYSUCKLE

Lonicera japonica

Southern honeysuckle, White honeysuckle

CAPRIFOLIACEAE Honeysuckle Family

SIZE
*Plant: Trailing or
    high-climbing vine.
Flower: 1½ inches,
    2-lipped, white
    fading to yellow.*

LEAVES
*To 3 inches, opposite,
    lance-shaped or
    oblong, evergreen.*

BLOOMS
March – November

A vigorous trailing or high-climbing vine, the alien Japanese honeysuckle has escaped from cultivation to blanket much of the eastern United States. Tough, woody stems often root at the nodes and form impenetrable mats in vacant lots and open woodlands across the Houston area. The spread is further aided by several species of birds that eat the berries and scatter seeds. Although useful to wildlife for its fruits and sheltering tangles of evergreen foliage, the plant has become a noxious and invasive weed in many locations. Japanese honeysuckle is rapidly crowding out other plants with its rampant growth and presents a threat to native vegetation.

The fragrant white flowers occur in pairs from the axils of the tough, opposite leaves and slowly fade to yellow on the second or third day. They are tubular and two-lipped, the upper lip with four lobes, the lower lip with a single narrow one. Five stamens project from the corolla tube. This common honeysuckle blooms throughout much of the year in Houston, from March through at least November.

The genus name honors Adam Lonitzer, a sixteenth-century German herbalist. Teas and poultices made from the plant are used for a wide variety of medicinal applications in its native Japan, but few have been tried in North America. Although the black berries provide food for a number of wildlife species, they are considered inedible for humans and may cause severe stomach upset. Fruits of several other native honeysuckles are listed as dangerously toxic.

AMERICAN ELDERBERRY

Sambucus canadensis

Common elderberry, Black elderberry, American elder

CAPRIFOLIACEAE Honeysuckle Family

SIZE
*Plant: 3–10 feet,
    shrubby, sometimes
    small tree.*
*Flower: ⅕ inch,
    5-lobed, in large
    clusters.*

LEAVES
*4–12 inches,
    compound, with
    5–11 leaflets.*

BLOOMS
May – July

Elderberry occurs as a woody shrub from three to ten feet tall, sometimes forming dense thickets in damp soil. We include it with the wildflowers because of its abundance along Houston roadways and in open places, and because it blooms while still relatively small. Its showy white flower clusters can scarcely be overlooked during May and June.

The pinnately compound leaves have five to eleven leaflets, each sharply serrated along the margins. Small five-lobed flowers occur in large, flattened compound clusters up to ten inches across and are followed by masses of purplish black berries.

The fruits have been widely used in making jelly and wine, and they provide food for many species of birds. However, the bark, roots, leaves, and green berries contain cyanide compounds and are mildly toxic; those toxins are destroyed by cooking. Flowers are sometimes eaten in pancakes and fritters. Elderberry stems are filled with white pith that can be easily removed, leaving a hollow tube from which children make whistles and flutes.

American elderberry has a long record of medicinal uses by various Indian tribes and early settlers. Poultices served as a treatment for sores and tumors, while decoctions of the flowers were taken for rheumatism and syphilis. Bark tea found wide use as a diuretic and laxative. Little information exists on the value of such treatments, but they were widely applied throughout the elderberry's range in eastern North America.

COMMON CHICKWEED

Stellaria media

Chickweed starwort

CARYOPHYLLACEAE Pink Family

SIZE
*Plant: Stems to 30
  inches, trailing,
  matted.
Flower: Very small,
  petals divided.*

LEAVES
*About 1 inch, opposite,
  oval.*

BLOOMS
November – May

An alien species native to Europe and western Asia, common chickweed has naturalized across much of the United States. It occurs in abundance in Houston and throughout the eastern third of Texas. Its merits depend on your point of view. Rickett notes that "*S. media* is the distressingly common weed of lawns, here and abroad." But Tull is more enthusiastic: "The winter growth of chickweed provides one of the tastiest wild greens in the state." She suggests tossing fresh plants in salads or cooking them in water.

Indeed, chickweed served a number of medicinal uses in Europe and was used to prevent and treat scurvy long before vitamins were known. Birds delight in the seeds and tender shoots, which have been fed to domestic chickens for centuries. Goldfinches and other winter finches in Texas often flock to lawns to feed on the greens when most other plants have wilted and died. Old names for chickweed in English, German, French, and Latin all translate as forms of "a morsel for the birds."

Common chickweed has weak spreading, matted stems with small opposite, oval leaves. It normally begins to invade lawns and fields in November and remains through the winter and early spring. Tiny white flowers have petals that are shorter than the sepals. Each petal is deeply divided, so that the five appear at first glance to be ten. On closer examination, each blossom is a charming white starburst, the source of the genus name, *Stellaria*.

GRASS PONY-FOOT

Dichondra carolinensis

Dichondra

CONVOLVULACEAE Morning-glory Family

SIZE
Plant: Trailing,
prostrate, branching.
Rooting at nodes to
form dense mats.
Flower: To ⅛ inch,
5-petalled,
inconspicuous.

LEAVES
1 inch, rounded, deeply
notched at base.

BLOOMS
March – June

Houston residents encounter pony-foot primarily as a weed in their lawns. A prostrate, creeping perennial, it branches and roots at the nodes to form dense mats in late winter and early spring. It blooms from March into May or June and then normally dies back, becoming dormant during the hot, dry summer. In slightly cooler climates, homeowners sometimes use it as a ground cover.

Rounded leaves are deeply notched at the base and have long, slender stalks. About one inch in diameter, they are sparsely hairy below. Tiny greenish white flowers have five sepals and five petals with downy outer surfaces. Because of its small flowers, pony-foot is seldom pictured in wildflower books, but the Houston homeowner is almost certain to encounter it in lawns and gardens. It also grows along moist roadsides and in open fields.

SILKY EVOLVULUS

Evolvulus sericeus

Silver morning glory, Creeping morning glory

CONVOLVULACEAE Morning-glory Family

SIZE
Plant: 2–12 inches.
  Erect or sprawling.
Flower: ½ inch,
  in leaf axils.

LEAVES
To 1 inch, narrow,
  downy below.

BLOOMS
April – October

The tiny silky evolvulus serves as a perfect example of the treasures that await the diligent wildflower enthusiast. A denizen of open fields and vacant lots, it grows no more than two to twelve inches tall and often sprawls among the grasses, where it is difficult to see. The delicate, funnellike flowers span only one-half inch but resemble in form the flowers of the larger morning glories. Normally white, they may also be pale bluish, according to some authors. Small, narrow leaves sometimes reach an inch in length. Dense silky hairs cover the stem and the undersides of the leaves; the uppersides of the leaves are smooth and hairless, providing the key to separation of this species from others in the genus.

A tropical perennial that ranges from Florida to California and southward to Argentina, silky evolvulus does not climb on other plants. *Evolvulus* means "rolled out" or "unrolled" in Latin, in contrast to *convolvulus*, "to entwine," the genus of the morning glories. *Sericeus* simply means "silky," in reference to the downy stems and undersides of the leaves.

SHOWY DODDER

Cuscuta indecora

Pretty dodder, Largeseed dodder,
Love-vine, Angel's hair, Strangle-weed, Witches' shoelaces

CUSCUTACEAE Dodder Family

SIZE
*Plant: Twining,
  slender vine on
  other vegetation.
Flower: ⅛ inch,
  5-lobed, in small
  clusters.*

LEAVES
*Absent or reduced to
  minute scales.*

BLOOMS
August – November

Dodder has long been considered a member of the morning-glory family, Convolvulaceae; however, most authors now place it in a family of its own. Two dozen species and named varieties of dodder occur in Texas, and all look much alike. Rickett notes that "few amateurs will want to undertake the formidable task of identifying the species; those that are sufficiently ambitious must tackle the technical manuals."

The smooth, twining yellow or orange vines are parasitic on other vegetation, an unusual trait among flowering plants. Sprouting from a seed, the tiny threadlike dodder seedling swings around until it touches a plant of another species and then proceeds to coil around it. Its own rudimentary root then shrivels and dies, while the dodder puts out suckers that penetrate the host and obtain nutrients from it. Dodder contains no chlorophyll, and the leaves are absent entirely or reduced to tiny scales. Some of the parasitic species prefer specific hosts, but most utilize a wide variety of other plants. By the time the flowers develop in late summer or early fall, dodder has lost all contact with the soil and has formed a tangled mat or canopy over its unwitting victims.

Individual waxy white flowers span little more than one-eighth inch and form small clusters along the threadlike stems. Five petals unite to form a small tube that is deeply lobed at the lip. Although the flowers usually go unnoticed, the yellowish masses of stems appear throughout the Houston area, sprawling over low vegetation in moist fields and along fencerows.

Dodders occur throughout the world, and medieval medicine claimed European species as treatments for epilepsy, leprosy, and syphilis. The Cherokee and other Native American tribes used poultices of dodder for bruises and wounds and made yellow dyes from the stems.

Cuscuta apparently arises from an Arabic word for the plants, but authors do not agree on the origin of "dodder." Some think it stems from the Old English verb *dadiren*, "to tremble," referring to the quivering stems. Others suggest an origin in the Germanic Frisian *dodd*, or "bunch," for the clusters of small flowers. A wide variety of fanciful common names exists in various parts of the country, all reflecting on the tangle of slender stems. "Love-vine" remains among the most common, although the smothering, parasitic habits of dodder hardly reflect well on the merits of love.

WHITE-TOPPED SEDGE

Rhynchospora colorata

White-topped umbrella grass, Umbrellagrass,
Whitetop, Star-rush, Ghost-grass

CYPERACEAE Sedge Family

SIZE
Plant: 12–32 inches.
Flower: Minute, but
supported by green-
and-white leafy
bracts to 6 inches
long.

LEAVES
Grasslike.

BLOOMS
April – August

Scores of sedge species occur throughout wetland habitats in the Houston area, and treatment of them goes far beyond the scope of this book. Most have inconspicuous flowers and will be lumped by casual observers with the grasses and rushes. White-topped sedge, however, has conspicuous green-and-white bracts below the globelike heads of tiny flowers and is certain to attract attention. It grows in abundance in wet ditches and fields and along bayous across the city.

Most current references apply the scientific name *Dichromena colorata* to white-topped sedge. However, Hatch, Gandhi, and Brown have merged that genus with the closely related *Rhynchospora*, and the latter taxonomy is followed here. Further work is needed to clarify the relationships.

R. colorata has three to six leafy bracts, with the white bases occupying one-tenth to one-third of their length. A second species, *R. latifolia*, also occurs in Southeast Texas, but appears to be infrequent in Houston. It normally has six to ten bracts, with white areas extending for at least half their length.

TEXAS BULL-NETTLE

Cnidoscolus texanus

Mala mujer, Tread-softly, Spurge-nettle

EUPHORBIACEAE Spurge Family

SIZE
Plant: 1–3 feet,
  spreading, often in
  colonies, armed with
  stinging hairs.
Flower: 1 inch, in
  terminal clusters,
  sexes separate.

LEAVES
3–6 inches, deeply
  3- to 5-lobed.

BLOOMS
April – November

A member of a large tropical genus that ranges sparingly into the southern U.S., Texas bull-nettle occurs throughout most of the state and can be found in fields and along roadsides in the Houston area. The branched, wide-spreading perennial grows from a deep taproot and can withstand the hottest, driest days of summer. Clusters of white flowers provide an attractive accent to Texas roadways, and Tull notes that the fragrant odor "competes with the finest perfumes." Be careful in your investigations, however, for bull-nettle is one of the most fearsomely armed of all our plants.

The entire plant bears stiff, stinging hairs that cause a painful, itching rash lasting for hours. Some people experience a severe reaction that may require treatment. Spanish-speaking people call it *mala mujer,* "bad woman." In spite of its nasty armament, bull-nettle produces large, tasty seeds utilized by many Indian tribes. Tull suggests that if suitably dressed in long pants and long sleeves, and wearing boots and gloves, one can pick the seed capsules with a pair of tongs and drop them into a paper sack. As the capsules ripen, they burst open, releasing the tasty nutlike kernels.

Broad, long-stalked leaves of bull-nettle are deeply lobed into three to five segments, each of which may be further lobed or toothed. The inch-wide white flowers bloom in terminal clusters, with male and female flowers separate but in the same cluster. There are no petals; five petallike sepals unite to form the tubular flower.

SNOW-ON-THE-PRAIRIE

Euphorbia bicolor

EUPHORBIACEAE Spurge Family

SIZE
Plant: 1–4 feet,
    branching, upright.
Flower: Minute,
    clusters surrounded
    by the upper
    white-edged leaves.

LEAVES
2–4 inches, alternate.

BLOOMS
July – November

Snow-on-the-prairie fills the fields and woodland clearings around Houston until they do, indeed, seem to be covered with drifting snow. This showy plant begins to bloom in late summer and reaches its peak in mid-September. What look like white flowers, however, are merely leafy bracts margined with white. The actual floral structures are far more complicated than they first appear. The true flowers are minute, with about thirty-five staminate (male) flowers and a single pistillate (female) flower clustered together in a cuplike receptacle. Five white, fleshy glands surround each cluster, giving the appearance of a five-petaled blossom. Those clusters, in turn, are surrounded by the white-edged leaves.

Although the branching, shrubby plants may reach three to four feet in height, snow-on-the-prairie is an annual. Some authors call it snow-on-the-mountain, but most Texas botanists reserve that name for *Euphorbia marginata*. The latter replaces *E. bicolor* from central Texas westward, and its white-margined bracts are oval in shape, rather than long and narrow.

The genus takes its name from Euphorbos, a Greek physician of the first century before Christ. "Spurge" comes from the Latin *purgare*, meaning to purge or cleanse, and the juice of many family members is regarded as a dangerous cathartic and emetic. Some people also find the milky sap of snow-on-the-prairie irritating to the skin.

SPOTTED SPURGE

Euphorbia maculata

Spotted euphorbia, Prostrate spurge

EUPHORBIACEAE Spurge Family

SIZE
*Plant: Stems to 20
  inches, branching,
  creeping.
Flower: Tiny complex
  of minute flowers
  surrounded by 4
  petallike glands.*

LEAVES
*To ½ inch, opposite,
  oblong, usually with
  purple spot along
  midvein.*

BLOOMS
May – December

Houstonians will encounter spotted spurge as a sprawling, creeping annual weed in lawns and gardens. It even emerges from cracks in sidewalks to spread in all directions from a tough, woody root. Oblong, half-inch leaves occur in pairs along the hairy stems and usually have an elongated purple spot along the midvein.

Examination of the white "flowers" with a magnifying glass, however, reveals an amazingly complex world. Spotted spurge bears tiny cuplike structures called "cyathia" at the nodes of short lateral, leafy shoots. Each cyathium is edged with four oblong glands, the petallike lobes usually mistaken for the petals of a single flower. Two to five minute staminate flowers arise within this gland-edged cyathium and surround a single pistillate flower. The latter eventually produces an ovoid seed capsule still flanked by the white lobes. While hardly an attractive wildflower, spotted spurge illustrates the doors of discovery that open upon close examination of many of our native plants.

More than sixty species of the genus *Euphorbia* occur in Texas. Some, like snow-on-the-prairie, *Euphorbia bicolor,* are large and showy, but most are smaller nondescript "weeds" that can be identified only by resorting to the technical manuals. Spotted spurge, however, is one of the more common species throughout most of Texas and across the eastern United States. It has been called *E. supina,* the "prostrate spurge," in several books.

ROUND-HEADED PRAIRIE CLOVER

Dalea multiflora

White prairie clover

FABACEAE Pea Family

SIZE
*Plant: 1–2 feet, slender
stems from woody
base.*
*Flower: Tiny, in
rounded terminal
cluster.*

LEAVES
*To 1½ inches, divided
into 3–9 small
leaflets.*

BLOOMS
May – July

This attractive plant will be found in many books under the scientific name *Petalostemum* (or *Petalostemon*) *multiflorum*. Botanists have recently merged that genus with *Dalea*, and the latter name is used in the newest Texas checklists.

Round-headed prairie clover is an upright perennial with several slender, branching stems one to two feet tall from a woody base. Leaves divide into three to nine narrow segments, each conspicuously dotted with glands below. The tiny, delicate flowers cluster in a rounded terminal head, each with five long stamens extending beyond the petals. The round flower cluster separates this species from other white prairie clovers with longer, columnar heads.

Abundant in the drier, sandy soils of central Texas, round-headed prairie clover ranges eastward to Harris County. We found it growing most frequently on the western edge of Houston, in the fields and along the roadsides in the Addicks area.

Flowers of prairie clover are unlike those of most legumes. Four of the five petals are loosely united with the tube of stamens and do not resemble the petals of the typical pea. Some authors consider them to be transformed stamens, a feature referred to in the former name *Petalostemum*. That, however, is primarily a matter of semantics, for many flowers have "petals" that are modified stamens, leaves, or other organs.

ILLINOIS BUNDLEFLOWER

Desmanthus illinoensis

Prairie mimosa, Illinois desmanthus

FABACEAE Pea Family

SIZE
Plant: 1–4 feet, erect or sprawling, bushy.
Flower: Tiny, with protruding stamens, in ball-like heads.

LEAVES
2 – 4 inches, twice divided.

BLOOMS
May – September

The upright or sprawling stems of Illinois bundleflower arise from a woody base. From one to four feet long, they lack the prickles that arm many of the similar Fabaceae. The leaves are bipinnately compound, or twice divided, the first divisions further separated into twenty to thirty pairs of small leaflets.

Tiny greenish white flowers have long white stamens protruding several times the length of the corolla, each of the five stamens tipped with yellow pollen. The crowded flower clusters thus give the effect of round, white, half-inch balls. Flat, curved seed pods also form dense clusters about an inch in diameter. One of the surest identification features of Illinois bundleflower, the fruiting heads are much sought for use in ornamental dried arrangements.

Bundleflower grows throughout the Houston area in fields and along sunny fencerows. High in protein, it provides an important browse for wildlife and for livestock. Foster and Duke also report that the Pawnee used a tea made from the leaves as a wash for itching.

"Illinois bundleflower" is a literal translation of the scientific name; *Desmanthus* stems from the Greek words for "bundle" and "flower." French botanist and explorer Andre Michaux first described the species from specimens collected in the Illinois Territory.

WHITE SWEET-CLOVER

Melilotus albus

Hubam, Melilot

FABACEAE Pea Family

SIZE
Plant: 2–8 feet, widely
branching.
Flower: ⅛–¼ inch,
in slender spikes.

LEAVES
3 narrow leaflets,
finely toothed on
margins.

BLOOMS
April – October

White sweet-clover is a bushy annual or biennial that grows from two to eight feet tall along Houston roadsides and in vacant lots, blooming sporadically from April until October. Leaves are divided into three narrow leaflets with finely toothed margins. The tiny flowers grow in numerous slender spikes from three to six inches long, each individual flower with the typical pea-blossom shape, the erect banner petal at the top.

Native to Eurasia, white sweet-clover was first recorded in Virginia in 1739, according to Bare. Cultivation began in Alabama in 1856. It was originally grown as a honey plant, and honey made from it has a light color and mild flavor. The genus name, in fact, comes from the Greek *meli*, meaning "honey." Plants were also used for natural dyes and in teas to treat several ailments.

Sweet-scented white and yellow sweet-clovers have been widely planted as hay crops and to rejuvenate the soil. However, moldy hay has been responsible for many deaths in cattle due to the presence of compounds called coumarins, which cause uncontrollable bleeding. From those coumarins scientists developed a compound known as warfarin for use in rodent poisons, and the compounds are also applied medicinally to prevent blood clotting.

WHITE CLOVER

Trifolium repens

White lawn clover, White Dutch clover, Ladino clover

FABACEAE Pea Family

SIZE
Plant: 4–10 inches,
  creeping stems
  forming mats.
Flower: ¼–½ inch,
  in globular 1-inch
  heads.

LEAVES
On long stalks,
  3 leaflets.

BLOOMS
February – October,
  dies back in
  midsummer.

An alien species introduced from Europe, white clover now occurs across the country. It is perhaps the most widely distributed of all the legumes, for it has spread throughout the temperate and subtropical regions of the world. City dwellers know it as an invasive weed in lawns, but white clover serves as an excellent fodder plant for pastures and is widely planted. Hardy, nutritious, and well-liked by livestock, it also improves the soil through nitrogen-fixing bacteria in its roots. An excellent honey plant as well, clover is pollinated primarily by bees. European folk medicine used the flowers in tea for rheumatism and gout, while American Indians made cloverleaf tea to treat colds, coughs, and fevers.

White clover forms extensive mats from creeping, perennial stems that root at the nodes. Small white or pale pinkish flowers form globular clusters on leafless stalks that normally rise above the surrounding foliage. Long-stalked leaves divide into three finely toothed leaflets, each leaflet marked with a pale V-shaped band. Occasional plants produce extra leaflets, the much-sought "four-leaf clovers" said to bring good luck.

COAST GERMANDER

Teucrium cubense

LAMIACEAE Mint Family

SIZE
Plant: 1–2 feet,
  branched from base.
Flower: ½–¾ inch,
  2-lipped. Stamens
  project through split
  upper lip.

LEAVES
To 1½ inches, deeply
  lobed.

BLOOMS
March – December

An extremely showy plant standing one to two feet tall, coast germander forms small colonies in saline and brackish soils around the upper reaches of Galveston Bay and along the Houston ship channel. It also occurs less frequently in fields and open woodlands, ranging well inland in Texas in spite of its name. Upright stems branch at the base and may branch again near the top, forming bushy clumps. Opposite leaves are lobed or deeply cut, particularly in the flowering portion of the stem.

The white flowers are two-lipped, as is typical of the mint family. However, the upper lip is deeply notched into two toothlike segments between which the stamens and pistil project upward. The middle lobe of the three-lobed lower lip is much broader than the others. Coast germander blooms sporadically from spring until fall.

The name "germander" is a corruption of the ancient Greek name for a related shrubby species. It passed from Greek through Medieval Latin and Old French to English, changing with each step. The genus, according to Healey, was named for Teucer, "a legendary king in the region of Troy," who used the plants medicinally.

WILD ONION

Allium canadense

Canada onion, Spring onion,
Canada garlic, Wild garlic

LILIACEAE Lily Family

SIZE
*Plant: 8–24 inches.
    Two varieties.
Flower: ¼ inch, in
    terminal cluster.
    Partially or
    completely replaced
    by bulblets in
    variety* canadense.

LEAVES
*6–18 inches, grasslike
    from bulb.*

BLOOMS
March – May

Flowers of wild onion range from white to deep rosy pink; however, those we studied in Houston tended to be whitish, with only pale pink shading. They become darker as they mature. Two varieties also occur, both blooming in the spring, and they are very different in their appearance. On first seeing them, the novice would doubt they are members of the same species.

Allium canadense var. *mobilense* has a terminal cluster of white or pink quarter-inch flowers borne on a slender, leafless stalk reaching eight to twenty-four inches. Long, grasslike leaves also rise from the small underground bulb that is covered by a fibrous network. This handsome variety occurs sparingly in vacant lots across the city and in the surrounding fields.

Allium canadense var. *canadense* appears to be more abundant along bayou banks within the city. Most of the flowers are replaced by aerial bulblets, and the remaining flowers normally wither without producing seeds. Instead, the bulblets propagate asexually, each giving rise to a new plant.

Allium is the Latin name for garlic and possibly derives from the Celtic *all,* meaning "pungent." Members of the genus have the flavor and odor of onions, and Dormon notes that wild onion can become a troublesome weed in cultivated crops. She reports that wheat, oats, and other grains may take on an onion flavor when harvested with the pungent plants. Various Indian tribes used crushed bulbs to relieve the pain of bee and wasp stings, and early explorers found the bulbs to be an effective cure for scurvy. Tull cites several ways to use wild onions in cooking. The *AMA Handbook of Poisonous and Injurious Plants,* however, lists all parts of the plant as potentially toxic and notes that "gastroenteritis is common in young children who ingest parts of *A. canadense.*"

FALSE GARLIC

Nothoscordum bivalve

Crow-poison, Yellow false garlic, Odorless onion

LILIACEAE Lily Family

SIZE
Plant: 8–16 inches.
Flower: To 1 inch
  across.

LEAVES
To about 16 inches,
  grasslike.

BLOOMS
Intermittent
  throughout the year.
  Most abundant in
  very early spring
  and late fall.

False garlic may well be the most abundant wildflower in Houston during the cooler months of the year. It springs up in lawns and fields from February into May and again in late fall. It also blooms intermittently after summer rains and through the winter if there is no killing freeze. Regarded by most homeowners as a lawn weed, it nevertheless provides a bright spot of color and serves as a nectar source for bees and butterflies when few other plants are blooming.

Also called "crow-poison," false garlic resembles the closely related wild onions, but it lacks the onion or garlic smell. The fibrous-coated bulb is inedible, and Delena Tull in *A Practical Guide to Edible & Useful Plants* notes, "I have found no information to indicate whether or not it truly is toxic, so we can only assume that it could cause poisoning."

Six to twelve white or cream-colored flowers cluster together in an umbel at the top of the leafless, foot-long stalk. Each ranges from one-half to one inch in diameter and has six petallike "tepals," a term used for the collective petals and sepals when all are alike. Reddish or greenish central stripes often ornament the outer surfaces of the tepals, while the stamens and ovaries are bright yellow. The flowers close on cloudy days or during cold weather, and the grasslike leaves might hardly be noticed among the grasses of the fields.

The genus name comes from the Greek words *nothos* and *skordon*, meaning "false garlic," while *bivalve* refers to the two membranous bracts that enclose the flower cluster during its early stages of development.

HALBERD-LEAVED ROSE-MALLOW

Hibiscus militaris

Scarlet rose-mallow, Smooth marsh-mallow, Halberd-leaved hibiscus

MALVACEAE Mallow Family

SIZE
Plant: To 6 feet,
  occasionally taller.
Flower: 6 inches, white
  or pink, with red
  center.

LEAVES
Spear-shaped, smooth
  above and below.

BLOOMS
May – November.
  Most common
  August – October.

An erect, shrubby native hibiscus with flowers spanning as much as six inches, the halberd-leaved rose-mallow can hardly be overlooked when present in the marshes of eastern Texas. Most references give the flower color as pale to deep pink, but we found the white form to be much more common in the Houston area, at least in the San Jacinto and Trinity river drainages east of the city. In those populations, this handsome rose-mallow has creamy white flowers with dark red centers.

The most recent Texas checklist by Hatch, Gandhi, and Brown suggests that this species, listed as *Hibiscus militaris* in other books, might more properly be called *H. laevis*. We have followed the majority, but the latter name may be favored in the future.

The halberd-leaved rose-mallow has a distinctive spear-shaped leaf with two lobes at the base. It takes its name from the halberd weapon of the fifteenth and sixteenth centuries, which had an axlike blade and spike mounted on the end of a long handle. The stem, leaves, and sepals are smooth, without the downy hairs that characterize many of the other *Hibiscus* species.

Swamp rose-mallow, *H. moscheutos*, occurs in much the same range and habitats as *militaris*, and it also has large white or pink flowers. The wider leaves of *moscheutos*, however, lack the basal lobes, and the stem, leaves, and calyx are covered with hairs.

Either of these two native species makes an attractive addition to the flower garden. Their large blooms equal those of the tropical hibiscus cultivars, and they prove hardy in Houston's climate, having adapted to conditions throughout the eastern half of the United States. Both species and selective hybrids are now becoming available from nurseries, especially those that offer native plants.

WHITE GAURA

Gaura lindheimeri

Lindheimer's gaura, Wild honeysuckle

ONAGRACEAE Evening-primrose Family

SIZE
*Plant: 2–5 feet,
    slender, upright or
    sprawling, much-
    branched,
    soft-hairy.*
*Flower: To 1 inch, all 4
    petals on upper side.*

LEAVES
*To 3 inches, narrow,
    alternate, stalkless.*

BLOOMS
April – November

The largest-flowered and showiest of the gauras, white gaura forms extensive colonies in open fields and along fencerows throughout the Houston area. The inch-wide flowers open at sunrise and close in the heat of the day, heralding the mornings from April through November with their fragrant scent. The delicate, distinctive blossoms are easily recognized, for they have all four petals arranged on the upper side, with the eight stamens drooping below. "They are like small white butterflies," Caroline Dormon wrote in *Flowers Native to the Deep South.*

The upright to sprawling stems of this slender perennial are much branched and reach two to five feet. Leaves measure up to three inches long and about one-half inch wide, alternate and stalkless, with scattered teeth along the margins. Upper leaves may be very small. The flowers appear in sparse terminal spikes or on short branches from the leaf axils. They turn pinkish and wilt rapidly in the sun.

This North American genus is centered in Texas, which has more than a dozen gaura species, and ranges from Canada to Guatemala. Although the genus is easy to recognize by its unique four-petaled flowers, species can be extremely difficult to distinguish. Identification often depends on exact measurements of flower parts and examination of the seed pods. Some area species are tall, rangy plants with tiny pinkish blooms.

White gaura was named for botanist Ferdinand Jakob Lindheimer, a German political refugee who immigrated first to Illinois and then settled in Texas. He and another great botanist, George Engelmann, provided plant specimens for Asa Gray of Harvard. Lindheimer collected tirelessly for thirteen years, particularly in the area bounded by Fredericksburg, San Antonio, and Houston, accumulating more than fifteen hundred species of plants that reached museums around the world. Nearly two dozen species were named in his honor. Lindheimer ended his collecting career in 1852 to become editor of a German-language newspaper in New Braunfels, but he remains one of the greatest names in Texas botany.

SPRING LADIES'-TRESSES

Spiranthes vernalis

Upland ladies'-tresses, Narrow-leaved ladies'-tresses,
Green-leaf ladies'-tresses

ORCHIDACEAE Orchid Family

SIZE
Plant: 6–20 inches,
  sometimes taller.
Flower: To ½ inch,
  in spiral on solitary
  spike.

LEAVES
To 12 inches, slender,
  grasslike.

BLOOMS
April – July

A number of orchid species occur in Texas, many of them in the forests and bogs of the Big Thicket. However, only the ladies'-tresses range regularly into the Houston area. The spiral arrangement of the flowers on the stalk accounts for the genus name, *Spiranthes*, as well as the common name. Rather than simply connoting a lock of hair, "tress" originally meant a braid. Several species of ladies'-tresses inhabit Southeast Texas. They can be difficult to distinguish, but *Spiranthes vernalis* is the most common. It occurs in moist areas throughout Houston but is usually overlooked.

Growing from a tuberous root, spring ladies'-tresses normally stands from six to twenty inches high, but plants up to three feet tall have been found. Slender, grasslike leaves sheath the stem, and numerous flowers spiral up the solitary terminal spike. The flaring lower lip of the flower is fleshy, crinkled along the edge, and sometimes marked with yellowish spots. A dense coating of fine hairs covers the stem and the bases of the flowers.

WHITE PRICKLY POPPY

Argemone albiflora subsp. *texana*

Texas prickly poppy, White pricklepoppy

PAPAVERACEAE Poppy Family

SIZE
Plant: 2–4 feet, very spiny.
Flower: 3–4 inches. With 6 delicate, crinkled petals.

LEAVES
To 8 inches, bluish green, lobed, spiny.

BLOOMS
April – June, sometimes later.

The large, delicate flowers of the prickly poppies belie their spiny, thistlelike foliage. Several species occur in Texas, including some with yellow and reddish blooms, but this white-flowered one is the most abundant and widespread. A southeastern species, it is represented in our state by the subspecies *texana*. *Argemone albiflora* is easily distributed by seed, and it forms large colonies in open fields. Plants frequently spring up in the Houston area in the disturbed soils along roadsides and railroad tracks.

Upright stems reach two to four feet in height and branch in the upper portions. The large, deeply lobed leaves are bluish green, often mottled with darker green patches. Sharp spines protect the wavy-edged leaves, inhibiting even cattle from grazing on the foliage. When broken, plants exude a latex sap that quickly turns bright yellow as it dries. The six-petalled flowers span up to four inches and are fragile and crinkled. They produce little nectar and are pollinated by bees and beetles that collect abundant pollen from the numerous yellow or reddish stamens. Beetles also consume the tender petals, leaving flowers ragged and less than photogenic.

The genus, *Argemone*, was apparently an ancient Greek name for some unknown plant that Pliny described as having an orange-colored juice. It could not have been one of the prickly poppies to which we now apply the name, however, for they are native only to the Americas.

POKEWEED

Phytolacca americana

Pokeberry, Poke, Great pokeweed, Scoke

PHYTOLACCACEAE Pokeweed Family

SIZE
Plant: 4–10 feet,
  branching, reddish
  stems.
Flower: ¼ inch,
  in long clusters.

LEAVES
4–12 inches, lancelike.

BLOOMS
July – October

A tall, branching, large-leaved plant, pokeweed reaches four to ten feet in height from a thick perennial root. The stems are reddish, and the four- to twelve-inch leaves taper at both ends. Long clusters of quarter-inch flowers have greenish white or pink petallike sepals; there are no true petals. The mature berries are dark purple and hang in drooping clusters. Pokeweed inhabits moist, open woodlands, thickets, and roadsides throughout the Houston area.

Many residents of Texas have eaten "poke salet," the cooked greens obtained from very young shoots gathered before they begin to turn pink. Boiled thoroughly in two changes of water, these greens are edible. All parts of the plant are potentially toxic to both humans and livestock, however, particularly the roots and larger leaves. The *AMA Handbook of Poisonous and Injurious Plants* notes that most poisonings occur from eating uncooked leaves in salads or from mistaking roots for parsnips or horseradish. Although mature berries appear to be relatively nontoxic, according to the handbook, it seems best to leave them for the many species of birds that consume them eagerly. Also, the juice of the plant can cause dermatitis.

The genus name, *Phytolacca,* comes from the Greek *phyton,* meaning "plant," and the modern Latin *lacca,* the latter derived from the Hindi *lakh,* for the dye obtained from the lac insect. Like those scale insects, pokeweed has been used as a red stain or dye. Indeed, the common name comes from the Algonquian Indian word *pokan,* which means any red-juiced plant. Various Native American tribes and early colonists also used pokeweed poultices for treatment of tumors, rheumatism, syphilis, and other maladies.

During James Knox Polk's presidential campaign, according to Durant, pokeweed sprigs were worn by his followers. It was later said that the plant got its name from our eleventh president, but, in truth, it was known as pokeweed long before Polk's political career began.

Some consider poke a noxious weed, but famed naturalist and author John Burroughs wrote glowingly of this common plant in his 1881 *A Bunch of Herbs:* "Pokeweed is a native American, and what a lusty, royal plant it is! It never invades cultivated fields, but hovers about the borders and looks over the fences like a painted Indian sachem. Thoreau coveted its strong purple stalk for a cane, and the robins eat its dark crimson-juiced berries."

SWAMP SMARTWEED

Polygonum hydropiperoides

Water smartweed, Water-pepper, Mild water-pepper

POLYGONACEAE Buckwheat Family

SIZE
*Plant: 1–3 feet, upright
or sprawling.
Flower: ⅛ inch, white
or pink petallike
sepals, in slender
spikes.*

LEAVES
*To 5 inches, alternate,
narrow, lancelike.*

BLOOMS
April – November

Nearly two dozen smartweeds and knotweeds occur in Texas, many of them in our area. Most are similar in appearance and can be identified only by careful attention to small differences in structure. Swamp smartweed and its close relatives were formerly placed in the genus *Persicaria* because they bear their flowers in slender spikes and lack a joint between the leaf blade and petiole present in species placed in *Polygonum*. Recently, however, Texas checklists have recombined the two genera under the latter name.

An annual or short-lived perennial, swamp smartweed grows abundantly in the wet mud or shallow water of streams, marshes, and ditches throughout the Houston area. Stems from one to three feet tall are usually erect, but they sometimes sprawl and root at the nodes to form dense colonies. Alternate leaves are long and narrow, while the flowers form slender, interrupted spikes. The tiny individual flowers lack petals and have white or pink petallike sepals. We include the species with the white flowers because those in the Houston area seem to be mainly white inside, although the outer sepals may be pale pink.

This species, *Polygonum hydropiperoides*, takes its name from the similarity to another species of our area, *P. hydropiper.* The latter name translates directly as "water-pepper," for the acrid, peppery taste of the leaves and seeds. Tull notes that they are so pungent that they raise blisters on the skin and should be used only as a spice, rather than as a salad or vegetable. Several species of *Polygonum* were used by Native American tribes in leaf teas for chills and fevers, while the poulticed leaves were applied to wounds. The genus name comes from the Greek *poly,* "many," and *gonu,* "joint," referring to the joints in the stems.

P. hydropiperoides is one of the most common species within the city and can be distinguished by the slender flower spikes and a fringe of stiff bristles on the sheaths of the stem joints.

TEN-PETAL ANEMONE

Anemone berlandieri

Southern anemone, Basket anemone,
Windflower, Granny's nightcap

RANUNCULACEAE Buttercup Family

SIZE
Plant: 6–12 inches.
Flower: To 1½ inches.
White, pink, blue, or
purple.

LEAVES
Mostly basal, deeply
divided or lobed.

BLOOMS
February – April

Blooming from February into April, ten-petal anemone ornaments lawns and fields like a breath of spring. The genus name stems from the Greek word *anemos*, meaning "wind," and Pliny asserted the flower could open only at the wind's bidding. To this day, "windflower" serves as a common name for various anemones in several parts of the country. The blooms close at night and during cloudy weather. According to Mary Durant, a Greek myth also claimed anemones sprang from the passionate tears shed by Venus over the body of the slain Adonis.

In spite of its common name, the ten to twenty "petals" of ten-petal anemone are not petals at all, but rather colored sepals. They vary from white through pink and pale blue to deep purple. Most of the plants found in Houston are white. The flowers are borne at the tips of six- to twelve-inch flower stalks that arise from bulblike perennial tubers. The resulting fruiting heads elongate into long, woolly, conelike cylinders of ripening ovaries. Basal leaves are deeply divided or lobed, and a whorl of smaller leaves occurs on the stem below the flower.

Anemone berlandieri is a recent name about which confusion still reigns. According to Hatch, Gandhi, and Brown, it replaces *A. heterophylla* and *A. decapetala* var. *heterophylla*, which have been used by other authors in the past. According to Johnston, however, it replaces *A. caroliniana*, the Carolina anemone that Hatch, Gandhi, and Brown treat as another distinct species.

Specimens from Houston that we examined appeared to be white-flowered forms of what was formerly keyed as *heterophylla* and is now called *berlandieri* by Hatch et al. and by Peterson and Brown. The species was named for Jean Louis Berlandier, a Swiss botanist who collected in Texas and Mexico from 1827 to 1830. Several other Texas plants also bear his name.

MACARTNEY ROSE

Rosa bracteata

Evergreen rose, Hedge rose, Prairie rose

ROSACEAE Rose Family

SIZE
Plant: Forming large masses, usually to 6 feet high. Stems with paired, recurved thorns.
Flower: 2–3 inches, 5 petals, many stamens.

LEAVES
2–4 inches, with 5–9 leaflets.

BLOOMS
April – July, less frequently until December.

A native of China, Macartney rose was introduced into cultivation in 1893, according to Robert Vines. Widely planted as a windbreak for cattle on the Texas coastal prairie, it has spread to become a noxious pest. The spiny, trailing or arching stems form tangled, impenetrable mounds up to six feet high and twenty feet across. Macartney rose occurs in scattered fields and thickets throughout the Houston area and becomes more abundant on the prairies farther south and west.

Five-petalled flowers span two to three inches and are subtended by large, leafy bracts, the source of the species name *bracteata*. Compound leaves divide into five, seven, or nine leaflets. Red fruits, or "hips," are hairy and globelike, up to an inch in diameter, with bracts below and five persistent sepals above.

Macartney rose might be confused with Cherokee rose, *Rosa laevigata*, which occurs more sparingly in the Houston area. The latter is also an Asian species that has escaped cultivation. It normally has only three leaflets, however, rather than the five to nine leaflets of Macartney rose.

"Rose" is an ancient name with no known origin. It is much the same in virtually all European languages. Some authors suggest it may have come from the Celtic *rhod*, meaning "red," but others suspect the color took its name from the flower. Many other words in current usage owe their roots to the rose.

SOUTHERN DEWBERRY

Rubus trivialis

Zarzamora, Wild blackberry

ROSACEAE Rose Family

SIZE
Plant: Long, slender,
*   trailing canes.*
*   Armed with curved*
*   thorns.*
Flower: 1 inch or
*   larger, 5 petals.*

LEAVES
Usually 3 or 5 leaflets,
*   coarsely toothed.*

BLOOMS
March – April

Dewberries grow prolifically along roadsides and fencerows throughout the Houston area and even spring up as weeds in lawns and gardens. The slender, trailing canes root at the tips and form tangled, prickly mats. Compound leaves usually have five leaflets on the older growth and three leaflets on the slender flowering stalks. The white, five-petalled blossoms appear singly and reveal their familial relationships in their roselike structure. Some wildflower books omit the dewberries and their relatives because they are woody-based semi-shrubs, but the abundant white flowers contribute greatly to Houston's floral beauty in the spring.

Southern dewberry can usually be identified by its low, sprawling growth habit; however, members of the genus *Rubus* are extremely difficult to separate. Robert Vines, in his monumental *Trees, Shrubs, and Woody Vines of the South-west*, notes that adequate coverage of the genus would call for the work of a specialist who had spent years studying the group. Disagreements still exist on appropriate nomenclature. Hatch, Gandhi, and Brown have recently assigned *Rubus trivialis* to R. *riograndis,* but Johnston does not follow that change. Since most books apply the former name, it has been continued here.

Delena Tull, in *A Practical Guide to Edible & Useful Plants*, describes many uses for the common dewberry. The leaves provide pleasant teas, while the canes can be used in basketry. Both the fruits and tender shoots prove useful as natural dyes. And Tull calls the dewberry "Texas' most popular wild berry," although she warns of the hazards of wading through prickles, chiggers, and poison ivy in their pursuit.

VIRGINIA BUTTONWEED

Diodia virginiana

Large buttonweed

RUBIACEAE Madder Family

SIZE
Plant: Stems to 2 feet,
  branching,
  sprawling.
Flower: ½ inch,
  4-lobed.

LEAVES
2–3 inches, opposite,
  narrow.

BLOOMS
May – October

Most homeowners in the Houston area encounter Virginia buttonweed as a pernicious weed in their lawns. Stems grow from a perennial root and reach two feet in length, branching and spreading through the grass until they form a tough mat. The narrow leaves are two to three inches in length, and the half-inch, trumpet-shaped flowers with four flaring lobes arise from the leaf axils. Leathery fruits are strongly six-ribbed and retain the two sepals that distinguish *Diodia virginiana* from rough buttonweed, *D. teres.* The latter usually has four sepals, or calyx lobes.

A representative of a largely tropical genus, Virginia buttonweed ranges from Texas and Florida northward to Missouri and New England. It inhabits swamps, meadows, and coastal prairies in the eastern third of our state and occurs throughout the Houston area in fields and yards. The genus name, according to Bare, comes from the Greek *diodos,* "thoroughfare," for they grow by the wayside.

CATCHWEED BEDSTRAW

Galium aparine

Cleavers, Goosegrass, Common bedstraw

RUBIACEAE Madder Family

SIZE
Plant: 1–3 feet, weak-stemmed, sprawling.
Flower: Less than ⅛ inch, in leaf axils.

LEAVES
To 1½ inches, in whorls of 6–8 around stem.

BLOOMS
March – May

Catchweed bedstraw will win no awards for floral beauty, but it occurs abundantly throughout the Houston area, in vacant lots and along roadsides and as a weed in lawns and gardens. The weak-stemmed plants reach one to three feet and often sprawl on other vegetation. Narrow leaves appear in whorls of six to eight around the four-angled stems, and both leaves and stems are covered with recurved prickles that stick to skin and clothes. The species takes one of its common names, "cleavers," from this ability to cling or "cleave." Tiny four-lobed flowers bloom in small clusters in the leaf axils.

Some nineteen *Galium* species occur in Texas, identified by such factors as range, number of leaves in each whorl, and details of the fruits. Catchweed bedstraw is one most likely to be found in Houston. Because this species is widespread in many parts of the world, botanists disagree on whether catchweed bedstraw is native to North America or has naturalized from Eurasia.

The fragrant foliage of another European species was used to stuff mattresses in medieval times; hence, "bedstraw." "Goosegrass" comes from its appeal as a food for geese. Herbal teas were widely taken for several ailments and as a "blood purifier," while the citric acid in the juice helped to prevent scurvy. Tull suggests using young growth of catchweed bedstraw as a potherb, since boiling or steaming softens the prickles. Natural-food advocate Euell Gibbons promoted the roasted fruits as a coffee substitute, although gathering the tiny capsules would be a tedious task.

Origins of the scientific name seem uncertain. Bare suggests Linnaeus may have had the Greek word *gala*, "milk," in mind when he named the genus, since a European species was widely used for curdling milk and making cheese. *Aparine* is an epithet used for centuries by botanists to mean "to catch or cling."

PRAIRIE BLUETS

Hedyotis nigricans

Fine-leaf bluets, Narrow-leaf bluets, Star-violet

RUBIACEAE Madder Family

SIZE
*Plant: 2–20 inches,
 branching in upper
 portions.*
*Flower: ¼ inch, 4-
 lobed. Color varies
 from white to pink
 or pale purple.*

LEAVES
*To 1½ inches, narrow,
 threadlike, opposite.*

BLOOMS
April – November

Prairie bluets was once classified as *Houstonia nigricans*, but that genus has now been merged with *Hedyotis,* forming a large complex of nearly three hundred species, many of which inhabit the Old World. Nineteen species are now known from Texas. Four varieties of prairie bluets are presently listed for the state, although the exact taxonomy needs further clarification. Most beginners will be satisfied with recognizing them as "bluets."

The flowers of prairie, or fine-leaf, bluets range from white to pink or pale purple. Most in the Houston area are pale enough to appear whitish at a distance, and the species has thus been included in this section. It occurs abundantly throughout vacant lots and along roadsides, even within the heart of the city. A tolerant, hardy perennial with a stout taproot, prairie bluets grows in a wide variety of dry soils.

Slender, delicate stems reach twenty inches in height and branch widely in the upper portions. Narrow, threadlike leaves appear in opposite pairs and often roll under along the margins. They turn black as they dry, accounting for the scientific name *nigricans.* Tiny flowers usually span no more than one-fourth inch and are borne in clusters at the ends of stiff branches. The four petals unite at the base to form a tube, with the stamens protruding well beyond the tube mouth. Although prairie bluets blooms primarily in spring, some flowers may occur through the summer into fall.

PARTRIDGE-BERRY

Mitchella repens

Two-eyed-berry, Running-box, Turkey-berry,
Twin-berry, Tea-berry, Squaw-vine

RUBIACEAE Madder Family

SIZE
Plant: Creeping, mat-
forming stems to 12
inches.
Flower: ½ inch, paired,
trumpet-shaped, 4-
lobed, densely hairy
on inner surface.

LEAVES
To 1 inch, rounded,
opposite pairs.

BLOOMS
May – July

This little creeping, mat-forming perennial prefers acid soils in open wood-lands. Brown has recorded it from Armand Bayou Nature Center, but it occurs more commonly in the northern, wooded portions of Houston and Harris County. Small, rounded leaves are evergreen and occur in opposite pairs.

The white to pale pink flowers are also paired, and their ovaries fuse to form a single round, red, berrylike fruit. Tubular, trumpet-shaped flowers normally have four corolla lobes, but one of those in the accompanying photograph has six lobes. The pretty little flowers are densely covered with short white hairs on the inner surface.

Found throughout the eastern half of North America, from Canada to Florida and Texas, partridge-berry is our sole representative of a genus named for John Mitchell (1680–1768). A physician as well as a botanist, Mitchell developed a treatment for yellow fever and saved thousands of lives during a Philadelphia epidemic. The species name, *repens*, means "creeping."

Partridge-berry provides an attractive ground cover beneath azaleas and other shade-loving, acid-soil shrubs, but it will not tolerate other conditions. It is also used extensively in terrariums. In spite of its name, partridge-berry has tasteless fruits that appear to be ignored by wildlife.

COMMON BALLOON-VINE

Cardiospermum halicacabum

Heart-seed, Heart-pea, Farolitos

SAPINDACEAE Soapberry Family

SIZE
*Plant: Sprawling,
  climbing stems to
  6 feet.*
*Flower: Less than
  ¼ inch, in sparse
  clusters on tendril-
  bearing stalks.*

LEAVES
*3 segments further
  divided into 3
  leaflets each.*

BLOOMS
June – November

Balloon-vine is an attractive sprawling, low-climbing annual vine that covers shrubs and fencerows in moist thickets and waste places throughout the Houston area. Slender, wiry, ribbed stems grow to six feet long and branch freely. The leaves are alternate and compound, dividing into three segments, each of which is further divided into three toothed leaflets.

Tiny flowers appear in small clusters on long, slender stalks, each stalk with paired tendrils that support the vine. The flowers have four petals, two larger than the others. The resulting balloon-like fruits are far more conspicuous than the flowers. Each inflated capsule contains three black seeds with a heart-shaped scar, giving rise to the genus name *Cardiospermum*, "heart-seed."

Several authors consider common balloon-vine to be a tropical species that has escaped and naturalized from cultivation. Wagner, Herbst, and Sohmer note in their *Manual of the Flowering Plants of Hawaii*, however, that although it is now widespread in tropical and subtropical regions around the world, it is probably native to the southern United States. They also describe its use as a magical remedy for dizziness in Hawaii, where it has been found since at least 1819. Hawaiians formerly wore the whole plant as a lei around their necks and then ate a bit of it before throwing it into the ocean.

LIZARD'S-TAIL

Saururus cernuus

Common lizard-tail, Water-dragon

SAURURACEAE Lizard's-tail Family

SIZE
*Plant: To 3 feet,
  perennial from
  rhizomes.
Flower: ⅛ inch,
  lacking petals and
  sepals, in elongated
  spike drooping
  at tip.*

LEAVES
*3–6 inches, heart-
  shaped,
  long-stalked.*

BLOOMS
April – August

Generally regarded as one of the most primitive of our flowering plants, lizard's-tail has flowers lacking both petals and sepals. Tiny individual flowers consist only of six to eight stamens and a single pistil, yet are extremely fragrant and attractive when arrayed along a crowded spike that droops at the tip. The genus name comes from the Greek words for "lizard" and "tail," while *cernuus* means "drooping" or "nodding" in Latin. As the seeds mature, the spike becomes erect.

The leaves of lizard's-tail are heart-shaped and long-stalked, growing alternately on the jointed stem that reaches three feet in height. The perennial plants spread from underground rhizomes to form dense colonies in the shallow water and wet mud of ditches and shaded ponds and marshes. A species that ranges across much of eastern North America, lizard's-tail occurs in the wooded areas of northern Houston and Harris County and in the San Jacinto and Trinity river bottoms to the north and east.

Poultices made from the roots of lizard's-tail were applied by Native Americans to wounds and inflammation, and a tea was brewed for stomach ailments. An Asian counterpart, *Saururus chinensis,* has also been used in traditional Chinese medicine, and it has recently been shown to contain a sedative compound with an unusual molecular structure.

CAROLINA HORSE-NETTLE

Solanum carolinense

Carolina nightshade, Ball-nettle, Horse-nettle

SOLANACEAE Nightshade Family

SIZE
*Plant: To 3 feet, stems
armed with yellow
spines.
Flower: 1 inch, petals
united in 5-lobed
star.*

LEAVES
*To 5 inches, lobed or
toothed margins,
yellow spines on
underside and
midrib.*

BLOOMS
April – October

A branching, coarse perennial up to three feet tall, Carolina horse-nettle spreads rapidly from creeping roots to form small colonies. Once established, it is difficult to eradicate, and it occurs commonly in fields and along roadsides throughout the Houston area. Caroline Dormon called it a "horrid thorny weed . . . a pest in every garden." The stems bear straight, yellowish spines, and the large lobed or toothed leaves also have yellow spines on the lower surface and along the midrib.

Although viciously armed, horse-nettle is an attractive wildflower. The five petals unite at the base to form a broad five-lobed star, with five stamens forming a central cone of yellow anthers. Flowers range in color from white to pale violet, but white appears to be by far the most common color in Houston. Ripened fruits hang in showy orange-yellow clusters like small tomatoes.

The berries of Carolina horse-nettle were once used for treating epilepsy and as a painkiller, as well as an aphrodisiac, according to Foster and Duke. Ripened berries fried in grease produced an ointment for dog mange. Native Americans gargled leaf tea for sore throats and drank the tea for worms, while using poulticed leaves for poison-ivy rash.

In spite of these medicinal applications, horse-nettle contains the toxic alkaloids shared by many of the Solanaceae, and all portions of the plant should be regarded as toxic. The berries have caused fatalities in children. Because of the widespread abundance of this and other poisonous plants, small children should always be cautioned not to eat unidentified berries.

AMERICAN NIGHTSHADE

Solanum ptycanthum

Common nightshade, Glossy nightshade, Hierba mora negra

SOLANACEAE Nightshade Family

SIZE
Plant: 1–3 feet,
   branching, smooth,
   spineless.
Flower: ⅓ inch,
   drooping, 5 petals
   curve backward.

LEAVES
2–4 inches, entire or
   wavy-margined,
   thin and smooth.

BLOOMS
March – November

This species has been called *Solanum americanum* by botanists through the years and will be so listed in most books currently in use. However, Hatch, Gandhi, and Brown (1990) now classify it as *S. ptycanthum,* reserving its former name for a coastal species previously referred to as *S. nodiflorum.* These two native species and *S. nigrum,* which was apparently introduced from Europe, compose a complex that has appeared under a variety of names.

Whatever scientific name is accepted, American nightshade remains a relatively easy species to identify in Houston, where it occurs abundantly as a weed in gardens and vacant lots and in the surrounding fields. While most of its genus bear sharp spines, American nightshade is unarmed; its stems and thin leaves are smooth to the touch. The pointed, oval or triangular leaves have untoothed margins, or are at the most wavy-edged. The starlike flowers are small and drooping, with five white petals curving backward and five stamens forming a yellow central core.

Leaves and green berries contain toxic alkaloids common to many of the Solanaceae, and most poisonings occur when children consume the immature fruits. Ripe, glossy black berries are apparently less harmful, but it is best to treat the entire plant as poisonous. Several historical medicinal uses have been documented for this native species and for *S. nigrum* in Europe.

WOODS CORN-SALAD

Valerianella woodsiana

Lamb's lettuce

VALERIANACEAE Valerian Family

SIZE
Plant: 6–20 inches,
  dichotomously
  branched.
Flower: 1/10 inch. In
  compact, squarish
  clusters.

LEAVES
To 2 inches, spatulate,
  slightly succulent.

BLOOMS
March – May

Corn-salad grows as a low annual from six to twenty inches tall. The stem forks to produce a pair of branches, then each branch gives rise to another pair, a growth form called "dichotomously branched." The leaves are opposite and somewhat succulent, with tiny hairs along the margins and on the lower surface of the midrib. These spatulate leaves are normally stalkless, and the upper ones may have shallow teeth at the base. Tiny funnel-shaped flowers have five irregular lobes and form dense, squarish, flat-topped clusters at the tips of the symmetrically branching stems. Developing fruits have three cells, but only one is fertile.

Five or six species of *Valerianella* occur in Texas; two are common in Houston, inhabiting moist ditches, bayou banks, and vacant lots. Woods corn-salad, *V. woodsiana,* and beaked corn-salad, *V. radiata,* can be safely separated only by minor differences in their fruits. Without microscopic examination and reference to a detailed key, both should simply be called "corn-salad." As Howard Irwin so aptly noted in *Roadside Flowers of Texas,* "The expression 'by their fruits ye shall know them' is perhaps more applicable here than among any other wildflowers."

TEXAS FROG-FRUIT

Phyla incisa

Sawtooth frog-fruit, Spatulate-leaved frog-fruit,
Wedge-leaf frog-fruit, Fog-fruit, Capeweed

VERBENACEAE Vervain Family

SIZE
Plant: To 1 foot,
  usually creeping.
Flower: Tiny. In
  elevated, close-
  packed heads.

LEAVES
To 2 inches, opposite,
  toothed near tip.

BLOOMS
March – November

There seems to be no clear consensus on the origin of the name "frog-fruit."
Most books avoid the obvious question entirely, while a few call members of the
genus "fog-fruit." Because several species inhabit damp, sandy soils along river
banks and lake shores, one might assume the name comes from their proximity
to frogs.

Older books place members of the genus *Phyla* with others now classified
in the genus *Lippia* and use the latter name. In his 1988 revision of the Texas
checklist, Johnston considers *Phyla incisa* to be a form of the variable *P. nodiflora*; however, Hatch, Gandhi, and Brown (1990) still list it as a distinct species.
Incisa has two to four pairs of coarse teeth on the leaf margins, while *nodiflora*
has five or more pairs of smaller teeth. Most specimens we collected in Houston
seem to fit *incisa*.

Texas frog-fruit grows abundantly throughout the Houston area, in open fields and along roadsides and bayou banks, and blooms through much of the year. The creeping perennial stems are four-angled and often purplish, and they root at the nodes to form dense mats. Opposite, stalkless leaves are wedge-shaped at the base and broadest beyond the middle, with incised teeth near the tip.

Tiny white (occasionally pale lavender) flowers with yellow centers cluster in dense, globelike heads at the tips of erect stalks. The flower heads elongate into longer cylinders as the flowers open upward. A closer look at individual flower structure reveals the frog-fruit's relationship to the verbenas and lantanas, but the similarity is not obvious at a casual glance.

COPPER-LILY

Habranthus tubispathus

Atamasco lily, Stagger-grass

AMARYLLIDACEAE Amaryllis Family

SIZE
Plant: 6–12 inches.
Flower: 1 inch across,
  trumpet-shaped.

LEAVES
Narrow, firm,
  grasslike. Arising
  after blooms.

BLOOMS
After summer rains.

One of the loveliest of Houston wildflowers, the copper-lily occurs in moist, open places after heavy rains. An uncommon species, it is nevertheless hard to overlook when in bloom. Those we photographed were discovered along the banks of Braes Bayou between Fannin and Greenbriar by Houston naturalist Robert Honig. Several large colonies with scores of plants bloomed during early September, but other authors list the bloom period as occurring from August to October and from June to November. Clair Brown, in *Wildflowers of Louisiana*, indicates it blooms in April. Indeed, flowering probably depends more on rainfall than on the season of the year.

The copper-lily was formerly known as *Habranthus texanus*, and some older references list it as *Zephyranthes texanus*. The common name "atamasco lily" comes from an Indian word meaning "stained with red" and has also been applied to white-flowered species in the eastern states. "Stagger-grass" refers to the fact that most members of the amaryllis family are toxic to livestock.

The flowering stem of the copper-lily comes from a deep bulb about an inch in diameter and appears before the narrow, grasslike leaves. From six to twelve inches tall, it bears a single golden yellow, trumpet-shaped flower that may be tinged with red on the outer surface. Opening early in the morning, the flower closes in the afternoon.

Correll and Johnston list the copper-lily as a Texas endemic, occurring from East Texas west to the Edwards Plateau and southward along the coast to the Rio Grande plain. Brown, however, notes that it is abundant in some locations in Louisiana. The latter may be traceable to escapes from cultivation.

PRAIRIE PARSLEY

Polytaenia nuttallii

Wild dill, Prairie parsnip

APIACEAE Parsley Family

SIZE
*Plant: 2–3 feet. Stem
    stout, stiff, branched.
Flower: ⅛ inch, in
    compound umbels.*

LEAVES
*To 8 inches, twice- or
    thrice-divided.*

BLOOMS
April – June

One of the larger members of the parsley family, prairie parsley stands two to three feet tall in open fields across the Houston area. The stout, upright biennial occurs even along bayou banks and in vacant lots throughout the inner city. Solitary stems branch widely in the upper portions and carry large leaves that are divided into broad segments, each of which is again divided and further lobed. Greenish yellow flowers form compound umbels; they are grouped in small clusters that combine to form larger ball-like clusters.

Leaves and seeds of prairie parsley can be used in much the same way as those of cultivated dill, according to Tull. It is one of the chief food plants for the caterpillars of the lovely black swallowtail, a butterfly that also lays its eggs on garden dill, fennel, parsley, and others of the family.

The genus name combines the Greek *poly,* "many," with *tainia,* "ribbon," referring to the crowded oil tubes in the fruits. The species honors Thomas Nuttall (1786–1859). Born in England, Nuttall came to the U.S. in 1808 and later served as curator of the Botanical Gardens at Harvard. He collected widely in the West and had several birds, as well as plants, named after him. Audubon wrote of Nuttall: "the scientific world is deeply indebted for many additions to our zoological and botanical knowledge which have resulted from his labors." Succeeding to a substantial inheritance, Nuttall later returned to England, but he is said to be the model for the naturalist, Old Curious, in Richard Henry Dana's *Two Years before the Mast.*

CREEPING SPOT-FLOWER

Acmella oppositifolia var. *repens*

ASTERACEAE Sunflower Family

SIZE
Plant: Creeping stems
  20–40 inches,
  branching and
  rooting at the nodes.
Flower head: ¾ inch.
  Rays few, short;
  disk flowers forming
  elevated cone.

LEAVES
1–3 inches, opposite,
  stalked, toothed on
  margins.

BLOOMS
July – December

Older books classify creeping spot-flower as *Spilanthes americana* var. *repens,* or simply as *S. repens.* However, the name we use now appears in the new Texas checklists by Johnston and by Hatch, Gandhi, and Brown. Spot-flower inhabits moist ditches and ponds throughout the southeastern United States, from Florida to eastern Texas, and occurs throughout the Houston area, where it blooms in the summer and fall.

Trailing, creeping stems of this wetland perennial branch freely and root at the nodes. Plants also spread from the rhizomes, forming dense colonies in muddy soils or shallow water. Only the flowering branches stand erect above the sprawling mat. The stems are often purplish and bear opposite, lance-shaped leaves with sharply toothed margins. Flower heads average three-fourths inch in diameter and contain both ray flowers and disk flowers. The orange-yellow rays are pistillate but sterile, while the small yellow disk flowers are perfect. They are closely packed on a cone-shaped receptacle.

BUSHY SEA OX-EYE

Borrichia frutescens

Sea oxeye, Sea-ox-eye daisy, Sea daisy

ASTERACEAE Sunflower Family

SIZE
Plant: 2–3 feet. Tough, brittle shrub.
Flower head: To 1½ inches, solitary. Rays yellow; disk greenish to brownish yellow.

LEAVES
1–2½ inches, opposite, gray-green, thick.

BLOOMS
April – December

Bushy sea ox-eye ranges along the coast from Virginia to Texas and south through Mexico and the West Indies. It is one of the most abundant plants of the Texas coast, forming dense stands on bay beaches and along the edges of saline and brackish marshes. In the Houston area it is particularly common on the upper reaches of Galveston Bay and along the Houston ship channel, where it blooms sparingly throughout most of the year.

A shrubby perennial two to three feet tall, sea ox-eye has brittle stems and opposite leaves. The gray-green leaves are also thick and leathery, typical of many seaside plants. Solitary flower heads appear at the tips of the branching stems. Yellow ray flowers are shallowly three-toothed at the tip; disk flowers range from brownish yellow to greenish yellow.

The genus honors seventeenth-century Danish botanist Ole Borch, whose name was Latinized to Borrichius. *Frutescens* means "shrubby."

LAWNFLOWER

Calyptocarpus vialis

Prostrate lawnflower, Straggler daisy, Hierba del caballo

ASTERACEAE Sunflower Family

SIZE
Plant: Weak,
  sprawling stems to
  2 feet long.
Flower head: ¼ inch,
  few yellow rays and
  disk flowers.

LEAVES
1–2 inches, opposite.

BLOOMS
February – December

Lawnflower would be largely overlooked if it were not, as the name suggests, a troublesome lawn weed. Native to Mexico, Central America, and the West Indies, it seems to have spread northward to colonize the Gulf Coast from Florida to Texas. Rickett notes that in Mexico it grows in the streets of the towns and takes its name, *vialis*, from *via*, meaning "way" or "street." Lawnflower is the only species in its genus.

Although related to the sunflowers and other large, showy species, lawn-flower has tiny flower heads no more than a quarter-inch across. Each contains a few yellow ray flowers and three or four yellow disk flowers. The solitary heads are borne on weak, branching stems that sprawl on the ground. Ovate leaves reach one to two inches in length and have serrate margins; they occur in pairs along the stem.

Lawnflower occurs in yards and fields across the Houston area. A hardy plant, it blooms virtually throughout the year.

BULL THISTLE

Cirsium horridulum

Yellow thistle, Spiny thistle

ASTERACEAE Sunflower Family

SIZE
Plant: 1–5 feet, from
    winter basal rosette.
Flower head: To 3
    inches, rays absent.

LEAVES
8–24 inches, lobed and
    toothed, spiny.

BLOOMS
March – June

Cirsium horridulum is, indeed, horridly armed with vicious spines. An abundant plant throughout the Houston area, it grows as a winter annual, forming large rosettes in open fields and along the roadsides. It begins blooming in March and continues into May or June, the thick flower stalk gradually lengthening until it stands up to five feet tall. The large leaves are irregularly lobed and toothed, the points ending in long, sharp spines.

Flowers of the bull thistle, or yellow thistle, vary from creamy white to yellow, rosy pink, or deep purple. The purplish form, typical of other thistles, predominates in most areas—from Maine along the Atlantic and Gulf coastal plains to East Texas and the Texas coast. However, most of the plants in Houston appear to be of the yellow strain, blending slowly into the purple eastward toward the Gulf. In Baytown, for example, both are common, while the coastal areas around Galveston and High Island have mostly purple bull thistles.

Unlike many of the Asteraceae, thistles have no ray flowers. The numerous disk flowers form a large flower head up to three inches across, surrounded by leafy bracts. Ripened seeds drift with the wind on downy parachutes, freely sowing pastures and fields.

Tull suggests several ways to utilize the edible roots, stems, and leaves in salads and as vegetables, but most people find the spiny armament too much to overcome. Those with sensitive skin can also develop dermatitis from the spines and hairs. Ajilvsgi notes that thistles were associated with magic in the Old World and were considered sacred to Thor, the god of thunder.

PLAINS COREOPSIS

Coreopsis tinctoria

Golden wave, Golden coreopsis, Garden coreopsis,
Cardamine coreopsis, Tickseed, Manzanilla silvestre

ASTERACEAE Sunflower Family

SIZE
*Plant: To 4 feet,
    slender,
    much-branched.
Flower head: 1¼
    inches. Ray flowers
    yellow with red at
    base; disk flowers
    reddish.*

LEAVES
*2–4 inches, once- or
    twice-divided into
    narrow segments.*

BLOOMS
*February – December,
    mostly in spring.*

Plains coreopsis blooms sparingly throughout the year, from February until December. However, it stages its major display in May, when it blankets fields and roadsides and lines the bayou banks throughout the Houston area. One of our most beautiful wildflowers, it lives up to another common name, "golden wave," and proves popular as a garden flower throughout much of the country.

The slender, rather delicate annual usually stands one to two feet tall, although it may occasionally reach four feet. Opposite leaves are once- or twice-divided into many narrow segments on the lower portions of the branching stems. Upper leaves may be entire and threadlike. Numerous flower heads are solitary at the tips of the slender branches. The yellow rays have reddish brown spots at the base and are three-toothed at the tip. Disk flowers are also reddish brown.

A dozen species of coreopsis occur in Texas, and several range into the Houston area. They can be difficult to distinguish, but plains coreopsis can usually be identified by its dissected leaves, its two-toned rays, and the presence of two rows of leafy bracts below the flower heads, the outer bracts much shorter than the inner.

Native Americans used root tea from coreopsis as a treatment for diarrhea.

The plants also rank among the most versatile of natural dyes, producing a wide range of red and yellow hues. This utility as a dye led to the scientific name *tinctoria*. The genus name stems from the Greek words *koris*, "bedbug," and *opsis*, meaning "appearance." The achenes, or "seeds," of some species were thought to resemble bedbugs, complete with two tiny antennalike "horns." This fancied resemblance also gave rise to the common name "tickseed." In spite of being named for a bedbug, plains coreopsis provides a beautiful sight as it forms golden waves across the fields of eastern Texas in the spring.

CLASPING-LEAVED CONEFLOWER

Dracopis amplexicaulis

Clasping coneflower

ASTERACEAE Sunflower Family

SIZE
Plant: 1–3 feet,
*   sometimes taller.*
Flower head: To 2
*   inches. Rays yellow,*
*   sometimes with*
*   reddish bases; disk*
*   reddish brown.*

LEAVES
2–4 inches, thick, clasp
*   stem.*

BLOOMS
April – June

Formerly placed in the genus *Rudbeckia* with the black-eyed susan and other coneflowers, the clasping-leaved coneflower now stands alone in the genus *Dracopis*. It can easily be recognized by its stalkless leaves that clasp the stem, a feature reflected in its specific name constructed from the Latin *amplexus,* "embracing," and *caulis,* "stem."

A common wildflower in moist locations throughout the eastern two-thirds of Texas, clasping-leaved coneflower blooms from April until early June on bayou banks and in vacant lots in many parts of Houston. It sometimes forms large, showy colonies. The stems branch in their upper portions, usually reaching a height of one to three feet. Flower heads are borne at the tips of the branches.

The five to nine yellow, drooping ray flowers are often deep reddish at the base. They are sterile and produce no fruits. Brownish, fertile disk flowers cover the central cone, which elongates as it matures.

CAMPHOR DAISY

Haplopappus phyllocephalus

Golden beach daisy

ASTERACEAE Sunflower Family

SIZE
Plant: To 2 feet, branching, sticky to the touch.
Flower head: 1½ inches, rays and disk yellow.

LEAVES
To 1½ inches, saw-toothed, thick, sticky.

BLOOMS
March – December

The camphor daisy is classified as *Machaeranthera phyllocephala* by some botanists; *Haplopappus phyllocephalus* by others. Hatch, Gandhi, and Brown follow the latter taxonomy, and that name is used here. Generic lines are not always cleanly drawn in this complex family, and such taxonomic changes are not uncommon.

Whichever scientific name is used, the observer should have no problem in identifying the highly aromatic camphor daisy. An inhabitant of sandy, saline or brackish soils, it ranges along the coast and across southern Texas. Its yellow flower heads ornament the fringes of Galveston Bay. An upright or sprawling annual reaching two feet, camphor daisy frequently lives through the winter and blooms throughout much of the year.

The freely branching stems and thickened leaves exude a resin that makes the plants sticky to the touch. Leaves are alternate, stalkless, and sharply toothed, extending upward on the flowering stems to clasp the flower heads. Both ray flowers and disk flowers are yellow. The saw-toothed leaves around the flower heads make camphor daisy immediately recognizable.

BITTERWEED

Helenium amarum

Bitter sneezeweed

ASTERACEAE Sunflower Family

SIZE
Plant: 6–24 inches,
  branching in upper
  portion.
Flower head: To
  1 inch. 5–10 yellow
  rays, 3-lobed at tip.
  Disk flowers yellow.

LEAVES
1–3 inches, numerous,
  narrow and
  threadlike.

BLOOMS
April – December

Bitterweed blooms from April through December in the Houston area. The six- to twenty-four-inch annual lines busy roadways and fills vacant lots and fields with mounds of yellow flowers, adding greatly to the color of the city. Bitterweed grows well in disturbed soils and is an indicator of overgrazing in pastures, where it proves highly unpopular. Although cattle normally avoid the bitterly aromatic plant, even small amounts eaten with other feed can alter the taste of milk. Several reports cite poisonings of horses and sheep. The scientific name comes from the Latin *amarus,* meaning "bitter."

Stems of bitterweed are deeply grooved and branch freely, bearing large numbers of narrow, almost threadlike leaves. The one-inch flower heads bloom profusely at the tips of slender stalks. Yellow ray flowers are three-lobed at the tip and droop downward from a dome-shaped central disk of yellow disk flowers.

PURPLE-HEADED SNEEZEWEED

Helenium flexuosum

ASTERACEAE Sunflower Family

SIZE
Plant: 16–40 inches,
  branching, stems
  winged.
Flower head: 1 inch.
  Rays yellow, orange,
  or reddish,
  sometimes lacking.
  Disk purple,
  globular.

LEAVES
1–3 inches, narrow,
  alternate, base
  descending stem as
  wings.

BLOOMS
May – June, occasional
  in fall.

A tall perennial reaching sixteen to forty inches, purple-headed sneezeweed occurs less frequently in Houston than the related bitterweed, *Helenium amarum.* It blooms through May and June in moist, open fields and woodland edges and along roadways, reblooming occasionally in the fall. The globelike head of disk flowers is reddish brown or purple, while drooping yellow ray flowers are frequently suffused with red or purple. Sneezeweeds in Houston often have dark orange rays. These ray flowers are sterile, and occasional plants have very tiny rays or lack them completely. Solitary flower heads appear at the tips of long stalks, forming a canopy of blooms above the leafy stems.

Upper leaves are narrow, alternate, and stalkless; larger lower leaves generally wither before the plant comes into bloom. The bases of the leaves extend down the branching stems, forming wings that serve to identify purple-headed sneezeweed as surely as do the flower heads.

Like the better-known bitterweed, sneezeweed is toxic to livestock, although animals usually avoid its bitter foliage. The common name comes from historic medicinal use of the dried and powdered flower heads in treating colds and congestion. Used as snuff to clear nasal passages, it causes violent sneezing. The scientific name, *flexuosum,* means "tortuous" or "zig-zag," referring to the bending of the stem at each leaf node.

SWAMP SUNFLOWER

Helianthus angustifolius

Narrow-leaved sunflower, Ribbon sunflower

ASTERACEAE Sunflower Family

SIZE
Plant: 3–6 feet.
Flower head: 2 inches.
  Rays yellow, disk
  reddish purple.

LEAVES
4–6 inches long,
  to ½ inch wide.
  Usually alternate,
  firm, margins rolled
  underneath.

BLOOMS
August – November

Swamp sunflowers grow in moist environments throughout the Houston area. An eastern species that occurs westward from the Atlantic to the Texas Gulf Coast, *angustifolius* forms colonies that ornament fields and woodland edges with patches of gold during the autumn months. The scientific name means "narrow-leaved." The firm, dark green leaves seldom measure more than a half-inch in width and are rolled under along the edges, a feature that readily distinguishes the species from the more robust, wider-leaved Maximilian sunflower and from the widely branching, broad-leaved common sunflower.

Swamp sunflower reaches a total height of three to six feet and has slender, upright stems that branch in the upper portions. The flower heads measure about two inches across and are borne at the tips of the long stems. In partial shade, plants tend to become lanky and sprawl on the ground; in full sun, they remain erect. This is a hardy, attractive perennial that should occupy a place in native flower gardens, perhaps as a background planting against a sunny wall or fence.

COMMON SUNFLOWER

Helianthus annuus

Mirasol, Kansas sunflower

ASTERACEAE Sunflower Family

SIZE
Plant: Normally 4–6 feet, sometimes taller. Much-branched.
Flower head: To 5 inches. Yellow rays, dark red or purple disk.

LEAVES
To 12 inches long. Broad, tapering to tip, rough and bristly.

BLOOMS
February – December

One can hardly avoid seeing the common sunflower anywhere in Houston. Although it is an annual, the large, bushy plant normally grows four to six feet tall and may reach more than eight feet. It springs up in fields and vacant lots and thrives in the disturbed soil along local freeways during construction projects. Beginning in late February or early March, it blooms throughout the year, until killed by a winter freeze.

Flower heads range up to five inches in diameter, with twenty to twenty-five bright yellow rays enclosing a central disk of numerous red to deep purple disk flowers. The stem may be more than an inch thick, and the large triangular leaves taper to a point at the tip and are coarsely toothed along the margins. Hairy stems and leaves feel rough and bristly.

The most abundant and widespread *Helianthus* species in Texas, the common sunflower occurs across much of North America. Spanish conquerors found sunflowers fashioned of gold in Aztec temples, and numerous Indian tribes cultivated them for thousands of years to use as food, medicine, and fiber, breeding selected strains to produce larger seeds.

Introduced to Europe in the late 1500s, the common sunflower was popularized in Russia and later returned to the United States as a commercial seed and oil crop. Cultivated hybrids, with their straight, sturdy, unbranched stems and platter-sized flower heads, scarcely resemble their wild ancestors, but they represent the only major crop that originated within present U.S. boundaries.

Although the seeds of the native common sunflower are much smaller than commercial strains, they provide a valuable food resource for many birds and other wildlife.

MAXIMILIAN SUNFLOWER

Helianthus maximiliani

Michaelmas daisy

ASTERACEAE Sunflower Family

SIZE
*Plant: 3–10 feet tall,
   usually with
   unbranched stems.
Flower head: 3–5
   inches, rays and disk
   yellow.*

LEAVES
*2–10 inches long,
   slender, often folded
   lengthwise.*

BLOOMS
September – October

The Maximilian sunflower is one of the largest and showiest of Houston's wild-flowers. Most abundant on the Edwards Plateau in central Texas, it also occurs throughout the north-central and southeastern portions of the state. It thrives in vacant lots and open fields on the outskirts of the city. Unlike the branching, broad-leaved common sunflower, Maximilian sunflower usually has several simple, unbranched stems arising from the fleshy root. The flower heads are borne on short stalks and combine to form a spire of gold along the upper portion of the stem. A perennial, Maximilian sunflower makes an attractive, tall bank of flowers and deserves far more popularity in cultivation. It does best in full sun against a fence or other background.

The leaves average two to four inches in length, but may be as long as ten inches on the lower portions of the plant. Narrow, pointed, and slightly toothed along the edges, they usually fold lengthwise along the midrib.

As with most other *Helianthus* species, Maximilian sunflower proves a useful wildlife food. Deer browse on the plants, and birds flock to the nutritious seeds. The species takes its name from German Prince Maximilian Alexander Philip of Neuwied, a naturalist who explored in South America from 1813 to 1817 and in North America in the 1830s.

GOLDEN-ASTER

Heterotheca subaxillaris

Camphorweed, Camphor-plant, Broadleaf gum-plant

ASTERACEAE Sunflower Family

SIZE
Plant: 1–3 feet,
occasionally to
6 feet. Much-
branched, densely
hairy.
Flower head: ½–¾
inch, rays and disk
yellow.

LEAVES
1–2 inches, rough,
sticky, coarsely
toothed. Upper
leaves clasping stem.

BLOOMS
August – November

Many authors list the golden-aster as *Heterotheca latifolia;* however, several botanists now consider plants assigned that name to be a variety of *H. sub-axillaris.* The species is highly variable, and most people will not choose to differentiate between the Texas forms.

An upright or sprawling, branching annual with densely hairy stems and leaves, golden-aster normally grows one to three feet tall, but may reach six feet on rare occasions. Rough, coarsely toothed leaves have gland-tipped hairs that exude a sticky resin. When crushed, the leaves smell strongly of camphor. Lower leaves are stalked but usually drop early in the season; smaller upper leaves are stalkless and clasp the stem, one of the distinctive features of this species. Both ray flowers and disk flowers are yellow.

Golden-aster grows abundantly in fields and along roadsides throughout the Houston area, normally flowering in late summer and fall. It forms dense stands and is usually not grazed by livestock, so ranchers regard it as a pest. Ajilvsgi suggests, however, that it makes an attractive addition to the wildflower garden if cut low in late summer. It then blooms profusely in low mounds until frost. Plants may also take that form along mowed roadsides across our region.

PRAIRIE DAWN

Hymenoxys texana

Texas bitterweed

ASTERACEAE Sunflower Family

SIZE
Plant: 2–8 inches.
Flower head: ¼ inch.
  Rays minute, disk
  yellow.

LEAVES
Basal rosette spatulate,
  toothed. Stem leaves
  narrow, entire.

BLOOMS
March – April

Placed on the endangered species list on March 13, 1985, prairie dawn holds the dubious distinction of being the only federally endangered plant in Harris County. Correll and Johnston noted in 1979 that it was "rare in sandy soils near Hockley and Houston, Harris Co., probably extinct (no known collections after 1900)." However, this tiny wildflower has been rediscovered in several locations in Fort Bend and Harris counties and occurs within the city limits on the western edge of Houston. Some populations are threatened by development.

Formerly known as Texas bitterweed, *Hymenoxys texana* was renamed to avoid confusion with more common plants called bitterweeds that cause livestock poisonings and spoil the milk of cows eating the plants. The U.S. Fish and Wildlife Service held a contest among schoolchildren in 1989 to choose the new name. As a result, we have a plant found nowhere else in the world, "prairie dawn."

Only two to eight inches tall, prairie dawn grows in poorly drained depressions or at the base of tiny mounds, called "mima mounds," in barren areas on open grasslands. Basal leaves are spoon-shaped and may have toothed margins, while smaller alternate leaves on the branching stem are narrow and untoothed.

Flower heads no more than one-fourth inch in length hold numerous tiny yellow disk flowers. Pale ray flowers around the perimeter are reduced to minute scales largely hidden by the phyllaries, the green bracts surrounding the flower head.

Prairie dawn is now being propagated successfully from seed at Harris County's Mercer Arboretum and Botanic Gardens, one of twenty-one institutions presently working with the national Center for Plant Conservation. (The San Antonio Botanical Center is the other one in Texas.) Headquartered at the Missouri Botanical Garden in St. Louis, the CPC was founded in 1984. The organization hopes to conserve native plant species by maintaining collections of stored seeds and living plants within the participating institutions. CPC estimates place the number of U.S. plants at significant risk of extinction at 4,400 species, roughly one-fifth of our country's native flora. Eight hundred may vanish within the decade without human intervention.

Texas is home to 114 of those species, 83 of which are called "high priority" species, in danger of extinction within the next few years. With current preservation efforts, prairie dawn may well survive as a unique local plant.

WEEDY DWARF-DANDELION

Krigia cespitosa

Dwarf dandelion

ASTERACEAE Sunflower Family

SIZE
Plant: 2–8 inches,
  branching, smooth.
Flower head: To
  ⅜ inch. Yellow rays
  5-toothed at tip.

LEAVES
To 2 inches, opposite,
  entire or shallowly
  lobed, some leaves
  on stem.

BLOOMS
March – June

Five *Krigia* species occur in eastern Texas, at least four of them in the Houston area. Weedy dwarf-dandelion is probably the most abundant, but all are similar in appearance. They differ in small details of the flower heads and in the presence or absence of leaves on the flowering stems. This species has long been treated as *K. oppositifolia*; however, recent research on the nomenclature indicates that *K. cespitosa* claims scientific precedence. Hatch, Gandhi, and Brown use the latter name in their 1990 Texas checklist.

A low annual, weedy dwarf-dandelion grows two to eight inches tall with smooth, branching, leafy stems. The bluish green leaves are opposite and narrow, tapering gradually to the base. Most have entire margins; some are shallowly lobed. The small flower heads contain only orange-yellow ray flowers, each ray finely five-toothed across its square tip. They open only in the morning hours during sunny weather and are much visited by butterflies and bees.

While these tiny plants do not attract attention when alone, they frequently form large, showy colonies that blanket sandy fields or roadsides. The species name, *cespitosa*, means "growing in dense clumps." The genus honors David Krig, a German physician, who was one of the first to collect plants in Maryland.

MANYSTEM FALSE-DANDELION

Pyrrhopappus multicaulis

Texas dandelion, Pata de leon

ASTERACEAE Sunflower Family

SIZE
Plant: 8–20 inches.
Flower head: To 2
  inches. Rays in 2 or
  3 rows, disk flowers
  absent.

LEAVES
2–6 inches, alternate,
  stalked, mostly in
  basal rosette. Small
  upper leaves usually
  lobed.

BLOOMS
February – June. Some
  in all months.

Few Houston wildflowers ornament area roadsides and fields longer than does the false-dandelion. The peak blooming season of this colorful annual continues from February until June, and smaller numbers of the showy flower heads appear throughout the summer. After late-summer rains, another flash of blazing yellow brightens the landscape through the cool autumn months.

The stalks of manystem false-dandelion rise to as much as twenty inches above a basal rosette of lobed leaves. A few smaller, alternate leaves appear on the branching stems. Flower heads measure up to two inches in diameter and contain two or three rows of ray flowers; disk flowers are absent. Opening in the morning, the blooms close about noon.

Carolina false-dandelion, *Pyrrhopappus carolinianus*, also occurs commonly in Southeast Texas, but it appears to be less frequent in Houston than *multicaulis*. The two are very difficult to separate, but *carolinianus* usually has unlobed leaves on the upper portion of the stem. Neither should be confused with the alien common dandelion, *Taraxacum officinale*. While well known farther north, the latter occurs less frequently in Houston, usually as a weed in lawns. Flower heads of common dandelion are borne singly on short, leafless stems above a basal rosette of leaves, an arrangement quite different than the taller, branching stems of false-dandelion.

The genus name of the false-dandelions, *Pyrrhopappus*, comes from the Greek words *pyrrhos*, "red," and *pappos*, "old man." From the latter, botanists named the pappus, the bristles or scales that represent the sepals around each tiny individual floret of the composites. These later become the "parachutes" attached to the fruits and are reddish or rust-colored on some of the false-dandelions. *Multicaulis* refers to the "many stems" of this species.

MEXICAN HAT

Ratibida columnifera

Upright prairie coneflower, Columnar prairie coneflower,
Long-headed coneflower, Redspike Mexican hat, Thimbleflower

ASTERACEAE Sunflower Family

SIZE

Plant: To 3 feet.
  Much-branched.
Flower head: 1–2
  inches. Rays yellow
  and/or dark red,
  drooping; disk
  reddish brown,
  columnar.

LEAVES

2–4 inches, divided
  into fine segments.

BLOOMS

March – November

Most books list Mexican hat under the scientific name *Ratibida columnaris;* however, Hatch, Gandhi, and Brown classify it as *R. columnifera* in their 1990 *Checklist of the Vascular Plants of Texas.* Johnston, in his 1988 update of the *Manual of the Vascular Plants of Texas,* notes that many present-day botanists believe Nuttall's use of the latter predates Sims's use of *columnaris.* "They may be correct," says Johnston.

Whichever epithet endures, Mexican hat remains one of the most abundant and charming of Texas' roadside flowers. It forms vast colonies across open fields and in ditches, and it occurs in scattered locations throughout Houston. A perennial, it is becoming popular in wildflower gardens, and cut flowers last for several days. It blooms throughout much of the year, from March through November, but seems to be most abundant in Houston in late May and early June.

The much-branched stems reach three feet in height and bear flower heads singly at the tips of the slender branches. Leaves are deeply divided into narrow, lacy segments. Four to ten sterile ray flowers droop down from the elongated central cone and show a wide variety of color forms, often on adjacent plants. Some are entirely yellow, while others are deep reddish brown. Most abundant is a form in which the rays are reddish at the base and golden yellow at the tip. Brownish disk flowers open progressively upward on the long, pale green central cone as it matures.

BLACK-EYED SUSAN

Rudbeckia hirta

Brown-eyed susan

ASTERACEAE Sunflower Family

SIZE
Plant: 1–3 feet, often forming mounds or small colonies.
Flower head: 2 inches. Yellow rays, dark brown disk.

LEAVES
Alternate, mostly on lower stems. Entire or slightly toothed, hairy.

BLOOMS
April – November

A dark, chocolate-brown central disk gives the popular black-eyed susan its common name. The yellow ray flowers sometimes have reddish bases and droop slightly from the flattened, cone-shaped disk. Most other *Rudbeckia* species have a longer disk and pendent rays, resulting in the name "coneflowers." The genus honors Olaus Rudbeck, a seventeenth-century botany professor at the University of Upsala in Sweden. *Hirta* comes from the Latin *hirtus,* meaning "hairy," for the stems and leaves of the black-eyed susan bear coarse, bristly hairs.

Black-eyed susan blooms from April through November in open fields and along roadsides throughout the Houston area. Stems branch near the middle, and the two-inch flower heads are borne at the tips of the branches, forming a golden mound from one to three feet high.

An annual or short-lived perennial, black-eyed susan is easily grown and has become popular in wildflower gardens. It deserves every gardener's attention, and several hybrid cultivars are now available. Flowers last several days, even if cut and placed in water, and they provide colorful accents in any planting scheme. Geyata Ajilvsgi notes in *Wildflowers of Texas* that the plant produces greenish and yellowish colors when used as a natural dye, and the dried leaves and flowers yield a pleasant tea.

CUTLEAF GROUNDSEL

Senecio tampicanus

Butterweed, Squaw weed

ASTERACEAE Sunflower Family

SIZE
*Plant: To 1 foot,
  sometimes taller.
Flower head: ½–¾
  inch, in clusters,
  rays and disk
  yellow.*

LEAVES
*2–8 inches, deeply
  divided, rounded
  lobes.*

BLOOMS
March – May

Cutleaf groundsel belongs to one of the largest and most widely distributed of all plant genera, with some two thousand species throughout the world. Fifteen species occur in Texas, many of them in the western part of the state. Most are identified by the shape of their leaves. The genus name, *Senecio,* comes from the Latin *senex,* "old man," an allusion to the grayish white pappus that becomes the "parachutes" on the ripened seed head. The same could be said, of course, for many others in the family Asteraceae.

Cutleaf groundsel has long been known as *Senecio imparipinnatus;* however, the name has recently been changed to *S. tampicanus.* It is one of the earliest of the yellow flowers in the spring, beginning in mid-March and blooming until May. Leaves are deeply divided into rounded lobes, which are in turn toothed or lobed. Small flower heads contain both ray and disk flowers. Borne on the tips of slender branches, they combine to form a large, showy, flattened cluster.

S. tampicanus closely resembles *S. glabellus,* more frequently called "butter-weed." The latter is also common along Houston roadways, and it differs in having the terminal leaf lobe much larger than the lateral lobes. There are other small differences in structure, but the two species are not easy to separate. Correll and Johnston indicate there are frequent intergrades between them.

Most of the *Senecio* species contain toxic alkaloids and have been suspected in livestock poisonings. Human deaths have occurred from using the leaves in herbal teas. Ingestion results in liver disease, for which there is no known cure.

In spite of their toxicity, groundsels were highly prized by Native Americans to use in poultices for wounds and abscesses. Ancient Greek and Arabian physicians also discovered the healing properties of Old World species. Thus, these attractive wildflowers trace their common name to a less-than-elegant beginning. "Groundsel" has evolved through a series of changes from the Anglo-Saxon *grundeswelge,* meaning "pus-absorber."

SIMPSON ROSINWEED

Silphium gracile

Slender rosinweed

ASTERACEAE Sunflower Family

SIZE
*Plant: To 5 feet. Single
  or few stems from
  base, sparingly
  branched.
Flower head: 3 inches.
  Rays yellow, disk
  yellow.*

LEAVES
*To 6 inches,
  rough-hairy.*

BLOOMS
June – September

Texas authors have long applied the name *Silphium simpsonii* var. *wrightii* to the rosinweed found in the Houston area. However, Correll and Johnston note in *Manual of the Vascular Plants of Texas* that "this can be interpreted as a relatively unstable taxonomic segregate" and that it is "intermediate between *S. asperrimum* and *S. gracile* and grades into both." Hatch, Gandhi, and Brown, in their more recent (1990) *Checklist of the Vascular Plants of Texas*, combine Simpson rosinweed with slender rosinweed, *S. gracile,* and that taxonomy is followed here. Members of the genus hybridize frequently and can pose problems in identification.

Simpson rosinweed might be mistaken for one of the large sunflowers, but the sturdy stems that reach five feet are sparingly branched, and the disk flowers are yellow. Several rows of broad, leafy bracts surround the base of the flower head. Lower leaves are up to six inches long and coarsely toothed; upper leaves are smaller and entire. Coarse, bristly hairs cover the entire plant, making it rough to the touch.

Disk flowers of this genus are infertile, and the flat achenes, or "seeds," develop only from the petallike ray flowers, producing several rows surrounding the disk.

The rosinweeds take their name from the resinous sap exuded from the stems and leaves. The sap was used medicinally by Native Americans, and children of early settlers used it as chewing gum.

Simpson rosinweed grows in many locations around the perimeter of Houston. We also found it blooming throughout the summer along Old Katy Road west of Loop 610.

TALL GOLDENROD

Solidago canadensis

Common goldenrod, Canada goldenrod, Field goldenrod

ASTERACEAE Sunflower Family

SIZE
*Plant: 3–7 feet,
  forming large
  colonies.
Flower head: ⅛ inch.
  Rays and disk
  flowers yellow.*

LEAVES
*To 6 inches.
  Numerous,
  alternate, stalkless,
  toothed near tip.
  Usually 3 main
  veins.*

BLOOMS
*September –
  November*

Tall goldenrod forms large colonies from underground rhizomes, filling fields and roadsides throughout the Houston area with a blanket of gold from September into November. Formerly called *Solidago altissima,* the local variety has now been reclassified as *S. canadensis* var. *scabra.* The most common goldenrod in Houston, it belongs to a varied species that occurs from Florida to Texas and northward into southern Canada. More than one hundred species make up the genus, and nearly one-third of them occur in Texas, along with a number of named varieties. Identification can be very difficult, for many look much alike.

Tall goldenrod is a stiff, upright perennial reaching three to seven feet. The numerous stems form clumps and branch in their upper portions. Lance-shaped leaves measure up to six inches long and one-half to one inch wide. Alternate and numerous along the stem, they have three main veins and are usually coarsely toothed near the tip.

Individual flower heads measure no more than one-eighth inch, but they contain both ray flowers and disk flowers. These yellow heads are borne on short branches along the upper side of longer, arching branches, combining to form a large terminal cluster.

Solidago means "to make whole," alluding to the curative powers of the goldenrods. Various Native American tribes and the early settlers brewed teas from the plants to treat stomach ailments, fevers, and snakebite. The roots were used to treat burns, and chewing flowers was said to relieve sore throats. Excellent natural dyes can also be made from the flowers and foliage, producing a range of yellow, gold, and green colors.

The pollen of goldenrods does contribute to allergies in close quarters; however, the plants often take the blame for serious autumn hay fever caused by the less obvious giant ragweed. Goldenrods have heavy pollen and are not wind-pollinated; thus, their pollen is not as widely distributed as that of the ragweeds.

Tall goldenrod provides a major nectar source for autumn butterflies, bees, and other insects. Fields are filled with whirring wings around the arching, golden heads. Monarch butterflies rely heavily on the flowers during migration to their winter quarters in the forests of Mexico.

SEASIDE GOLDENROD

Solidago sempervirens

Seacoast goldenrod

ASTERACEAE Sunflower Family

SIZE
Plant: 2–6 feet.
Flower head: ¼ inch.
  Rays and disk
  flowers yellow.
  Often in slender
  spikes.

LEAVES
Thick and succulent.
  Basal leaves to 6
  inches, long-stalked;
  stem leaves smaller,
  narrow, clasping.

BLOOMS
September –
  November

Seaside goldenrod is the only *Solidago* species to thrive in saline marshes and on the dunes along Texas beaches. However, it also inhabits moist ditches and fields farther inland and appears throughout most of the Houston area. Once listed as *S. mexicana*, seaside goldenrod is now classified as *S. sempervirens,* with several varieties occurring from Newfoundland southward along the Atlantic and Gulf coasts. Correll and Johnston list all plants in Texas as variety *mexicana,* but Hatch, Gandhi, and Brown attribute both that variety and the nominate variety *sempervirens* to our area of the state.

Seaside goldenrod grows to a height of six feet, but many of the local populations reach no more than two feet. The erect stems are usually solitary and un-branched, terminating in slender yellow spikes. Individual quarter-inch flower heads contain both ray flowers and disk flowers and are borne in one-sided clusters. Smooth-margined basal leaves attain a length of at least six inches and taper into long, slender stalks, sometimes appearing almost grasslike. Narrow upper leaves are much smaller and clasp the stem. The leaves are thick and succulent, quite unlike those of most other goldenrods. In addition to a single prominent midrib, they are covered by a characteristic lacy network of small veins.

Because of its shorter stature and less invasive nature, as compared with the more abundant tall goldenrod, seaside goldenrod makes a good addition to the native wildflower garden, especially one planted to attract autumn butterflies. The nectar-rich flowers bloom from September through November.

PRICKLY SOW-THISTLE

Sonchus asper

Spiny-leaved sow-thistle, Achicoria dulce

ASTERACEAE Sunflower Family

SIZE
*Plant: 1–6 feet,
  branching in upper
  portion.*
*Flower head: To
  1 inch. Dandelion-
  like, contains only
  ray flowers.*

LEAVES
*2–8 inches, lobed,
  spiny. Rounded
  basal lobes clasp
  stem.*

BLOOMS
Most months

"The sow-thistles are as unbeautiful as their name: disagreeable and trouble-some weeds," says Harold Rickett, in his multivolume *Wild Flowers of the United States: Texas.* Introduced from Europe, alien sow-thistles have invaded most of the United States and occur throughout Texas. Dispersed by the breeze on silky-parachuted seeds, the annuals spring up everywhere in disturbed soil and bloom throughout most of the year. A nuisance in croplands, lawns, and gardens, they even grow from sidewalk cracks in downtown Houston.

The flowering stalk of prickly sow-thistle rises from an early basal rosette of leaves and may reach six feet, although it is usually much shorter. Leaves measure two to eight inches, with lobed margins tipped with sharp spines. On the middle and upper portions of the plant, the leaves clasp the stem with large, rounded lobes, or "ears." Flower heads are borne on short stalks, mostly at the top of the plant. Lacking disk flowers, sow-thistles have one-inch heads of numerous ray flowers, much like those of the dandelions.

Common or smooth sow-thistle, *Sonchus oleraceus,* occurs less frequently in Houston. It resembles *asper,* but the spiny, clasping "ears" of the upper leaves are sharply angular, rather than round.

In spite of their bitter, milky sap, sow-thistles have been fed to livestock, including ducks and geese, for centuries in Europe. The less than elegant name comes from the plant's reported appeal to pigs. Tull also reports that either *Sonchus* species "provides a reasonable, though bitter, potherb." However, she suggests using the young basal leaves in winter and early spring, for she notes that after buds form, the plants become too bitter to eat.

COMMON DANDELION

Taraxacum officinale

ASTERACEAE Sunflower Family

SIZE
Plant: Low-growing.
Flower head: 1–2
*   inches. Solitary on*
*   hollow, leafless*
*   stem. Yellow ray*
*   flowers only.*

LEAVES
2–10 inches, margins
*   lobed. Basal rosette*
*   only.*

BLOOMS
Almost all year in
*   Texas.*

Originally native to Eurasia, the common dandelion has naturalized across much of North America. It prefers disturbed soil and has become a persistent weed in lawns and pastures in the northern and eastern parts of the country. However, the common dandelion is far less abundant in Houston than the taller manystem false-dandelion, *Pyrrhopappus multicaulis.*

While the false-dandelion has branching stems bearing small leaves, common dandelion produces only a basal rosette of leaves from its deep taproot, and its flower heads are solitary on hollow, leafless stalks. The two- to ten-inch leaves are normally wider at the tip than at the base and have numerous lobes along the margins. "Dandelion" comes from the French *dent de lion,* "tooth of the lion," a name apparently derived from the leaf shape.

The parachuted fruits of the dandelion are as familiar as the yellow flowers. The numerous stalked achenes, or "seeds," have white, feathery bristles that form a rounded head when mature and then disperse on the wings of the wind. What small child can resist picking such a fruiting head and blowing on it to send the parachutes aloft? This practice has earned the dandelion the name "blowballs" in some areas of the Southeast.

The dandelion's scientific name, *officinale,* stems from its medicinal uses. First mentioned in the writings of Arab physicians in the early Middle Ages, it then appeared as a useful medicinal plant in the herbals of Europe. Indeed, common dandelion occupied a place in the *U.S. Pharmacopoeia* from 1831 to 1926 and in the *National Formulary* until 1965. It was used for liver, gallbladder, kidney, and bladder ailments; however, some people suffer contact dermatitis from the milky latex sap.

For centuries Europeans have also considered the dandelion a tasty edible. Young spring leaves make a vitamin-rich potherb if boiled in several changes of water to remove the bitter juices, and the roasted taproot serves as a substitute for coffee. Many have enjoyed golden dandelion wine, made by fermenting the flower heads.

Thus, while some homeowners have cursed the common dandelion, others have sung its praises as a food and medicine. A "weed" is only a wildflower that grows where it is not welcome.

GREEN-THREAD

Thelesperma filifolium

Divided green-thread, Fine-leaved thelesperma

ASTERACEAE Sunflower Family

SIZE
*Plant: 8–20 inches,
  occasionally taller.
Flower head: 1½
  inches. On slender,
  leafless stalks. 8
  yellow rays; disk
  purple-brown.*

LEAVES
*1–4 inches, finely
  divided into
  threadlike segments.*

BLOOMS
February – December

An annual or short-lived perennial, green-thread occurs in scattered locations throughout the Houston area, preferring sandy soils in fields and along roadsides. It blooms sporadically through much of the year. The opposite leaves are one- to three-times divided into narrow, threadlike segments, giving rise to the name "green-thread" and to the epithet *filifolium*, which means "thread-leaved." The genus takes its name from the Greek words for "nipple" and "seed," referring to projections on the achenes of some species.

Stems of green-thread often branch at the base and again in the upper portions, forming dense clumps topped by flower heads borne on slender, delicate stalks. There are usually eight yellow ray flowers that begin to droop soon after opening. Each ray is three-lobed at the tip. Disk flowers are purplish brown.

FRINGED PUCCOON

Lithospermum incisum

Narrow-leaved puccoon, Narrow-leaf yellow gromwell

BORAGINACEAE Forget-me-not Family

SIZE
Plant: 8–12 inches, hairy.
Flower: 1½ inches long, trumpet-shaped, with fringed lobes.

LEAVES
To 4 inches, narrow, with rolled edges. Stem leaves smaller.

BLOOMS
Usually March – April, occasional in winter.

This attractive perennial grows sparingly in fields and along roadsides across the Houston area. It blooms primarily in March and April, but some plants may bear flowers even during the winter months. Although several puccoon species occur in Texas, *Lithospermum incisum* is distinctive in having the lobes of the flower incised, or fringed, and often ruffled. Strangely, many of these large blossoms are sterile. In late spring and early summer the plants bear "cleistogamous" flowers that are tiny and never open. These, however, are fertile.

The hairy stems rise from a cluster of narrow basal leaves, the edges of which roll under. Stem leaves are smaller but become more profuse as the plant grows and the basal leaves wither. The trumpet-shaped flowers attain a length of one and one-half inches and form a compact terminal spike.

Lithospermum means "stone-seed" in Greek, referring to the hard, stony fruits. According to Bare, "puccoon" is an Omaha-Ponca Indian name for the plants. The roots of fringed puccoon were used by the Indians and settlers to produce a red dye, and a number of early medicinal applications have also been documented. Recently, the root was investigated as a possible source of new drugs. Many of the early folk medicines had their origins in fact. Cultures around the world frequently use plants of the same genus or family for identical purposes, giving credence to claims made for them, however unscientific those claims may seem.

WILD MUSKMELON

Cucumis melo var. *dudaim*

Dudaim melon, Smell melon

CUCURBITACEAE Gourd Family

SIZE
*Plant: Coarse, trailing
   stems to several feet.
Flower: 1 inch,
   5-lobed.*

LEAVES
*2–5 inches, rough,
   margins finely
   toothed.*

BLOOMS
April – December

This little melon is apparently a native variety of the muskmelon, or canta-loupe, which was imported from Asia for cultivation. It ranges across much of coastal, southern, and central Texas and occurs in scattered locations through-out the Houston area. It blooms from spring until fall, and the yellow fruits are conspicuous among the sprawling, trailing vines.

Angular stems bear alternate leaves that are broadly rounded or kidney-shaped. Both stems and leaves are covered with bristly hairs and feel rough to the touch. One-inch yellow flowers and simple tendrils grow from the leaf axils. Fruits range up to three inches in length and two inches in diameter. Bright yellow with brown marbling when mature, they have an extremely strong, musky odor.

MELONETTE

Melothria pendula

Drooping melonette, Green melonette,
Creeping cucumber, meloncito

CUCURBITACEAE Gourd Family

SIZE
Plant: Slender,
  climbing vine.
Flower: ⅓ inch,
  5-lobed.

LEAVES
1–2 inches, sometimes
  larger. Broadly
  5-angled.

BLOOMS
April – November

A slender, delicate vine from a perennial root, melonette climbs over shrubs and fences along streams and marshes and in damp thickets. We found it to be fairly common east of Houston in the floodplains of the San Jacinto and Trinity rivers. One- to two-inch leaves are broadly five-angled or lobed, and the small yellow flowers arise from the leaf axils. Male and female flowers are separate but on the same vine. The former occur in small clusters; the latter are usually single, with the ovary below the corolla.

Fruits seldom measure more than one inch in length and one-half inch in diameter, but they droop on slender stalks. Green with whitish spots, they slowly turn black with time. The fruits are not edible, and Tull notes they have been responsible for accidental poisonings. *Melothria* is a classical name for a wild vine; *pendula* means "drooping."

JOINT-VETCH

Aeschynomene indica

FABACEAE Pea Family

SIZE
Plant: To 8 feet,
 much-branched.
Flower: ⅓ inch,
 creamy yellow with
 reddish veins.

LEAVES
2–4 inches, pinnately
 compound, many
 small leaflets.

BLOOMS
Most frequent August
 – September,
 occasional May –
 December.

Joint-vetch grows as a weak-stemmed, widely branching perennial up to eight feet tall, dying back to the underground portion of the stem in winter. An uncommon plant in eastern Texas, it inhabits the shallow water or mud of ditches and marshes. We found it blooming in August and September around the upper portions of Galveston Bay, particularly in the Trinity River floodplain.

Alternate, compound leaves are divided into nineteen to seventy-five or more tiny leaflets that get progressively smaller toward the tip. They are odd-pinnate, with a single leaflet at the tip producing an odd number when added to the alternating leaflets along the stalk. Small pealike flowers have an erect banner petal and smaller pairs of wing and keel petals. Borne in small clusters in the leaf axils, the flowers are creamy yellow with reddish veins. Flattened two-inch seed pods are constricted and jointed between the seeds, fragmenting into separate one-seed sections when mature.

PLAINS WILD INDIGO

Baptisia bracteata

Whitestem wild indigo, Creamy wild indigo, Nodding indigo, Large-bracted wild indigo, Plains false indigo

FABACEAE Pea Family

SIZE
*Plant: 12–30 inches,
  forming bushy
  mound.
Flower: ¾ inch, in
  long horizontal or
  drooping clusters,
  interspersed with
  leafy bracts.*

LEAVES
*3 leaflets, with 2 leafy
  stipules at base.*

BLOOMS
March – May

Texas' plains wild indigo has long been classified as *Baptisia leucophaea* by botanists. However, many now consider it merely a variety of *B. bracteata*, a similar species from the southeastern states. Hatch, Gandhi, and Brown have combined the two under the latter name, and we follow that taxonomy here.

A perennial from a tough, woody root, plains wild indigo branches to form low, bushy mounds in fields and open places throughout much of the Houston area, blooming from March into May. The leaf has three spatulate leaflets from one to four inches long, but two broad, leaflike stipules where the leaf stalk joins the stem make it appear to have five leaflets. A leafy bract also subtends each of the flowers in the long raceme, or flower cluster.

The flowers are pale creamy yellow, and the clusters curve downward or extend horizontally from near the base of the plant. The appearance is quite different from the following species, *B. sphaerocarpa*, which has upright racemes of bright yellow flowers. The ripe fruits are hard, inflated pods about two inches long.

Plains wild indigo would make an attractive addition to the wildflower garden, but after the blooming season the entire plant turns gray or black. It eventually breaks off at the ground to blow away as a tumbleweed.

GREEN WILD INDIGO

Baptisia sphaerocarpa

Bush-pea, Wild indigo, Yellow wisteria,
Upright wild indigo, Round-fruited baptisia

FABACEAE Pea Family

SIZE
Plant: To 3 feet, bushy.
Flower: To 1 inch,
  bright yellow, in
  upright spikes.

LEAVES
Dark bluish green, 3
  leaflets, upper stem
  leaves often with 1
  or 2 leaflets.

BLOOMS
April – May

Green wild indigo is a tough, bushy perennial forming mounds up to three feet high. Leaves are a dark bluish green and have three leaflets. They lack the broad, leafy stipules of the previous species, *Baptisia bracteata*. Leaves on the upper stem are often reduced to only one or two leaflets. Large flowers up to one inch in length are bright yellow and form long, slender, upright racemes that extend above the foliage. These glowing spires appear quite different from the drooping racemes of paler creamy flowers displayed by *bracteata*.

The fruits of green wild indigo are woody, globelike pods, giving rise to the name *sphaerocarpa*, which means "spherical-fruited." The genus name comes from the Greek *baptisis*, "a dipping," as in the dyeing process. Roots of several of the *Baptisia* species have been used to produce blue dyes, but the commercial indigo dyes came originally from plants of a different genus, *Indigofera*.

Native Americans used wild indigo roots, seeds, and leaves for a number of medicinal applications; however, the plants contain toxic alkaloids. All parts of the plants should be considered poisonous.

White false indigo, *Baptisia alba*, also occurs on the upper Texas coast. Formerly called *B. leucantha*, it has upright spikes of pure white flowers. Although abundant along the coast near Winnie and High Island, where it blooms beside its yellow counterpart, it does not seem to appear with any regularity near Houston.

PARTRIDGE PEA

Chamaecrista fasciculata

Prairie senna, Showy senna, Bee-flower

FABACEAE Pea Family

SIZE
*Plant: 1–4 feet, slender
or branched.
Flower: To 1½ inch,
5 unequal petals.*

LEAVES
*Pinnately compound,
8–15 pairs of small
leaflets.*

BLOOMS
June – November

Botanists have long classified the partridge pea as *Cassia fasciculata;* however, members of that genus have recently been divided between the genera *Chamae-crista* and *Senna.* The showy partridge pea is now listed in the former by Johnston and by Hatch, Gandhi, and Brown. At least four varieties occur in various parts of Texas.

A smooth, upright annual, partridge pea blooms in Houston from June into November. The slender stems are usually unbranched in dense stands but branch readily when not crowded, reaching a height of one to four feet. This attractive legume prefers open, sunny locations and grows abundantly in fields and vacant lots and along roadsides and bayous throughout the Houston area.

The asymmetric, five-petalled flowers have smaller upper petals and a large, broad lower one. The former have red spots at the base. There are ten stamens, varying from yellow to deep purple, and the pistil curves to the side oppo-site those stamens. Flowers grow in small clusters in the leaf axils but mature sequentially, so that only one in each cluster is open at a time. They wilt by midday.

Pinnately compound leaves have eight to fifteen pairs of small leaflets that are slightly sensitive, closing partially to touch and at night.

A poor nectar producer, partridge pea attracts bees that collect pollen, and it depends on them for pollination. Nectar is produced, however, in small glands at the bases of the leaves and is taken by ants, wasps, and flies. Steady streams of ants visit these nectar glands and may provide some protection for the plant by attacking other creatures that eat the leaves. Several species of yellow sulfur butterflies lay eggs on the partridge pea, and their caterpillars consume the foliage.

Flat, narrow seed pods from two to three inches long open with explosive force on warm, dry days, expelling shiny black seeds that provide an important food for several species of birds. Like many other legumes, partridge pea also contributes nitrogen to the soil.

BLACK MEDIC

Medicago lupulina

Black medick, Black bur-clover, Nonesuch

FABACEAE Pea Family

SIZE
*Plant: Stems to 2 feet,
    forming creeping
    mats.*
*Flower: Tiny, 10–50 in
    ¼-inch rounded
    clusters.*

LEAVES
*3 leaflets, long-stalked,
    cloverlike.*

BLOOMS
March – December

An alien from Europe, the cloverlike black medic is now widespread throughout most of North America. It occurs abundantly as a weed in Houston lawns and along roadsides and bayous. A low, creeping annual, it forms dense mats and has some value as a cattle and wildlife food in pastures. The best-known member of the genus is the purple-flowered alfalfa, *Medicago sativa*, which is widely planted as a fodder crop. Black medic and other local members of the genus all have yellow flowers.

Leaves are divided into three leaflets, each finely toothed on the margins. Ten to fifty tiny flowers grow in a dense, cylindrical cluster no more than a quarter of an inch long. They are quickly replaced by small black, coiled seed pods with prominent veins. These characteristic fruits have no prickles, a feature that distinguishes *Medicago lupulina* from the following species, *M. polymorpha*.

Lupulina means "little hops," an apparent reference to the clusters of tiny fruits that resemble those of hops. According to a reference in Prior's *Popular Names of British Plants*, as quoted by Bare, "This is the species recognized in Ireland as the true shamrock."

BUR-CLOVER

Medicago polymorpha

FABACEAE Pea Family

SIZE
*Plant: Stems to 20
  inches, sprawling,
  mat-forming.
Flower: Tiny, in
  clusters of 3 to 5.
  Forming spiny,
  spiral fruits.*

LEAVES
*3 leaflets, cloverlike,
  with long-toothed
  stipules at base of
  leaf stalks.*

BLOOMS
February – June

Like the previous species, black medic, bur-clover occurs as a common weed in Houston lawns and along bayou banks and roadways. It differs, however, in several easily recognizable details. The three leaflets are more prominently toothed on the margins, and large, leafy stipules at the base of the leaf stalks are strongly fringed with long teeth. Small flower heads usually contain only three to five yellow flowers, rather than the ten or more displayed by black medic. The resulting fruits form spiny spirals, giving rise to the name "bur-clover."

The genus *Medicago* contains many species native to Europe, Asia, and northern Africa. All of the Texas species were introduced, and many have spread widely across North America. In general, they provide useful fodder crops, but they can be invasive weeds in lawns and gardens.

The genus name comes from the Greek *medike*, used by Dioscorides for a plant that was introduced to Greece from Media, an ancient country in what is now Iran. Authorities differ on the identity of that original plant. Some call it a "grass," others suggest it was a kind of clover, or perhaps alfalfa. Its namesakes have traveled widely to colonize most of the world.

Bur-clover's specific name, *polymorpha*, means "many forms." The one found in Houston and throughout Texas is variety *vulgaris*. Some authors have erroneously called it *M. hispida*.

ANNUAL YELLOW SWEET-CLOVER

Melilotus indicus

Sour clover, Indian clover, Alfalfilla

FABACEAE Pea Family

SIZE
Plant: 12–20 inches.
Flower: ⅒ inch,
  pealike, in slender
  spike.

LEAVES
3 narrow leaflets,
  finely toothed on
  margins.

BLOOMS
March – October, most
  common in spring.

This yellow-flowered legume grows abundantly along Houston roadways and bayous and in vacant lots, blooming mainly in the spring but continuing sparingly into fall. An annual reaching twelve to twenty inches, it closely resembles yellow sweet-clover, *Melilotus officinalis*. The latter, however, stands up to five feet tall and has larger blossoms on the flowering spikes. Individual flowers of *M. indicus* measure little more than one-tenth of an inch. Both are Eurasian plants that have been widely introduced, but the taller yellow sweet-clover remains much less common in East Texas and along the coast.

Originally native to the Mediterranean area, annual yellow sweet-clover, or sour clover, produces tiny pealike flowers in slender spikes two to three inches long. Leaves have three rather fleshy leaflets that are slightly toothed along the margins. A fragrant plant with the scent of new-mown hay, it has been widely planted as a honeybee plant and hay crop and to enrich the soil.

TROPICAL NEPTUNIA

Neptunia pubescens

Prairie neptunia, Sand neptunia

FABACEAE Pea Family

SIZE
*Plant: To 20 inches,
 creeping, prostrate.
Flower: Minute, 20–30
 flowers in ½-inch
 cluster.*

LEAVES
*Twice divided, many
 tiny leaflets.*

BLOOMS
April – November

A prostrate perennial with creeping stems, tropical neptunia grows in vacant lots and fields and along bayou banks and roadsides throughout the Houston area. The leaves are doubly compound; a leaf divides into three or four pairs of segments, and each segment divides again into fifteen to thirty-five pairs of tiny leaflets fringed with minute hairs. The sensitive leaves close at night and fold quickly when touched.

Half-inch flower heads appear on short stalks above the foliage, each round head containing twenty to thirty flowers. The five petals and five sepals are scarcely visible on individual flowers, for ten long stamens protrude far out of each corolla. It is these collective stamens that produce the round yellow head. At the base of the cluster, however, are flowers with wider, petaloid stamens. The unusual yellow structures lack anthers and are sterile.

A related species, *Neptunia lutea*, is also found in our area. Called yellow neptunia, or yellow puff, it differs from *N. pubescens* in having no flowers with petaloid stamens at the base of the cluster. There are thirty to sixty flowers in each head, and all the stamens are alike. Each leaf segment of yellow neptunia contains only eight to eighteen pairs of leaflets.

Although *N. lutea* is the species usually covered in wildflower books, we found *N. pubescens* to be far more common within the city. The yellow flower heads of tropical neptunia occur from spring until fall, producing clusters of flat seed pods.

RATTLEBUSH

Sesbania drummondii

Rattle bean, Poison bean, Siene bean,
Drummond rattlebox, Coffee bean

FABACEAE Pea Family

SIZE
Plant: To 10 feet,
* perennial from*
* woody base.*
Flower: ½ inch, in
* elongated hanging*
* clusters.*

LEAVES
Once-divided, 20–50
* leaflets.*

BLOOMS
May – October

The perennial rattlebush branches widely and grows to ten feet from a woody base, dying back in winter and sprouting early in the spring. It prefers wet ditches and fields, as well as the margins of ponds and streams, and grows abundantly throughout the Houston area. It flowers from May into October.

Half-inch yellow or orange-yellow flowers have the typical pea-flower shape and bloom in elongated, pendant clusters from the axils of the leaves. Alternate and compound, the four- to eight-inch leaves divide once into twenty to fifty leaflets.

Large four-sided, four-winged pods contain several seeds that rattle when mature and dry. Deaths among cattle, sheep, and goats have occurred from various *Sesbania* species, and Tull documents at least one child fatality from eating the seeds of rattlebush. Reportedly, the seeds were used as a substitute for coffee during the Civil War, leading to the popular name "coffee bean." That use, however, seems highly suspect because of the known toxic nature of the plant. Toxicity might be reduced by boiling, but experiments seem ill-advised. While most poisonings occur from the seeds, all parts of the plant should be considered potentially poisonous.

The genus *Sesbania* takes its name from *sesban,* an ancient Arabic name for a related plant. *Drummondii* honors English botanist Thomas Drummond, who collected in Texas in 1833–34. According to Vines, Drummond collected extensively near Galveston, where rattlebush is particularly common.

WILD COWPEA

Vigna luteola

Deer pea

FABACEAE Pea Family

SIZE
Plant: Trailing,
  twining stems to 10
  feet.
Flower: To 1 inch, in
  small clusters.

LEAVES
3 leaflets, each 1–3
  inches long.

BLOOMS
April – November,
  most common in
  fall.

Wild cowpea belongs to a tropical and subtropical genus found around the world. It is a close relative of the cultivated cowpea—also called black-eyed-pea and cream-pea—which was introduced from the Old World as a food plant. The latter species, *Vigna unguiculata*, usually has purplish flowers and produces a much larger seed pod.

Wild cowpea has yellow flowers in sparse clusters on long stalks. The "standard," the wide upper petal, measures nearly an inch across. Leaves are trifoliate, with three lance-shaped leaflets from one to three inches long. The densely hairy stems trail and twine over other vegetation, sometimes forming mats in wet fields and along the edges of marshes and ponds. *V. luteola* reportedly blooms from April through November, but we found it most common in early autumn, particularly east of Houston along Galveston Bay.

The genus *Vigna* honors Dominico Vigna, a seventeenth-century botany professor at Pisa in Italy. *Luteola* simply means "yellowish."

SOUTHERN CORYDALIS

Corydalis micrantha

Scrambled eggs

FUMARIACEAE Fumitory Family

SIZE
*Plant: To 1 foot,
  occasionally taller.
Flower: ¾ inch, several
  in slender spike.*

LEAVES
*Alternate, finely
  dissected.*

BLOOMS
February – April

This pretty, delicate wildflower belongs to a family that contains such longtime garden favorites as bleeding-heart and Dutchman's-breeches. Some authors call the Fumariaceae the bleeding-heart family. Older references placed all of these strangely shaped wildflowers in the poppy family, the Papaveraceae.

Southern corydalis is a winter annual that appears sparingly in Houston as a "weed" in gardens and disturbed soil. It blooms early in the spring, and Ajilvsgi describes it covering large areas in fall-plowed fields "with an almost solid sheet of yellow. . . ." Three varieties occur in eastern Texas, and other species range into the central and western portions of the state.

Normally about twelve inches tall, southern corydalis has alternate leaves divided into five to seven segments, each segment then divided twice more. The yellow flowers have four petals, the outer two wrapping around the inner two. The upper petal extends backward into a long, rounded spur. Several flowers are interspersed with leafy bracts on a slender spike.

The genus *Corydalis* takes its name from an old Greek word for the European crested lark. The long spur of a European species was thought to resemble the hind claw of the bird, an analogy that also gave us the "larkspurs" of an entirely different family. *Micrantha* means "small-flowered."

Roots of Asian *Corydalis* species have been used in several medicinal applications, and Chinese studies show that alkaloids obtained from the genus act as muscle relaxants and painkillers. The plants are potentially toxic, however, and should be admired only for their delicate beauty.

YELLOW BLUE-EYED GRASS

Sisyrinchium exile

Small-flowered blue-eyed grass, Fairy stars

IRIDACEAE Iris Family

SIZE
Plant: 2–7 inches.
Flower: ¼ inch. 6
  yellow tepals, with
  red-brown central
  ring.

LEAVES
Slender, grasslike.

BLOOMS
April – May

This tiny wildflower stands only two to seven inches tall in Houston lawns and vacant lots, blooming mainly in April and May. When abundant, it presents a charming scene, living up to the fanciful name "fairy stars." Much smaller than most members of the genus, it is yellowish rather than the customary blue, with a reddish brown ring in the center of the flower. The short stem has narrow, flattened wings, and the leaves are grasslike. Three sepals and three petals look alike and are called "tepals."

Sisyrinchium was the name of an unidentified plant mentioned by Pliny in the first century. It now serves as the genus name for several species of blue-eyed grass that hybridize readily and can be extremely difficult to separate. According to Correll and Johnston, *S. exile* hybridizes with another small species, *S. rosulatum*, in our area. Yellow blue-eyed grass is considered a native of South America, but it occurs in the U.S. from Florida to southeastern Texas.

SPOTTED BEEBALM

Monarda punctata

Horsemint, Spotted horsemint, Yellow horsemint, Dotted monarda, Spotted wild-bergamont, Perennial sandy-land sage, Painted mint

LAMIACEAE Mint Family

SIZE
*Plant: 1–3 feet,
  branching,
  clump-forming.
Flower: To 1 inch, in
  several whorls
  around the stem.*

LEAVES
*1–4 inches, opposite,
  lancelike, shallowly
  toothed.*

BLOOMS
April – August

Because spotted beebalm prefers dry, sandy soils, it occurs less frequently in Houston than the widespread lemon beebalm, *Monarda citriodora*. However, its attractive flowers and unusual form make it worth the search. A hairy-stemmed perennial that branches in the upper portions, it often forms clumps one to three feet tall and blooms from April into early August. Spotted beebalm is a highly variable species, with nine varieties listed for Texas. They differ in minor floral details and in the length and position of the hairs on the leaves.

The yellow, inch-long flower is spotted with purple. Tubular and two-lipped, it has a gaping mouth with two stamens arching downward from below the narrow upper lip. Several flowers combine in a whorl, and there are two to seven whorls in a flowering spike, each subtended by a set of conspicuous leafy bracts. The bracts are usually yellowish or creamy with a purple tinge. Lance-shaped leaves up to four inches long have toothed margins and taper into short stalks. These leaves are paired on opposite sides of the square stem typical of the mints.

The genus was named for Nicholas Monardes, a sixteenth-century Spanish physician and botanist who took special interest in the plants of the New World. Several Native American tribes used leaf tea from spotted beebalm for colds, fevers, stomach cramps, and coughs. A highly aromatic herb with the scent of thyme, the species is a source of the antiseptic drug thymol, an ingredient of cough syrups. When the commercial thyme fields in Europe were destroyed during World War I, spotted beebalm was grown in the United States as a substitute. Thymol is now made synthetically, and spotted beebalm has reverted to its original use as a nectar plant for butterflies and other insects.

BERLANDIER'S FLAX

Linum berlandieri

LINACEAE Flax Family

SIZE
Plant: 6–12 inches,
  branching in upper
  portions.
Flower: ¾ to 1¼
  inches, reddish
  center.

LEAVES
1 inch, narrow,
  alternate, stalkless.

BLOOMS
March – September

Abundant in fields and vacant lots throughout the Houston area, Berlandier's flax has long traveled under the name "stiff-stem flax," *Linum rigidum* var. *berlandieri*, one of four Texas varieties in that species. Recent work, however, indicates that it deserves species status of its own, and Hatch, Gandhi, and Brown classify it as *L. berlandieri* var. *berlandieri* in their 1990 *Checklist of the Vascular Plants of Texas.* The variety is distinctive in having a brick-red center to the yellow or dull orange flower.

The stiff, wiry stems reach six to twelve inches and branch freely in their upper portions. Small, slender leaves are alternate, stalkless, and stiff. Delicate, five-petalled flowers normally span three-quarters to slightly more than an inch and are borne in open clusters at the tips of the branches.

Linum is the Latin name for flax. An Old World species, *L. usitatissimum*, was cultivated in Mesopotamia more than four thousand years ago and may date back even farther. Besides serving a number of early medicinal uses, it yielded cloth, thread, and oil. Linen and linseed oil come from commercial flax, as their names indicate.

CAROLINA JESSAMINE

Gelsemium sempervirens

Yellow jessamine, Yellow jasmine, Poor-man's rope,
Evening trumpet-flower, Carolina wild woodbine,
Jamin amarillo, Madreselva

LOGANIACEAE Logania Family

SIZE
Plant: Sprawling,
  high-climbing
  woody vine.
Flower: To 1½ inches,
  funnel-shaped,
  5-lobed.

LEAVES
To 3 inches, opposite,
  on short stalks.

BLOOMS
February – April

Spring is at least on the way when the Carolina jessamine begins to bloom. Beginning in February, or even in January during warm winters, the bright yellow trumpets ornament woodland edges and thickets throughout the Houston area, particularly north and east of the city. The high-climbing, perennial vines with slender, wiry stems cover fencerows and clamber over shrubs, blanketing them with evergreen foliage. Carolina jessamine may reach the tops of tall pines or form dense mats as it trails across the ground. It is frequently planted as an ornamental vine.

Leaves are opposite and up to three inches long, tapering to the tip. Waxy yellow flowers appear in small clusters from the leaf axils. One to one and one-half inches long, the flowers are funnel-shaped with five flaring lobes. The genus name, according to Vines, comes from the Italian name for jessamine, *gelsomino. Sempervirens* means "ever-green." In spite of its common names, Carolina jessamine is not related to other cultivated plants called jessamine or jasmine; most of those are members of the olive and nightshade families.

All parts of the plant contain toxic alkaloids. Adult poisonings occurred early in the century when the roots of Carolina jessamine were used in medicinal preparations for deadening pain and reducing spasms. The root was also used as a folk remedy for cancer. Foster and Duke report child deaths from eating a single flower, and other poisonings have resulted when children sucked nectar from the fragrant flowers. Honey produced from the nectar may also be toxic. Because Carolina jessamine is common throughout eastern Texas and because it is widely planted as an ornamental vine, children should be cautioned about its toxic character.

ARROWLEAF SIDA

Sida rhombifolia

Axocatzin

MALVACEAE Mallow Family

SIZE
*Plant: 2–4 feet, woody
in lower portions.
Flower: ¾ inch. 5
asymmetric petals.*

LEAVES
*1–3 inches,
diamond-shaped,
toothed.*

BLOOMS
Throughout the year.

Arrowleaf sida grows abundantly throughout the Houston area, inhabiting fields and fencerows and springing up even in backyard flower gardens. An erect to sprawling, shrubby annual or perennial, it reaches two to four feet and blooms almost throughout the year. Somewhat woody stems bear alternate, short-stalked leaves one to three inches long and about half as wide. Dark green above, they are paler below, with short, grayish hairs. The sharply toothed leaves are wedge-shaped at the base and broadest in the middle, giving them a diamond shape that accounts for both the common name and the scientific epithet *rhombifolia*.

Only about three-fourths of an inch across, the flowers are not showy, but they possess a delicate beauty. Creamy to orange-yellow, they may be reddish in the center. Each of the five overlapping petals is strangely asymmetric, with a long lobe on one side at the base. Stamens unite in a short column, betraying the sida's relationship with the hibiscus and other mallows.

ANGLE-STEM WATER-PRIMROSE

Ludwigia leptocarpa

Angle-stem ludwigia

ONAGRACEAE Evening-primrose Family

SIZE
*Plant: To 6 feet, freely
 branched.
Flower: ¾ inch, 5–6
 petals and sepals.*

LEAVES
*To 7 inches, lancelike,
 usually hairs on
 veins.*

BLOOMS
August – October

The genus *Ludwigia* contains approximately eighty species that occupy wet, open habitats throughout the tropical and warm temperate regions of the world. The largest variety occurs in North and South America. Texas hosts fourteen different species, most of them in the eastern portion of the state. Classification often depends on the number of stamens and sepals and on small details of the seed capsules. One group has the same number of stamens and sepals; another has twice as many stamens in two rings.

The genus was named in honor of Christian Ludwig, an eighteenth-century professor of medicine at Leipzig, Germany. Ludwig was also a botanical explorer, collector, and writer. Common names used for many of the similar species include water-primrose, primrose-willow, and seedbox.

Angle-stem water-primrose, *Ludwigia leptocarpa*, grows in water-filled ditches and along the edges of marshes and ponds. We found it in the eastern portion of the Houston area, along the upper reaches of Galveston Bay. A tall, freely branching plant with angular stems, it blooms from August through October. Flowers are more numerous and smaller than those of the more common shrubby water-primrose, *L. octovalvis*. The leaves are lancelike, from one to seven inches long, with dense hairs along the leaf veins and on the branches.

Most references state that *L. leptocarpa* has five sepals and five petals and note parenthetically, "rarely six." However, we found many of the plants in our area consistently to have six of each, as shown in the accompanying photograph. There are twice as many stamens. The slender, elongated seed capsules curve gently upward, tipped by the residual triangular sepals.

SHRUBBY WATER-PRIMROSE

Ludwigia octovalvis

Narrow-leaved water-primrose, Primrose-willow

ONAGRACEAE Evening-primrose Family

SIZE
Plant: To 4 feet,
  branching.
Flower: 1–1½ inches, 4
  petals and sepals.

LEAVES
1–6 inches, narrow.

BLOOMS
July – October

Shrubby water-primrose appears to be the most abundant and widely distributed *Ludwigia* species in the Houston area. It inhabits wet ditches and the edges of marshes and ponds, sometimes reaching a height of four feet from a branching base. Because of its watery habitats, it easily endures midsummer heat and drought, blooming from July through October. *L. octovalvis* ranges across the southern half of Texas and throughout the warmer regions of the world.

Flowers are larger than those of the previous species, *L. leptocarpa,* averaging one to one and one-half inches across. Solitary on stalks from the leaf axils, they have four sepals and petals and eight stamens, the latter arranged in two series around the raised central disk. The resulting thin-walled, slender seed capsules are cylindrical and from one to two inches long, topped by the residual sepals. Leaves one to six inches in length are short-stalked and narrowly lance-shaped.

URUGUAY WATER-PRIMROSE

Ludwigia uruguayensis

Hairy water-primrose

ONAGRACEAE Evening-primrose Family

SIZE
Plant: 3 feet, erect
* stems above floating*
* or sprawling*
* vegetation.*
Flower: 1½–2 inches, 5
* or 6 petals and*
* sepals.*

LEAVES
1-4 inches, alternate,
* slender, hairs on*
* veins beneath.*

BLOOMS
June – September

A tropical species, Uruguay water-primrose ranges from the southeastern states to the Texas coast and southward through Central and South America to Argentina. It grows as an aquatic perennial in water-filled ditches and ponds, particularly east of Houston near Galveston Bay. The sprawling, floating stems root at the nodes in the muddy bottom and send up erect, hairy flowering stems to a height of three feet.

Alternate, slender leaves are sharp-pointed and up to four inches long. The flowers appear on solitary stalks from the axils of the upper leaves. Larger and brighter yellow than the flowers of the preceding common species, *Ludwigia octovalvis*, they normally have five petals and five sepals. Occasional flowers with six petals and sepals are found, and the accompanying photograph shows one flower with five, another with six. Each has twice that number of stamens. Tough, woody seed capsules are covered with downy hairs and reach one-half to one inch in length.

CUT-LEAVED EVENING-PRIMROSE

Oenothera laciniata

Downy evening-primrose, Sinuate-leaved evening-primrose,
Cutleaf evening primrose

ONAGRACEAE Evening-primrose Family

SIZE
Plant: 4–18 inches,
  erect or sprawling.
Flower: ½–1 inch.
  4 petals.

LEAVES
1–2 inches. Deeply
  lobed, toothed, or
  merely wavy-
  margined.

BLOOMS
March – November,
  most common in
  spring and fall.

The pink-flowered showy evening-primrose, *Oenothera speciosa,* is by far the
most abundant of the *Oenothera* species in Houston. However, nearly three
dozen evening-primroses occur in Texas, many of them bearing yellow flowers.
O. laciniata is perhaps the most common of the local yellow species, growing in
sandy soils and disturbed ground throughout the area. The downy plants range
from four to eighteen inches tall and have small flowers no more than an inch
across. They bloom sporadically through most of the year, but seem to prefer
the cooler spring and autumn months.

The four-petalled, pale yellow flowers open in the evening and wither the
next morning in the sunshine, turning pink as they age. They are borne singly
in the leaf axils, and plants seldom have more than one or two flowers open
at a time. Leaf shape varies dramatically, from deeply lobed (the meaning of
laciniata) to merely toothed or wavy-margined.

Many of the evening-primroses are locally called "buttercups"; however,
that name more properly applies to members of the genus *Ranunculus* in an entirely different family. Buttercups have five waxy yellow petals, while evening-
primroses always have four petals and vary in color from yellow to white or
pink.

Yellow Wood-Sorrel

Oxalis dillenii

Dillen's oxalis

OXALIDACEAE Wood-sorrel Family

SIZE
*Plant: To 15 inches,
  usually lower,
  mound-forming.
Flower: ½ inch,
  5 petals.*

LEAVES
*Long-stalked, 3 leaflets,
  cloverlike.*

BLOOMS
February – November

Yellow wood-sorrel grows abundantly throughout the Houston area in many different habitats. However, it is most often noticed as a weed in lawns and gardens. A perennial that may reach fifteen inches in height, but is usually much shorter, it branches at the base, creeping to form small mounds. The cloverlike leaves are long-stalked and have three leaflets that fold downward at night and during cloudy or cool weather.

Wood-sorrel blooms virtually throughout the year, particularly in the spring and fall. Five-petalled yellow flowers grow in small clusters on long stalks above the foliage. They open only on warm, sunny days and hang downward when closed. The long seed capsules are held upright.

The genus name comes from the Greek word for "sharp" and refers to the sour taste caused by crystals of oxalic acid. People who enjoy wild foods like to toss *Oxalis* leaves in green salads, but this must be done in moderation. Too much oxalic acid can cause stomach problems, and the plants can be toxic even to livestock when consumed in large quantities.

The species honors Johann Jakob Dillen (1684–1747), a German-born botany professor at Oxford.

YELLOW PASSION-FLOWER

Passiflora lutea

PASSIFLORACEAE Passion-flower Family

SIZE
Plant: Trailing or
climbing stems to 10
feet.
Flower: 1 inch,
greenish yellow.

LEAVES
To 4 inches, wider than
long, broadly
3-lobed.

BLOOMS
May – September

The yellow passion-flower is a miniature edition of the better-known purple passion-flower, or "maypop," *Passiflora incarnata.* A slender perennial vine, it trails on the ground or climbs by means of coiled tendrils from the leaf axils. Although seldom noticed, it grows in moist, shady woods and thickets from Pennsylvania to Kansas and south to Florida and Texas. Common in the Houston area, it frequently springs up uninvited in yards and gardens. *P. lutea* makes a delightful addition to a sheltered corner, blooming almost continuously from May until September.

Greenish yellow flowers measure no more than an inch across. The five petals and five sepals are hidden beneath the threadlike filaments of the unique corona, the "crown of thorns" in the analogy to Christ's passion. Five stamens unite at the base to form a column around the three-styled pistil. Borne singly or in pairs on long, slender stalks, the flowers give rise to purplish black fruits one-half inch long.

Leaves of the yellow passion-flower are thin and pale green or bluish green. Wider than they are long, they have three blunt lobes.

COMMON PURSLANE

Portulaca oleracea

Pusley, Pussley, Verdolaga

PORTULACACEAE Purslane Family

SIZE
Plant: To 12 inches,
  prostrate, branching
  stems.
Flower: ¼ inch,
  usually 5-petalled.

LEAVES
To 1 inch, succulent,
  spatulate.

BLOOMS
May – November

Common purslane is a succulent plant with much-branched, sprawling stems, sometimes with a reddish hue. The fleshy, spatulate leaves are scattered along the foot-long stems and cluster at the growing tips. Small, five-petalled yellow flowers bloom singly in the leaf clusters, opening in the morning sun and closing within a few hours. An alien that has become established widely in North America, purslane can be a troublesome weed in gardens, its broken stems rooting quickly to produce new plants. In Houston it springs up occasionally even in vacant lots surrounded by towering downtown office buildings.

An extremely nutritious edible plant, common purslane has been cultivated for at least two thousand years in India and for centuries in Europe. Leaves and stems are pickled, used raw in salads, or cooked with other greens. The tart taste, however, comes from large quantities of oxalic acid, and consuming too much can lead to poisoning. Europeans also made poultices of purslane for sores and inflammation, and settlers in America used poultices and teas for a number of medicinal applications.

CAROLINA BUTTERCUP

Ranunculus carolinianus

RANUNCULACEAE Buttercup Family

SIZE
*Plant: 10–20 inches,
trailing.*
*Flower: ½–1 inch.
5 petals.*

LEAVES
*Cleft into 3 leaflets,
each lobed or cleft
further.*

BLOOMS
February – April

About fifteen species and several additional varieties of buttercups occur in the state, many of them in East Texas and along the coast. Identification rests on the detailed use of scientific keys, and the casual wildflower observer may be content to simply call the plants "buttercups." This species, for example, is listed as *Ranunculus hispidus* var. *nitidans* by Hatch, Gandhi, and Brown in their 1990 *Checklist of the Vascular Plants of Texas.* Other books retain its former name, *carolinianus.*

A perennial that grows from thick, fibrous roots, Carolina buttercup produces trailing branches that root at the nodes. Basal leaves have long stalks and are deeply cleft into three leaflets, each of which is further lobed or cleft. This leaf shape, typical of several species, gives the buttercups their alternate name, "crowfoot." Stem leaves remain smaller but have a similar shape.

Flowers are borne at the tips of the stems and have five shiny yellow petals. The waxy, buttery patina comes from a specialized layer of cells just beneath the surface and makes members of the genus easy to recognize.

Early buttercup, *Ranunculus fascicularis,* is similar to *R. carolinianus,* but the abundant hairs on the stem are appressed rather than pointing outward.

The genus name is the diminutive of the Latin *rana,* meaning "frog." Several of these floral "little frogs" inhabit marshes, stream beds, and moist woodlands where amphibians also abound. Buttercups bloom primarily in the spring.

Yellow-Flowered Mecardonia

Mecardonia vandellioides

Prostrate mecardonia, Prostrate water hyssop,
Stalked water hyssop

SCROPHULARIACEAE Snapdragon Family

SIZE
*Plant: To 16 inches,
    usually smaller.
Flower: ¼–½ inch,
    2-lipped, 5 lobes.*

LEAVES
*½–1 inch, sessile,
    sharply toothed
    toward tip.*

BLOOMS
March – November

Mecardonia, or water hyssop, is one of the delightful discoveries one makes when carefully examining wet ditches and the edges of ponds and marshes for the smaller flora so often overlooked. The perennial plants stand erect or sprawl, often rooting at the lower nodes to form colonies in moist habitats throughout the Houston area. A white-flowered species, *Mecardonia acuminata*, occurs more sparingly in eastern Texas.

Yellow-flowered mecardonia has small, opposite, stalkless leaves in pairs on the four-angled stem. Only one-half to one inch long, the leaves are oval or spatulate and sharply toothed outward from the middle. Solitary flowers are borne on long, slender stalks arising from the axils of the upper leaves, each stalk with two leaflike bracts at its base. Pale yellow with purple veins, the flowers are two-lipped. The upper lip has two united lobes that are bearded at the base; the lower has three lobes that spread more widely.

Members of a largely tropical group centered in South America, mecardonias have been placed in the genus *Bacopa* by some authors.

CUT-LEAF GROUND-CHERRY

Physalis angulata

Southwest ground-cherry, Lanceleaf ground-cherry,
Purple-vein ground-cherry, Husk-tomato

SOLANACEAE Nightshade Family

SIZE
Plant: To 3 feet, much-
  branched,
  smooth.
Flower: ½ inch,
  bell-shaped.

LEAVES
To 4 inches on long
  stalk, irregularly
  toothed.

BLOOMS
May – October

Several varieties of *Physalis angulata* have been named, the complex ranging across most of Texas. Cut-leaf ground-cherry occurs as a common weed throughout Houston, springing up in gardens and vacant lots and along the roadsides. The smooth, angular stems are usually without the hairs that characterize many other *Physalis* species and branch freely to produce low, herbaceous bushes up to three feet tall. Most plants, however, will be considerably smaller.

The alternate leaves have long stalks and blades up to four inches long, the margins usually deeply and irregularly toothed. Half-inch, bell-shaped flowers grow singly on long, slender stalks from the leaf axils or in stem forks. Pale yellow, they lack the dark spots in the center displayed by other species. The corolla is shallowly five-lobed, and the five stamens have bluish anthers.

The fruit of the ground-cherry is a round berry contained within the inflated calyx. Although small during the flowering season, the calyx, the combined sepals, extends and inflates into a large "bag" to contain the fruit. The genus name, *Physalis*, comes from the Greek *physa*, meaning "bladder." That of *P. angulata* is ten-ribbed and more than an inch long.

Hybrid ground-cherries are widely cultivated for fruits that are popular in preserves. Another imported species, called Chinese lantern, has a red husk and is grown as an ornamental for use in dried arrangements. Ripe berries of most of the ground-cherries are apparently edible, but many are mealy and tasteless. Such sampling is ill-advised, however, for the green berries and the leaves are dangerously poisonous. Fatalities among children who ate unripe berries have been documented. Such a phenomenon is not unusual among members of the nightshade family. Many produce edible ripe fruits but have poisonous foliage and green fruits.

BEACH GROUND-CHERRY

Physalis cinerascens

Starry-hair ground-cherry, Seaside ground-cherry

SOLANACEAE Nightshade Family

SIZE
*Plant: To 3 feet, stems
   sprawling and
   trailing, covered
   with star-shaped
   hairs.*
*Flower: ½–¾ inch,
   widely bell-shaped,
   yellow with purple
   spots in center.*

LEAVES
*1–3 inches, oval,
   margins wavy.*

BLOOMS
March – November

In spite of its common name, beach ground-cherry ranges across the entire state. Plants deserving of the name belong to the variety *spathulifolia,* which grows in sandy soils along the Gulf Coast. Variety *cinerascens* inhabits more loamy soils inland through Texas. The former, with longer leaves and larger flowers, seems to occur more abundantly east of Houston along Galveston Bay. The latter is widely distributed throughout our area. Both were formerly placed in the species *Physalis viscosa* and will be found under that name in older books.

"Starry-hair ground-cherry" might be a more appropriate name, since *P. cinerascens* is characterized by a dense covering of minute branching, star-shaped hairs. Sprawling, trailing stems reach a length of three feet and bear one- to three-inch leaves with wavy margins. Long-stalked flowers grow from the leaf axils, giving rise to the husk-covered fruits typical of all the ground-cherries. The yellow, bell-shaped flowers open widely and have purple spots at the bases of the five fused petal lobes.

The genus *Physalis*—a name derived from the Greek *physa,* meaning "bladder"—contains about a hundred species, most in North and South America. Texas hosts sixteen species and many more named varieties, some of which can be difficult to identify. All, however, can be recognized as ground-cherries by the flower form and by the distinctive fruits.

FALSE-MINT

Dicliptera brachiata

ACANTHACEAE Acanthus Family

SIZE
Plant: 1–2 feet, erect
or sprawling. Thin,
angular stems.
Flower: ¾ inch,
2-lipped.

LEAVES
To 4 inches, opposite,
with long petioles.

BLOOMS
July – October

Less than an inch long, the lovely pink to purple flowers of false-mint are easily overlooked in the moist, shady river bottoms and along the woodland edges where they are fairly common from July through October. The erect or sprawling perennial plants grow one to two feet tall and have thin, angled stems that are often hexagonal in cross section. They branch widely, and the species name *brachiata* means "branched at right angles."

The opposite leaves taper gradually into long petioles and have thin blades relished by many species of insects. Flowers are deeply two-lipped, both lips narrow and usually unlobed. Two stamens project from the mouth of the corolla. Flowers occur singly or in small clusters from the leaf axils, the clusters subtended by two to four pairs of leafy bracts. The genus, which contains about 150 tropical and subtropical species around the world, takes its name from the Greek *diclis*, "double folding," and *pteron*, "wing," referring to the appearance of the bracts.

SEA-PURSLANE

Sesuvium portulacastrum

Prostrate sea-purslane, Shore purslane, Cenicilla

AIZOACEAE Carpetweed Family

SIZE
*Plant: Creeping stems
to 6 feet, rooting at
nodes.*
*Flower: To 1 inch. 5
sepals, petals absent.*

LEAVES
*1–2 inches, opposite,
fleshy, succulent.*

BLOOMS
March – December

Sea-purslane thrives on saline, sandy soils and occurs along portions of Galveston Bay and on the coastal beaches. A creeping perennial that roots at the nodes, it frequently forms mats several feet in diameter and blooms throughout most of the year. Fleshy, succulent leaves appear in pairs on the brittle stems and may turn yellow or reddish with age.

Flowers are borne singly on short stalks from the leaf axils and have no petals. The five sepals are greenish on the outer surface, a rich rose or lavender on the inner surface. Stamens are numerous. The resulting seed capsule opens by means of a conical lid to expose the shiny black seeds.

According to Wagner, Herbst, and Sohmer, the genus *Sesuvium* takes its name from the land of the Sesuvii, a Gallic tribe. *Portulacastrum* refers to the similarity to members of the related genus *Portulaca*.

American Basket-Flower

Centaurea americana

Basket flower, Star-thistle, American knapweed,
Powderpuff thistle, Thornless thistle,
Shaving brush, Sweet sultan, Cardo del valle

ASTERACEAE Sunflower Family

SIZE
Plant: 3–6 feet,
  branched in upper
  portion.
Flower head: 2–3
  inches. Disk flowers
  only.

LEAVES
2–3 inches, slender,
  alternate, stalkless.

BLOOMS
May – August

This plant of many names is one of Houston's most handsome wildflowers. A southwestern species that ranges across much of Texas, it occurs in open fields and along woodland edges, blooming from May to August. Frequently cultivated, it occupies a large, mainly Old World genus with such garden favorites as cornflower and bachelor's-button. Although the flower heads vaguely resemble those of the thistles, the stem and foliage are not armed with spines.

Basket-flower normally stands three to six feet tall and forms dense colonies covered with three-inch flower heads ranging in color from pink or rose to darker lavender. The thick, upright, leafy stems are ridged and branch in their upper portions. Lancelike leaves are alternate and stalkless. The huge flower heads contain only disk flowers. Outer florets are much longer and darker than the center ones, their long lobes giving a fringed appearance. A cup of prickly bracts that looks like a finely woven basket surrounds the flower head.

The genus was named after the centaurs of Greek legend. According to Durant, the philosopher Theophrastus, writing a history of plants in about 288 B.C., attributed great healing powers to one of the European species. It supposedly healed the wounds of Chiron, the centaur who had been felled by the poisoned arrows of Hercules. Durant notes, however, that no medicinal uses of *Centaurea* are known, and Theophrastus probably meant to give credit to a plant of the gentian family.

INDIAN BLANKET

Gaillardia pulchella

Firewheel, Blanket flower, Showy gaillardia, Rose-ring gaillardia

ASTERACEAE Sunflower Family

SIZE
Plant: 1–2 feet high,
branched at the base
and sometimes
sprawling.
Flower head: 1–2½
inches.

LEAVES
Smooth-edged to lobed,
hairy, 1–3 inches
long.

BLOOMS
February – December

Indian blanket is a common annual that often covers large areas in fields and vacant lots. Its hardy nature and attractive red-and-yellow flowers make it a popular garden plant as well, and seed packets are readily available. It blooms almost throughout the year in Houston, with the showiest display in late spring.

As with all members of the sunflower family, what appears to be a single blossom is actually a head of many tiny ones. The petallike ray flowers are usually red with yellow, three-lobed tips. The red or deep purple center contains many tiny, tubular disk flowers. Each is a perfect, self-contained blossom with all the reproductive parts, but the entire flower head functions as a unit in attracting pollinators.

The genus honors Gaillard de Marentonneau, an eighteenth-century French botanist. *Pulchella* comes from the Latin diminutive of *pulcher*, meaning "beautiful."

ROSE PALAFOXIA

Palafoxia rosea

ASTERACEAE Sunflower Family

SIZE
*Plant: 1–2 feet, widely
   branched. Slender,
   wiry stems covered
   with short hairs.*
*Flower head: 1 inch,
   with 12–25 disk
   flowers only.*

LEAVES
*To 3 inches, narrow,
   alternate.*

BLOOMS
June – November

At least seven species and several named varieties of palafoxias occur in Texas. A few have conspicuous ray flowers, but most lack the rays and have only disk flowers. The latter species can be difficult to identify without resorting to the technical manuals and keys; however, *Palafoxia rosea* is the species most frequently encountered in the immediate Houston area, where it prefers sandy soils in fields and along woodland edges.

Rose palafoxia has thin, wiry stems and slender branches that reach one to two feet. The leaves are narrow and alternate. They, like the stems and branches, are covered with short hairs. Flower heads measure about one inch across and contain from twelve to twenty-five disk flowers, each with five widely spreading lobes. The pink to deep rose heads occur on short stalks to form loose terminal clusters during late summer and fall.

The genus *Palafoxia* is limited primarily to the southwestern states and Mexico. Bare notes that it takes its name from Jose de Palafox y Melzi (1780–1847), a noted Spanish general and defender against the armies of Napoleon. Wagner, Herbst, and Sohmer, however, state that the origin is not clear. They suggest the genus might also have been named for Juan de Palafox y Mendoza (1600–1659), a renowned prelate.

Rose palafoxia and its close relatives produce ample quantities of nectar and pollen and are visited by numerous insects, especially beetles and butterflies. Easily grown from fall-sown seed, according to Ajilvsgi, they deserve attention as massed plantings in wildflower gardens.

PURPLE PLUCHEA

Pluchea odorata

Marsh-fleabane, Salt-marsh fleabane, Canela

ASTERACEAE Sunflower Family

SIZE
*Plant: 1–3 feet. Stiff,
 hairy annual.
Flower head: ¼ inch,
 in flat-topped
 clusters. Tubular
 disk flowers only.*

LEAVES
*2–6 inches, alternate,
 margins usually
 toothed.*

BLOOMS
*May – December.
 Most abundant in
 July – September.*

Purple pluchea, or marsh-fleabane, appears under the scientific name *Pluchea purpurascens* in most books currently in use. However, Hatch, Gandhi, and Brown now assign it to *P. odorata*. Although many publications list its habitat as the saline and brackish marshes of the southern states, it occurs in wet soils across virtually all of Texas.

Three closely related species—*P. camphorata, P. foetida,* and *P. rosea*—also occur within our area; however, *P. odorata* is the most abundant. The species differ in minor details of leaf shape and attachment and in the color of the flower heads, *odorata* having the deepest purple color. The scientific names of the various species and such common names as "camphorweed" and "stinking pluchea" reflect the aromatic foliage. Medicinal uses have been documented. Ajilvsgi also notes that the leaves of purple pluchea are used in Mexico for herbal tea. The genus honors Noel Pluche (1688–1761), a French naturalist.

A stiff, upright annual, purple pluchea reaches three feet and branches in the upper portions of the stem. Leaves vary in length from two to six inches and are alternate and short-stalked. Leaf margins usually are shallowly toothed. Small flower heads up to one-quarter inch high have no ray flowers but contain sev-

eral series of tubular disk flowers, the outer ones lacking stamens. The crowded, short-stalked clusters form large, flat-topped terminal masses as they mature, adding patches of bright color to the green of marsh edges and creek banks in summer and fall. The massed flower heads are frequently used in dried flower arrangements.

The fragrant flowers attract numerous bees and butterflies and perform well in cultivation. Like many of our native plants, purple pluchea makes a useful addition to the summer garden.

TEXAS IRONWEED

Vernonia texana

ASTERACEAE Sunflower Family

SIZE
*Plant: 1–3 feet,
   slender, slightly
   branched.*
*Flower head: ½ inch,
   in loose terminal
   clusters. About 20
   disk flowers; ray
   flowers absent.*

LEAVES
*2–5 inches, reduced
   above. Alternate,
   sessile, narrow,
   sparsely haired
   beneath.*

BLOOMS
*June – October.
   Mainly July –
   August.*

An erect, slender perennial, Texas ironweed grows one to three feet tall with unbranched or sparsely branching stems. The narrow, linear leaves range from two to five inches long on the lower stem but are much smaller toward the top. Roughly hairy on the upper surface, the leaves are usually pitted on the under surface and have sparse hairs along the veins. Margins are mostly smooth but may be slightly toothed. Another species common in the Houston area, Missouri ironweed, *Vernonia missurica*, has broader leaves that are densely hairy beneath.

Flower heads occur in loose terminal clusters and contain about twenty tubular disk flowers, which are deeply lobed. All are bisexual and fertile. The phyllaries, or bracts, surrounding the flower head are tinged with reddish purple.

The genus *Vernonia* contains nearly a thousand species around the world. Hybridization is common among many of the species, and identification can be difficult. The name honors William Vernon, an early English botanist who traveled in North America before his death in 1711.

CROSS-VINE

Bignonia capreolata

Quarter-vine

BIGNONIACEAE Trumpet-creeper Family

SIZE
Plant: Woody,
high-climbing vine.
Flower: 2 inches, in
clusters of 2–5.
Reddish orange
outside, yellow
inside.

LEAVES
Opposite, 2 leaflets
with tendril,
evergreen.

BLOOMS
March – May

One of our most beautiful native vines, cross-vine inhabits rich, moist wood-lands throughout the southeastern states and occurs commonly in eastern Texas. It is frequently planted as an ornamental. A section cut through the woody stem reveals a cross of soft tissue, hence the common name.

The high-climbing, evergreen vine has opposite leaves up to six inches in length, although they are usually smaller. Each compound leaf has two oval leaflets. This arrangement of two leaflets on each side of the climbing stem makes cross-vine readily identifiable even when not in bloom. Between the paired leaflets is a third leaflet modified into a branching tendril.

Clusters of two to five two-inch flowers arise from the leaf axils. Dark reddish orange outside and yellow inside, the corolla is trumpet-shaped and broadly five-lobed. Fruits are elongated, flattened capsules that split to liberate the winged seeds.

The genus and family were named for Abbé Jean Paul Bignon, the court librarian to King Louis XV. The species name *capreolata* means "winding" or "twining."

COMMON TRUMPET-CREEPER

Campsis radicans

Trumpet-vine, Cow-itch vine, Foxglove-vine,
Trumpet-honeysuckle, Devil's-shoestring

BIGNONIACEAE Trumpet-creeper Family

SIZE
Plant: Woody vine,
climbing to 30–40
feet.
Flower: 3–4 inches,
trumpet-shaped,
with 5 flaring lobes.

LEAVES
Opposite, pinnate,
7–13 leaflets on
foot-long rachis.

BLOOMS
May – October

Trumpet-creeper grows abundantly across much of the eastern United States and through the eastern half of Texas. In Houston it occurs in almost every small woodland lot and along the bayou banks. Many people plant or encourage it on backyard fences, where it provides an attractive backdrop with its bright green leaves and large, trumpet-shaped red-orange flowers. Pollinated chiefly by hummingbirds and long-tongued bees, trumpet-creeper is encouraged as a hummingbird nectar plant; however, it can easily get out of control in a small yard. The woody, deciduous vine climbs to thirty feet or more by means of aerial holdfast rootlets arising from the stems.

The opposite leaves are odd-pinnately compound, with seven to thirteen leaflets along the foot-long central stalk. References differ on the reason for the name "cow-itch vine." Some authors state trumpet-creeper is not poisonous but is frequently confused with poison ivy, while others assert the foliage causes contact dermatitis.

TRUMPET HONEYSUCKLE

Lonicera sempervirens

Coral honeysuckle, Evergreen honeysuckle, Woodbine

CAPRIFOLIACEAE Honeysuckle Family

SIZE
Plant: Twining or low-climbing vine to 18 feet.
Flower: 2 inches, tubular, in whorls around stem.

LEAVES
To 3 inches, elliptical, evergreen. Terminal leaves unite to encircle stem.

BLOOMS
March – May

Trumpet, or coral, honeysuckle is a lovely twining or low-climbing perennial vine that ranges across the eastern U.S. and into East Texas. It occurs widely throughout the Houston area along fencerows and woodland edges, but it is much less invasive than the introduced Japanese honeysuckle, *Lonicera japonica*. Trumpet honeysuckle proves highly desirable as an ornamental vine and attracts ruby-throated hummingbirds, whose spring migration through Houston coincides with the plant's March to May blooming period. In addition to the native variety carried by several native-plant nurseries, horticultural forms are also available. The foliage is at least partially evergreen.

Slender, red tubular flowers, usually with yellowish throats, grow in several whorls around the tips of the stems, forming interrupted clusters. These five-lobed flowers produce red berries relished by cardinals and other birds. The opposite leaves are green and smooth on the upper surface, whitish and slightly downy below. The upper one or two pairs of leaves unite at the base to form a single unit encircling the stem tip from which the flowers appear.

The genus of the honeysuckles, *Lonicera*, honors sixteenth-century German herbalist Adam Lonitzer. *Sempervirens* refers to the evergreen foliage.

SALT-MARSH MORNING GLORY

Ipomoea sagittata

CONVOLVULACEAE Morning-glory Family

SIZE
*Plant: Long, twining
stems climbing on
other vegetation.
Flower: 3–4 inches,
funnel-shaped.*

LEAVES
*2–4 inches,
arrowhead-shaped.*

BLOOMS
April – October

As its name implies, the salt-marsh morning glory inhabits coastal saline and brackish marshes. In the Houston area it occurs primarily along the upper reaches of Galveston Bay and the ship channel and in the San Jacinto and Trinity river drainages east of the city. One of the largest of the native morning glories, it has rose to reddish purple, funnel-shaped flowers up to four inches across. Long, narrow lobes at the base of the leaf extend backward to give each leaf an arrowhead shape; hence, the name *sagittata*.

The herbaceous, perennial vines trail and climb, twining tightly around other plants and forming large colonies as they spread from creeping roots. The genus name, *Ipomoea*, comes from Greek words meaning "wormlike," referring to the twisting stems. The showy, attractive flowers open early in the morning and usually close by noon, a trait of many morning glories that gives them their common name.

SHARP-POD MORNING GLORY

Ipomoea trichocarpa

Tie vine, Wild morning glory, Coastal morning glory

CONVOLVULACEAE Morning-glory Family

SIZE
Plant: Trailing,
*   twining stems to*
*   15 feet.*
Flower: To 2 inches,
*   funnel-shaped.*

LEAVES
1–4 inches, heart-
*   shaped or 3- to*
*   5-lobed.*

BLOOMS
April – December

Approximately forty species of morning glories occur in Texas, some of them originating in Mexico, the West Indies, or the southeastern states. Sharp-pod morning glory, however, is one of the most abundant and widespread in the state, and it is the species most likely to be found in Houston. While the larger salt-marsh morning glory inhabits marshes east of the city, *trichocarpa* can be found throughout the area. A rampant, aggressive plant, it covers fences on the Katy prairies and climbs over shrubs along Galveston Bay. Rooted in cracks in concrete or asphalt, it may even shroud power poles along busy city streets.

The herbaceous, perennial vine grows from a tuberous root, and the stems reach fifteen feet in length. It can be a troublesome weed in cultivated crops. Leaves vary from heart-shaped to deeply three- or five-lobed, and funnel-shaped flowers are rosy lavender with darker centers. The lip of the funnel has five shallow lobes, indicating its origin from five fused petals. As with many *Ipomoea* species, the flowers open in the morning and wither by midday.

Marshall Johnston, in his 1988 update of the *Manual of the Vascular Plants of Texas*, reassigns *I. trichocarpa* to *I. cordatotriloba*. Other authors have not yet done so, and the older name is retained here.

BUTTERFLY PEA

Centrosema virginianum

Coastal butterfly pea, Climbing butterfly pea,
Spurred butterfly pea

FABACEAE Pea Family

SIZE
Plant: Trailing,
 twining vines to 6
 feet.
Flower: 1½ inches,
 with large banner
 petal, hangs "upside
 down."

LEAVES
Alternate, long-stalked,
 compound. 3 leaflets
 to 2½ inches.

BLOOMS
March – November.
 Most abundant July
 – September.

This large, attractive wildflower fits no single color category. Some authors place it with the red and pink flowers; others, with the blue. In fact, the color varies from a deep rose-pink through shades of lavender to violet-blue. Nor is there a consensus on the form of the common name. Some authorities call it "butterfly pea," others hyphenate it as "butterfly-pea," indicating the lack of uniformity in nomenclature.

A sprawling, twining herbaceous vine, butterfly pea has alternate, long-stalked leaves on stems up to six feet long. Each compound, trifoliate leaf has three elongated leaflets three-quarters to two and one-half inches in length. The vines are fairly common in Houston-area fields and along fencerows and woodland edges, occurring most frequently in sandy soils.

The delicate flower has the typical pea-blossom shape, but the banner, or standard, petal is much larger than the others, spreading to as much as one and one-half inches. Flowers appear singly or in small clusters in the leaf axils and hang upside down, with the large banner petal pointing downward instead of upward. Opening in the morning, the flowers wither quickly in the hot sunshine of the Houston summer. Fruits are slender, flattened pods from one to five inches long. As the halves split open, they form twisted spirals.

CORAL BEAN

Erythrina herbacea

Eastern coral bean, Cherokee bean, Cardinal-spear,
Mamou, Colorin

FABACEAE Pea Family

SIZE
*Plant: Perennial shrub
to 6 feet, sprouting
from large root.
Flower: 2 inches,
slender, in large
spike.*

LEAVES
*Alternate, long-stalked,
with 3 leaflets.*

BLOOMS
April – June

This thorny, perennial shrub occurs along the southeastern coastal plain from North Carolina to Texas and is widespread in the sandy soils of open woodlands and thickets throughout the Houston area. It is also widely planted as an ornamental, as are some of its tropical relatives. The latter species are also used in Central and South America as living fenceposts and as shade trees for coffee plantations.

Coral bean dies back to its large root during winter freezes and sends up new stems in the spring, often reaching a height of six feet. Alternate leaves, borne on prickly petioles, have three leaflets, each broadly triangular and lobed at the base.

The bright scarlet, two-inch flowers grow in showy terminal spikes. Although they have the typical five-petalled pea structure, they appear tubular because the long banner petal folds to enclose the shorter wing and keel petals. As might be expected, the blooms attract hummingbirds during spring migration.

The long, dark pods split open to reveal seeds as brilliantly scarlet as the flowers. Once commonly strung as beads, the seeds are extremely poisonous. All parts of the plant contain toxic alkaloids, but the seeds are most likely to be consumed by children. The toxins produce reactions similar to those of curare, and Tull reports the ingestion of a single seed can cause serious illness. Tropical species are widely used as rat poisons.

The large genus takes its name from the Greek *erythros,* meaning "red." *Herbacea* refers to the herbaceous nature of our local coral bean, in contrast to the woody trees and shrubs found farther south.

DOWNY MILK PEA

Galactia regularis

FABACEAE Pea Family

SIZE
Plant: Prostrate or
twining vine to
3 feet.
Flower: ⅓ inch, in
sparse racemes.

LEAVES
3 oval leaflets, each
1–1½ inches long.

BLOOMS
June – August

Many authors, including Correll and Johnston, separate this species into two distinct taxa, *Galactia regularis* and *G. volubilis,* based on growth habit and the amount of downy hair on the stems and on the underside of the leaves. The most recent Texas checklist by Hatch, Gandhi, and Brown, however, combines the two forms under the name *G. regularis,* and we follow that taxonomy here.

Downy milk pea is a delicate, herbaceous vine that frequently sprawls prostrate on the ground but may occasionally twine on other plants. Compound leaves have three long-oval leaflets rounded at both ends. Each leaflet measures one to one and one-half inches long.

Reddish purple flowers occur in small racemes from the leaf axils and average no more than one-third inch long. Examined closely, however, they are extremely attractive.

The genus name *Galactia* derives from the Greek word for "milk." According to Rickett, Patrick Browne, an Englishman who named this mainly American genus, mistakenly thought that the plants had milky juice. The error is continued in the name "milk pea," for which there is no common substitute.

SCARLET PEA

Indigofera miniata

Coast indigo

FABACEAE Pea Family

SIZE
Plant: Sprawling, trailing perennial to 4 feet.
Flower: ½ inch, in slender axillary spikes.

LEAVES
5–9 leaflets arranged alternately. Leaflets ½–1 inch, grayish, hairy.

BLOOMS
April – September

Scarlet pea grows throughout much of eastern Texas, occupying sandy soils in lawns, pastures, and open woodlands. We found it particularly common in vacant lots on the west side of Houston. A delicate sprawling, trailing vine, it has much-branched stems one to four feet long and gray-green foliage covered with short hairs. The compound leaves have five to nine leaflets arranged alternately, rather than in pairs, on the central leaf stalk, an unusual configuration among the Fabaceae.

Flowers vary in color from salmon pink to brick red and grow in spikes from the leaf axils. As they develop, the flower spikes become much longer than the leaves. The banner petal of the typical pea flower is held erect.

The genus name *Indigofera* means "indigo-bearing," and two larger species of the genus provided the commercial indigo dyes before such natural products were largely replaced by synthetics. Both of those species, *I. tinctoria* of southern Asia and *I. suffruticosa* from the West Indies and tropical America, were formerly cultivated in the southern states and now grow wild. The latter occurs in our area, but it is an erect, shrubby plant easily distinguished from our native scarlet pea. The species name of scarlet pea, *miniata*, means "cinnabar-red," referring to the flower color.

POWDERPUFF

Mimosa strigillosa

Herbaceous mimosa

FABACEAE Pea Family

SIZE
Plant: Trailing stems
  to 6 feet long.
Flower: Tiny, in
  globelike heads
  about ¾ inch in
  diameter.

LEAVES
Doubly compound,
  sensitive to touch.

BLOOMS
April – November

Powderpuff is one of the most common wildflowers in Houston, blooming from April through November. The perennial base sends out sprawling annual stems up to six feet long that form tangled mats on the ground along roadsides and bayou banks and in vacant lots across the city. Individual pink flowers are very tiny, but they cluster in showy, globelike heads about three-quarters of an inch in diameter. The long pink stamens tipped with yellow pollen give the flower heads a delicate beauty and the appropriate common name "powderpuff."

This creeping, herbaceous *Mimosa* resembles a related genus, *Shrankia,* called the sensitive briars. The latter, however, have stems armed with vicious, re-curved spines. Powderpuff stems may have stiff bristles, but they are not nox-ious to the touch.

The leaves are bipinnately compound, divided into four to eight pairs of seg-ments called pinnae (featherlike), and each of those is again divided into ten to fifteen pairs of tiny leaflets. The entire structure constitutes a single leaf.

Sensitive to stimuli, the leaves seem to wilt at the slightest touch, as if they possess a nervous reflex. At the base of each leaflet is a swelling made up of thin-walled cells filled with water. When touched, a chemical signal is trans-mitted through the leaf, and the water in the swellings moves into intercellular spaces and nearby cells. The resulting loss of turgor causes the leaflets to droop. The process occurs with amazing rapidity, and leaves may begin to close in as little as a tenth of a second. Recovery requires a much longer period of time.

BLADDER-POD

Sesbania vesicaria

Bag-pod

FABACEAE Pea Family

SIZE
*Plant: Erect annual to
10 feet.
Flower: ½ inch, orange
to red, in pendant
racemes from leaf
axils.*

LEAVES
*To 9 inches. With 10–
20 pairs of oblong
leaflets.*

BLOOMS
August – October

Bladder-pod is an erect, shrubby annual up to ten feet tall, although it is usually lower. Less widely distributed than the perennial rattlebush, *Sesbania drummondii,* it nevertheless occurs in moist soils along roadsides and bayou banks and may even spring up in the newly disturbed soils of roadway construction projects. The flowers are orange or red, and the inflated seed pods are rounded in cross section. In contrast, rattlebush has yellow flowers and four-angled seed pods.

Compound leaves of bladder-pod reach nine inches in length and are divided into ten to twenty pairs of narrow, opposite leaflets. The leaves and the slender flower clusters that hang from the leaf axils provide food for at least two species of large weevils. The beetles quickly riddle the tender leaflets, leaving them with a scalloped appearance.

The genus takes its name from *sesban,* an Arabic name for one of the species. *Vesicaria* refers to the bladderlike pod. Apparently native to the West Indies, bladder-pod has spread across the southern states. Like other *Sesbania* species, all parts of the plant contain toxic alkaloids, and the seeds are dangerously poisonous to both humans and livestock.

AMBERIQUE BEAN

Strophostyles helvula

Trailing wild bean

FABACEAE Pea Family

SIZE
*Plant: Herbaceous,
 annual vine to
 8 feet.
Flower: ⅝ inch, in
 compact cluster on
 erect stalk. Banner
 petal erect, keel
 sickle-shaped.*

LEAVES
*3 leaflets, each bluntly
 3-lobed or
 egg-shaped.*

BLOOMS
June – September

Amberique bean has long been known as *Strophostyles helvola* and is so listed in most publications now in print. Bare noted, however, that the reference was unclear, since *helvolus* means "light yellow." More recently, Johnston acknowledged that Linnaeus originally spelled the specific epithet *helvula*. Johnston chose not to correct the spelling in his checklist; however, Hatch, Gandhi, and Brown adopted *helvula* in their 1990 listing of the vascular plants of Texas. We follow that revised nomenclature here.

Amberique bean ranges from the Canadian border southward to Florida and Texas and occurs in widely scattered parts of the Houston area, preferring sandy and disturbed soils along bayou banks and roadsides. It is also common on coastal and bayside beaches. A trailing or climbing vine reaching eight feet in length, it has long-stalked, compound leaves. The three leaflets are broadly egg-shaped or pear-shaped, often with broad lobes at the base.

Dark pink to purplish flowers are borne in compact clusters atop long, upright stalks from the leaf axils. The banner petal is broad and upright; the keel petals are united into a narrow, curved beak that is darker at the tip. The style curves to conform to the enveloping keel, giving rise to the genus name *Strophostyles*, formed from the Greek words *strophe* and *stylos*, meaning "twining pillar."

Nine of the ten stamens are united in a sleeve around the style; the tenth is free, providing access to nectar glands at the base of the pistil. When bees press down on the keel to reach the nectar, the column springs up to douse them liberally with pollen.

PERSIAN CLOVER

Trifolium resupinatum

Reversed clover

FABACEAE Pea Family

SIZE
Plant: To 18 inches, erect or sprawling.
Flower: Less than ¼ inch; in small, open heads.

LEAVES
3 leaflets.

BLOOMS
March – June

Although native to the Old World, Persian clover has been widely introduced in North America. Correll and Johnston call it a "rare roadside escapee" in eastern Texas, but it now grows abundantly along some Houston roadsides and bayou banks. An annual, it blooms from March until June.

Leaves of the upright or sprawling plant are divided into the three leaflets typical of *Trifolium* species, each leaflet one to two times as long as wide. Rose to purple flowers form small, few-flowered heads. Individual flowers are unique in twisting at the base so that the largest petal, called the banner, is on the bottom rather than on the top as in most other clovers and members of the pea family. These "upside-down," or resupinate, flowers give Persian clover the name *re-supinatum*. At maturity a spiny, balloonlike calyx encloses the seed pods.

CENTAURY

Centaurium pulchellum

GENTIANACEAE Gentian Family

SIZE
Plant: 4–10 inches,
erect, branching in
upper portions.
Flower: Small, 5-lobed,
forming terminal
clusters.

LEAVES
To ¾ inch, opposite,
sessile.

BLOOMS
May – August

Centaury is not listed among Texas species by Correll and Johnston and was apparently first found in Hardin County in 1972. It has now spread throughout East Texas and along the upper coast, however, and we found it to be common on the west side of Houston, particularly along Clay Road and in the Addicks Reservoir area. It blooms through the summer, from May until August.

The genus was named for the centaur of Greek mythology. This half man, half horse reputedly used a plant of the genus to heal a wound caused by an arrow of Hercules. Although the name is mythical, there is no denying the beauty of the plant as reflected in the specific epithet *pulchellum*, which means "pretty" or "beautiful."

A slender perennial standing only four to ten inches tall, centaury has opposite leaves that clasp the stem. Lower stem leaves are elliptical and up to three-quarters of an inch long; upper leaves are smaller and narrow. The little pink to dark rose flowers are five-lobed and trumpet-shaped. Borne on short stalks at the ends of the branches and from the upper leaf axils, they form a showy cluster at the top of the plant.

Other *Centaurium* species occur farther west and south in Texas, and the various forms can be difficult to identify. Most common in Houston, however, is *pulchellum*, a relatively new immigrant to our state.

MEADOW PINK

Sabatia campestris

Prairie rose-gentian, Pink prairie gentian, Pink star, Texas star

GENTIANACEAE Gentian Family

SIZE
*Plant: Erect annual, to
  20 inches.
Flower: 1–1½ inches,
  5 rose-colored petals
  with yellow central
  star.*

LEAVES
*To 1½ inches, opposite,
  clasping stem.*

BLOOMS
April – July

One of our prettiest spring wildflowers, meadow pink blooms from April into June or July throughout the Houston area. An annual, it reseeds readily and forms colonies along roadsides and bayou banks and in vacant lots across the city. Its habitat is reflected by the specific name *campestris*, meaning "of the fields." The genus honors eighteenth-century Italian botanist Liberatus Sabbati.

Ajilvsgi suggests that meadow pink should be used more extensively in garden plantings, praising the color and long-lasting quality of its sweet-scented blooms. For best results, she notes, the seeds should be planted in early fall in a raked area and left uncovered.

The upright, four-angled stems grow to twenty inches and branch sparingly in the upper portions, bearing opposite, stalkless leaves that are broadest at the base and clasp the stem. Five-petalled flowers appear at the ends of the branches and on long stalks from the leaf axils, spanning slightly more than an inch. They range in color from pink to deep rose and have a yellow central star, as if mirroring the five pollen-laden stamens.

Meadow pink provides an excellent example of the reproductive strategy called proterandry, in which the pollen is shed before the stigma of the flower is receptive, thereby assuring cross-pollination. When the flower opens, the two branches of the elongated style lie flat and twist together to conceal the stigmatic surfaces. Later, after the anthers have dispersed their pollen, the style uncoils and becomes erect, exposing the stigmata to fresh pollen carried by insects from other flowers.

CAROLINA GERANIUM

Geranium carolinianum

Carolina cranesbill, Crane's-bill, Wild geranium

GERANIACEAE Geranium Family

SIZE
*Plant: 6–24 inches,
    erect or sprawling,
    much-branched,
    densely hairy.
Flower: ¼ inch,
    5-petalled.*

LEAVES
*Rounded, on long
    stalks. Cut into 5–9
    lobed segments.*

BLOOMS
*March – May. Begins
    in January if no
    winter freeze.*

Both the family and the genus of this abundant Houston wildflower take their names from the Greek *geranos,* or "crane." The long, erect seed capsule was thought to resemble the bill of a crane, and the simile gives us the common as well as the scientific names. Carolina geranium occurs virtually throughout the contiguous United States and across most of Texas. It and several other members of the genus *Geranium* are native, while the florists' "geraniums" grown in pots and gardens originated in Africa and belong to the genus *Pelargonium.*

An annual or biennial, Carolina geranium has downy stems that branch freely to form low mounds. It grows as a weed in lawns, fields, and disturbed areas throughout Houston, blooming in early spring. Long-stalked leaves have rounded blades that are deeply cut into five to nine narrow segments, each of which is further toothed or lobed. In summer the leaves turn various shades of yellow, red, and purple, providing colorful accents even after the blooming season is over.

Quarter-inch pink or whitish flowers are paired in small clusters at the tips of the branches, the flower stalks subtended by narrow bracts. Each of the five petals is notched at the tip. The crane's-bill seed capsule opens from the base when mature, each segment curling upward like a coiled spring, expelling a seed with explosive force.

Native geraniums were widely used by American Indians and early settlers for a variety of ailments ranging from toothache to gonorrhea. The plants were particularly useful as an astringent or styptic in stopping the bleeding from open wounds.

HENBIT

Lamium amplexicaule

Clasping henbit, Henbit dead-nettle

LAMIACEAE Mint Family

SIZE
Plant: 4–18 inches.
Flower: ½ inch.
 Narrow tube;
 2-lobed, flaring lips.

LEAVES
1 inch. Lower on long
 stalks; upper
 clasping stem.

BLOOMS
February – April

A native of Europe, henbit has naturalized throughout North America. It grows abundantly as a "weed" in Houston lawns and fields and can be troublesome in cultivated crops. Should you encounter it in your lawn or garden, however, examine it closely. Although small, this is a truly charming plant, too beautiful in form and color to be casually tossed aside.

The upright or sprawling plant branches freely near the base and stands four to eighteen inches tall. Opposite, rounded leaves have scalloped edges and are conspicuously veined. Lower leaves have long stalks; upper ones clasp the stem, the reason for the name *amplexicaule*.

Delicate half-inch flowers are narrowly tubular, flaring into two lobed lips. Pinkish or reddish purple, they are flecked with darker spots. Whorls of flowers encircle the stem, each tier subtended by leaflike bracts.

Several references describe henbit as blooming throughout the year, but it grows primarily as a winter annual in Houston yards. Seeds germinate in the fall, and the plants mature through the winter to flower in early spring. Most plants die in the summer heat. The earliest blossoms may not open at all. Because the anthers and stigmas are close together and mature at the same time, individual flowers self-pollinate while in the bud. Later flowers then open for cross-pollination. They provide an early nectar source for bees and small butterflies before most other wildflowers open in the spring.

LEMON BEEBALM

Monarda citriodora

Lemon-mint, Horsemint, Plains horsemint

LAMIACEAE Mint Family

SIZE
Plant: To 2½ feet.
Flower: ¾ inch long, in
interrupted whorls
around the stem.

LEAVES
Opposite, slender,
often with serrated
edges.

BLOOMS
April – October. Most
abundant in late
May and early June.

This distinctive plant blooms most profusely across Houston in late May and early June. It is particularly abundant along the banks of the bayous, where it forms almost solid stands. The two-lipped flowers grow in several whorls, each supported by leafy bracts, resembling a multitiered Oriental pagoda. As with all members of the mint family, the stem is square in cross section.

Flowers can be white or pink, often with purple spots; the bracts are tinged with purple. Most of the beebalm in Houston is pale in color, but some patches of a deep purple strain occur in scattered locations. The latter probably result from seeding with commercial varieties of wildflower seed.

The genus name, *Monarda*, was applied by Linnaeus in honor of Nicholas Monardes, a sixteenth-century Spanish physician who wrote on medicinal plants of the New World. The species, *citriodora*, refers to the lemon fragrance of the plant. An aromatic tea can be brewed from the dried leaves.

INTERMEDIATE FALSE DRAGON-HEAD

Physostegia intermedia

Pale false dragon-head, Intermediate lion-heart,
Intermediate obedient-plant

LAMIACEAE Mint Family

SIZE
Plant: 1–5 feet.
*Flower: ¾ inch. On
   erect, slender spike.*

LEAVES
*2–4 inches, opposite,
   narrow, margins
   wavy.*

BLOOMS
April – June

This attractive member of the mint family forms large colonies in wet ditches and marshy areas around Houston, often growing directly in standing water. It begins blooming in April and is through by early June.

The solitary, slender stems usually stand about three feet tall but may reach five feet on occasion. Only a few pairs of opposite leaves clasp the square stem. The leaves attain a length of two to four inches and are narrow and almost grasslike, with wavy margins. Individual flowers attach directly to the stem and form an erect, slender spike. Three-quarters of an inch long, the flowers have two distinct lips and an inflated throat that is rosy pink or lavender outside and spotted with darker rose-purple inside.

Several other species of *Physostegia* occur in eastern and coastal Texas, and they can be difficult to distinguish. Most have larger flowers than *intermedia*. The genus name comes from the Greek *physa,* "bladder," and *stege,* "covering," referring to the inflated calyx that covers the ripening fruits. Our species resemble the Eurasian dragon-heads of the genus *Dracocephalum,* named for their gaping mouths. Hence, "false dragon-head." They also gained the name "obedient-plant" because the flowers remain in place, as if on command, when pushed to the side.

TROPICAL SAGE

Salvia coccinea

Scarlet sage, Red sage, Texas sage,
Indian fire, Mirto, Mejorana

LAMIACEAE Mint Family

SIZE
Plant: 1–3 feet,
  upright, hairy, stem
  4-angled.
Flower: 1 inch,
  2-lipped, in
  interrupted spike.

LEAVES
To 2½ inches, opposite,
  stalked, sharply
  toothed.

BLOOMS
March – December

An upright, sparsely branched perennial to three feet tall, tropical sage occurs in scattered locations throughout the Houston area. It is also widely planted to attract hummingbirds and butterflies and spreads rapidly to colonize new habitats. Although normally considered native to the coastal plain from South Carolina to Florida and Texas and then southward through the West Indies and tropical America, its origins are uncertain. A few authors suggest it may have been widely naturalized from South America.

The stalked leaves are paired on the four-angled stem and have sharply toothed margins. Bright red or deep scarlet flowers appear in interrupted termi-nal spikes. One inch long, the flowers are two-lipped, the upper lip narrow and unlobed, the lower lip much broader and strongly lobed. Hardy in cultivation and sprouting from a woody base, tropical sage blooms profusely throughout much of the year.

The genus takes its name from the Latin *salvare,* "to heal," in reference to the medicinal properties of some species. It is the largest genus in the mint family, with more than seven hundred species around the world. Twenty-three species are now listed for Texas, but *Salvia coccinea* is the only red-flowered one growing wild in the Houston area. The specific name *coccinea* simply means "red" or "scarlet."

PINK MINT

Stachys drummondii

Drummond betony, Drummond hedge-nettle, Wound-wort

LAMIACEAE Mint Family

SIZE
Plant: To 2 feet,
  square-stemmed,
  hairy.
Flower: ½ inch,
  2-lipped, in
  interrupted spikes.

LEAVES
To 4 inches, opposite,
  long-stalked,
  margins with
  rounded teeth.

BLOOMS
February – June,
  occasionally longer.

Pink mint grows as an upright annual or biennial, reaching a height of two feet. The square stem typical of the mint family is hairy and branched. Long-stalked, opposite leaves are ovate in shape with rounded teeth on the margins.

Pink or lavender flowers appear in whorls in the leaf axils, forming a long terminal spike. Distinctly two-lipped, the flower has a hooded upper lip that is often notched and a longer, broadly three-lobed lower lip. The genus name is the Greek word for "spike," referring to the flower arrangement. The specific name honors Thomas Drummond, an English botanist who collected extensively in Texas in 1833–34.

Pink mint is not common in the immediate Houston area, occurring mainly to the east along Galveston Bay. However, it may form extensive colonies in partly shaded fields and along woodland edges. An attractive plant, pink mint would be an excellent addition to the wildflower garden. Ajilvsgi notes that it is "easily raised from seed sown in November."

Most plants bloom between February and June; however, some may flower in the fall, extending the blooming season through the winter if there is no killing freeze. With its ample supply of nectar and pollen, pink mint serves as an early food source for bees, butterflies, and other insects.

AMERICAN GERMANDER

Teucrium canadense

Wood-sage, Wild basil

LAMIACEAE Mint Family

SIZE
*Plant: To 3 feet, hairy,
    forming dense
    colonies.*
*Flower: To ¾ inch,
    2-lipped. Stamens
    and pistil project
    through split upper
    lip.*

LEAVES
*To 4 inches, opposite,
    stalked, toothed,
    hairy.*

BLOOMS
April – November

Although not an abundant wildflower in the Houston area, American germander occurs sparingly along the upper reaches of Galveston Bay and in wet
soils near inland marshes and streams. The branching stems form dense colonies from creeping rhizomes and reach three feet in height. Soft, downy hairs

cover the stems and lower surfaces of the leaves, at times giving this attractive perennial a silvery appearance. The opposite, lance-shaped leaves have toothed margins.

Flowers range in color from pale pink to lavender with darker purple spots, fading to yellowish with age. They occur in dense terminal spikes that elongate as the flowers open upward along the stem. American germander ranges from Canada to Florida, Texas, and Arizona. Found throughout most of our state, it is an important honey plant.

The two-lipped flower has a deeply cleft upper lip through which the reproductive parts protrude. When newly opened, the four stamens arch up and over the flower, dusting the back of a bee with pollen as it lands on the lower lip to extract nectar from the corolla tube. Their pollen expended, the stamens become erect. The style then arches down and exposes the stigma to bee-carried pollen from other fresh flowers, assuring cross-pollination by the hungry bees.

The genus *Teucrium* takes its name from Teucer, a legendary king of Troy. "Germander" entered our language along a tortuous path from the ancient Greek *chamaedrys,* a "low shrub," according to Bare. In later Greek it became *chamandrya,* and it passed into Medieval Latin as *germandra.* Old French transformed it into *germandree,* and the name then became "germander" in English. Such complex origins are common in all of the natural sciences.

American germander has a long history of medicinal applications among Native Americans and early settlers. Leaf tea was used as a diuretic and for lung ailments and worms. Externally, the leaves served as an antiseptic dressing.

TOOTH-CUP

Ammannia coccinea

Purple ammannia

LYTHRACEAE Loosestrife Family

SIZE
*Plant: To 2 feet, stem
    square, smooth.
Flower: ⅛ inch,
    stalkless, 4-petalled,
    in leaf axils.*

LEAVES
*To 2 inches,
    occasionally longer.
    Opposite, slender,
    clasping stem with
    basal lobes.*

BLOOMS
*April – November.
    Mainly in late
    summer and
    early fall.*

Tooth-cup occurs sparingly in the shallow water or mud of roadside ditches, ponds, and marshes across the Houston area but is most common to the north and east of the city. The tiny flowers are easily overlooked; however, once discovered, their bright color and intricate form make them worthy of close examination.

The sharply four-angled stems branch in the upper portions and reach two feet in height, sometimes sprawling and spreading from the thickened base. Opposite leaves are long and slender, clasping the stem with large earlike lobes on each side so as to nearly encircle the stem. Once recognized, this combination of square stem and clasping, linear leaves makes tooth-cup easy to identify.

Flowers appear in small, stalkless clusters from the leaf axils and are little more than an eighth of an inch across. The four deep pink to purple petals drop quickly, leaving the persistent four-angled, toothed calyx. When mature, the capsule is globelike and filled with yellow or reddish seeds. Some authors give the blooming season as April through November; however, the population in our area seems to flower mainly in late summer and early fall.

This little-known genus contains about thirty species in the tropical and warm temperate regions of the world. The source of the name is apparently in doubt. Wagner, Herbst, and Sohmer state that it honors P. Ammann (1634–91), a German botanist at Leipzig. Bare, however, cites Johann Ammann (1699–1741), a Russian professor of natural history in St. Petersburg. The specific epithet *coccinea* refers to the color of the flowers.

WINE-CUP

Callirhoe involucrata

Slim-lobed poppy-mallow, Low poppy-mallow

MALVACEAE Mallow Family

SIZE
Plant: To 3 feet, hairy,
*   sprawling, and*
*   trailing.*
Flower: To 2½ inches,
*   deeply cupped.*

LEAVES
1–2 inches. Cleft into
*   5–7 narrow, lobed*
*   segments.*

BLOOMS
February – June

The flowers of wine-cup, or poppy-mallow, resemble fragile chalices filled with deep red wine. The five delicate petals remain strongly cupped and are white at the base. Borne on long, hairy stems that sprawl and trail vinelike across fields and vacant lots, they must be included among the most beautiful of all Houston wildflowers. Leaves are usually divided into five to seven narrow palmate segments, each of which is further toothed or lobed.

Several members of this exclusively North American genus inhabit Texas, but *involucrata* occurs most widely across the state and is most common in the Houston area. All are easily recognized by their wine-colored blooms.

Callirhoe was the name of an ocean nymph in Greek mythology, while the species name refers to the involucre, a ring of leafy bracts directly below the calyx of the flower.

Several Indian names for the wine-cups meant "medicine," for the plants were widely used. According to Janet Bare, Native Americans made drinks to treat intestinal pains, and they inhaled burning roots for colds and bronchial ailments.

SALT MARSH-MALLOW

Kosteletzkya virginica

Seashore mallow, Coastal mallow,
Virginia hibiscus, Wild hollyhock

MALVACEAE Mallow Family

SIZE
*Plant: To 6 feet,
    branching,
    shrublike, covered
    with shaggy hairs.
Flower: 2–3 ½ inches,
    5-petalled, stamens
    forming central
    column.*

LEAVES
*To 6 inches, alternate,
    stalked, toothed,
    hairy.*

BLOOMS
June – November

This tall, showy perennial inhabits the wet, often saline soils along the coast from Long Island southward to Florida and westward around the Gulf of Mexico to Texas. In our area it occurs east of Houston in the ditches and brackish marshes surrounding Galveston Bay. In recent years, however, it has also become popular as an addition to the wildflower garden, where it displays its large pink flowers throughout the summer months.

The upright, branching stems reach six feet in height and form dense clumps when given enough moisture and sunlight. Alternate, gray-green leaves have long stalks and are densely hairy. Coarsely toothed on the margins, they may also have pointed basal lobes.

Five-petalled pink flowers open widely, spanning from two to as much as three and one-half inches. The many stamens are united into a long column surrounding the style, indicating the close relationship to the hibiscus and other well-known mallows. The fruits, however, are flat rings containing one-seeded segments, more like those of the cultivated hollyhocks than the hibiscus species.

A small genus of about thirty species found mainly in tropical America and Africa, *Kosteletzkya* takes its name from Bohemian botanist V.F. Kosteletzky. *Virginica* simply refers to the type locality from which the species was named.

TURK'S-CAP

Malvaviscus arboreus var. *drummondii*

Drummond wax-mallow, Texas mallow, Red mallow,
Mexican-apple, Scotch-purse

MALVACEAE Mallow Family

SIZE
*Plant: Woody
perennial, usually
to 3–4 feet.
Flower: ¾–1½ inches,
remaining partially
closed, stamen
column projects
beyond petals.*

LEAVES
*2–5 inches, as wide
as long, coarsely
toothed, often
broadly 3-lobed.*

BLOOMS
*Throughout the year,
mainly spring and
fall.*

Many botanical authors prefer the name "Drummond wax-mallow" for this bright, beautiful perennial shrub, but it is perhaps most widely known as "Turk's-cap." The form that occurs throughout eastern Texas is presently classified as a variety of the more widely distributed *Malvaviscus arboreus*, but that consensus may soon change. Johnston notes that "there is considerable evidence that our Turk's-cap should be considered a distinct species under the homotypic synonym *Malvaviscus drummondii*." While early monographs treated the genus as a single species with many varieties extending from Texas through South America, more recent works have begun to separate the forms.

Turk's-cap grows naturally in open woodlands and thickets throughout the Houston area and is also widely cultivated to attract hummingbirds and butterflies. It blooms throughout the year until a hard freeze but is most prolific in spring and fall.

The woody, much-branched stems bear alternate, stalked leaves that are densely hairy beneath. As wide as they are long, the leaves are coarsely toothed on the margins and are often shallowly three-lobed.

Turk's-cap takes its name from the resemblance of the flower to a Turkish fez. The five petals never open completely, remaining spirally wrapped at the base to form a long tube. As with other members of the Malvaceae, the stamen filaments unite to form a column that extends beyond the partially open petals. Flowers appear from the leaf axils or in terminal clusters.

The fruits are red and slightly flattened, not unlike a tiny apple. Although edible either raw or cooked, they contain large seeds and only a small amount of mealy flesh. Tull, however, praises the jelly made from the fruits and also lists other ways to use the edible flowers and young leaves. She suggests drying the flowers for use in herbal tea.

The genus name *Malvaviscus* means "sticky mallow." The subspecies, or species, is a tribute to English botanist Thomas Drummond, who collected widely in Texas and for whom many of our local plants are named.

SHOWY EVENING-PRIMROSE

Oenothera speciosa

Pink primrose, Mexican primrose, Buttercup, Amapola

ONAGRACEAE Evening-primrose Family

SIZE
Plant: To 18 inches,
branching and
sprawling.
Flower: To 3 inches.
4 petals.

LEAVES
Toothed or wavy-
edged, alternate,
to 3 inches long.

BLOOMS
March – July,
occasional in fall.

Few other wildflowers are as widespread across Houston as the evening-primrose. It occurs in abundance along freeways and bayous, in vacant lots, and in lawns and boulevards throughout the city. The large, delicate flowers complement the floral display of bluebonnets and paintbrush in early spring, but the blooming season also extends into summer.

The four-petalled blossoms range in color from deep rose-pink to white. Because the perennial plants spread to form extensive colonies with similar genetic traits, the color within a colony usually remains consistent. So, too, does the tendency for individual flowers to open either in the evening or in the morning; they close in the heat of the day.

This attractive species is often called simply "primrose," but another family of true primroses more properly claims that name. The evening-primroses are distinguished by having only four petals. Many Texans call the plant "buttercup," but that name, too, is more properly applied to an entirely different group of plants with waxy yellow petals. *Oenothera*, the genus of the evening-primroses, was a name used by Pliny in the first century for a plant reputed to produce sleep when its juice was consumed with wine, according to Janet Bare in *Wildflowers and Weeds of Kansas*.

VIOLET WOOD-SORREL

Oxalis violacea

OXALIDACEAE Wood-sorrel Family

SIZE
Plant: 4–16 inches, forming colonies.
Flower: ¾ inch, 5 petals.

LEAVES
Long-stalked, 3 leaflets, reddish below.

BLOOMS
March – May. August – October without leaves.

This species illustrates the problems encountered in arranging flowers by color. While color serves as a convenient aid for the nonspecialist, not all species fit the artificial slots created for them. Some books place violet wood-sorrel with the blue flowers; others, with the red. Because this particular flower seems nearer the reddish end of the spectrum, we have followed the latter course.

Violet wood-sorrel occurs in abundance throughout fields and open, sunny woodlands across the Houston area. Springing up as a weed in lawns and gardens, its attractive flowers and foliage make it a candidate for cultivation. However, this low perennial spreads by off-shoots from the scaly bulbs and by underground runners to form invasive colonies that quickly get out of hand.

Long-stalked leaves have three leaflets that are broadly notched at the tips. Bright green above, they are reddish purple underneath. The five-petalled flowers appear in small clusters on long stems, opening one at a time. Both the flowers and the cloverlike leaves close at night and on cool, cloudy days.

Violet wood-sorrel blooms prolifically in the spring, usually from March through May, and then dies back. It may bloom again in late summer or fall without leaves.

As with other *Oxalis* species, the tart, sour leaves are sometimes used in salads. Children frequently chew on the leaves and stems, calling the plant "rabbit-grass." Too much oxalic acid, however, can lead to stomach upsets.

SHAGGY PORTULACA

Portulaca pilosa

Moss-rose, Chisme, Rose purslane

PORTULACACEAE Purslane Family

SIZE
Plant: 2–8 inches,
  forming mounds
  or mats.
Flower: To ½ inch,
  5-petalled.

LEAVES
To ½ inch, narrow,
  thick, and succulent.
  Tufts of curly white
  hairs in leaf axils.

BLOOMS
May – December

Now classified as *Portulaca pilosa*, shaggy portulaca was formerly called *P. mundula* by many authors. A small but beautiful annual wildflower found sparingly in sunny, open locations, it prefers sandy or gravelly soils. It closely resembles the much larger commercial moss-rose, *P. grandiflora*, introduced from South America for widespread cultivation. Succulent, sprawling stems reach eight inches in length and branch to form low mounds or mats. The deep rose-red, five-petalled flowers span about one-half inch and grow in small clusters subtended by a whorl of six to ten thick, narrow leaves. Tufts of kinky, woolly white hairs appear with the flowers and in the leaf axils.

The root of the name *Portulaca* seems uncertain, for it dates far back into history and was used for related Eurasian species. Niering and Olmstead assert it means "little gate," from the seed capsule that opens with a lid. Healey suggests an origin in the Latin *porto*, "to carry," and *lac*, "milky," referring to the milky sap. Bare takes a safer stand; she assigns it an "unknown meaning."

SCARLET PIMPERNEL

Anagallis arvensis

Common pimpernel, Poor-man's weather glass,
Hierba del pajaro

PRIMULACEAE Primrose Family

SIZE
Plant: Branching
  stems to 1 foot.
  Sprawling.
Flower: To ½ inch. 5
  salmon to red petals.

LEAVES
Opposite, oval,
  stalkless, to 1 inch.

BLOOMS
March – May, less
  common through
  November.

An alien plant introduced to the U.S. from Europe, scarlet pimpernel is one of many small but delightful annual wildflowers the casual observer might easily overlook. Low and sprawling, it grows in abundance in vacant lots and fields and along the bayou banks throughout Houston. Five-petalled flowers vary from salmon to bright red and grow singly at the tips of the branching stems and in the leaf axils. Several references report blue forms and white forms as well as red, but we have never encountered them in the Houston area. Scarlet pimpernel blooms most profusely from March through May but may also flower again in the fall after heavy rains.

Authors do not agree on the origin of the name. Durant believes it comes from the Latin *piperinella*, "little peppers," because the fine, round, bulletlike seeds resemble pepper seeds. Rickett says "pimpernel" is a corruption of a Latin word meaning "featherlike" that was applied to several species.

Regardless of its archaic origins, a wealth of folklore surrounds the scarlet pimpernel. Pliny asserted that the juice of the plant, "applied with honey, disperses films upon the eyes, bloodshot in those organs resulting from blows and argema." It was also recommended as a cure for melancholy. Actually, juice of the leaves may cause a mild rash on sensitive skin.

Pimpernel was considered a magical plant in Ireland. One has only to hold it in the hand, the legend goes, to understand the language of the birds.

The English name "poor-man's weather glass" is sometimes used in this country as well. It stems from a belief that the plant opens its flowers to the bright, sunny sky and closes them at the approach of bad weather.

Baroness Emmuska Orczy made the lovely wildflower famous outside the botanical world with her 1905 classic, *The Scarlet Pimpernel.* "The scarlet pimpernel, Mademoiselle," said Sir Andrew to Suzanne, "is the name of a humble English wayside flower; but it is also the name chosen to hide the identity of the best and bravest man in all the world."

PRAIRIE GERARDIA

Agalinis heterophylla

Prairie agalinis

SCROPHULARIACEAE Snapdragon Family

SIZE
Plant: To 3 feet.
Flower: ¾–1 inch,
   5-lobed.

LEAVES
½–2 inches. Lower
   cleft; upper small
   and narrow.

BLOOMS
August – November

Prairie gerardia is another of those wildflowers that defy color categories. Flowers vary from light pink to orchid or purple, but the hues appear closer to the reddish purples than to the blue. Several *Agalinis* species occur in eastern Texas, and they differ only in minor details. Because they cannot often be separated by the novice in the field, most people lump them simply as "gerardias." Members of this genus were incorrectly placed in the genus *Gerardia* at one time, and the name remains as a common epithet in spite of their reclassification.

The upright or sprawling three-foot stems of prairie gerardia are smooth and frequently angled. Numerous slender, wiry branches bear small, narrow leaves; lower leaves may be cleft into three narrow lobes. This variety in leaf form gives the species the name *heterophylla*. Funnel-shaped flowers arise from the leaf axils and are indistinctly two-lipped, with five broad, flat lobes. Darker purple spots and yellowish streaks ornament the throat, perhaps serving as "targets" for the bees and butterflies that find *Agalinis* species so attractive.

Prairie gerardia occurs commonly in open fields and woodland edges throughout the Houston area. It blooms primarily from August through November, although some may be found as early as June. During the fall, it serves as the major foodplant for late broods of the buckeye butterfly, and those beautiful insects with the large eye-spots on their hind wings add greatly to the charm of a gerardia patch on a warm, sunny October afternoon.

TEXAS PAINTBRUSH

Castilleja indivisa

Indian paintbrush, Entireleaf paintbrush, Scarlet paintbrush

SCROPHULARIACEAE Snapdragon Family

SIZE
Plant: 8–16 inches.
Flower: 1 inch,
* surrounded by red*
* bracts.*

LEAVES
Slender, alternate,
* hairy, entire or*
* slightly lobed at*
* base.*

BLOOMS
March – May,
* occasional in other*
* months.*

This showy plant resembles a brush dipped in red paint. One of our earliest spring flowers, it first appears in March along Houston roadsides to add its splendor to the colorful palette that also includes bluebonnets, pink evening-primroses, and yellow false-dandelions. The intense red-orange color is actually due to leaflike bracts surrounding the tubular, greenish yellow flowers. Occasionally a plant with yellowish or cream-colored bracts can be found.

Many similar paintbrushes occur across the country, and botanists have identified nine or ten in Texas. Most are perennials, but this most widely distributed of the state's species normally grows as an annual. Semiparasitic on other plants, particularly grasses, Texas paintbrush penetrates their roots and obtains part of its nutrients from the unwitting hosts. The genus takes its name from Spanish botanist Juan Castillejo of Cadiz.

WEST INDIAN LANTANA

Lantana camara

Common lantana, Alfombrilla, Hediona

VERBENACEAE Vervain Family

SIZE
*Plant: 3–5 feet,
sometimes taller.
Much-branched,
woody shrub.
Flower: ¼ inch, each
4-lobed, in compact
heads.*

LEAVES
*2–4 inches, opposite,
stalked, hairy,
margins finely
toothed.*

BLOOMS
May – December

West Indian lantana is native to tropical America, escaping from cultivation to spread throughout Texas. It occurs in scattered locations across the Houston area. The erect or sprawling woody perennial normally reaches three to five feet in height but may be taller. Leaves are opposite, stalked, and finely toothed on the margins.

Flower color varies from yellow to pink or red, the variability further complicated by the introduction of countless new hybrids. Typically the individual florets open creamy yellow and turn pink as they mature. Showy, headlike spikes do not elongate as the flowers open gradually from the outside inward, but they become a deeper pink. Each tiny flower is trumpet-shaped, with four unequal lobes.

Texas lantana, *Lantana horrida,* is a native species that occurs commonly in southern and central Texas. It appears to be less abundant in the Houston area than the introduced *L. camara*. Texas lantana has larger, coarser teeth on the leaf margins and flowers that open bright yellow-orange and turn reddish.

Both of these species and the numerous cultivars are welcome additions to the wildflower garden, providing one of the best of all nectar sources for attracting butterflies. Birds also eat the black, fleshy fruits. Immature fruits are extremely toxic and have caused deaths among children, pets, and livestock. It is not clear whether the ripe fruits are less toxic, but no deaths have been reported from their ingestion. It is best, however, to leave them strictly alone. Hairs on the stems and leaves of lantanas may also cause a rash on sensitive skin.

Lantana was the early Latin name for plants now placed in the genus *Viburnum*. The name was transferred to those we now call lantanas by Linnaeus, perhaps because of a similarity in the inflorescences of the two unrelated groups. *Camara* stems from a Latin word meaning "to arch," referring to the arching stems.

LANCE-LEAVED WATER-WILLOW

Justicia ovata var. *lanceolata*

ACANTHACEAE Acanthus Family

SIZE
Plant: To 12 inches, branching, forming colonies.
Flower: ⅜ inch, 2-lipped, in slender spikes from leaf axils.

LEAVES
1–4 inches, lanceolate, opposite, stalkless.

BLOOMS
March – June, occasional in fall.

This small but pretty wildflower occurs sparingly in moist woodlands and thickets and along the margins of streams and ponds throughout the Houston area. It was formerly classified as *Justicia lanceolata*, and it appears under that name in most books currently in use. However, authorities now consider this form from eastern Texas to be a variety of *J. ovata* found in the southeastern states. The genus name honors James Justice, an eighteenth-century Scottish horticulturist. *Ovata* and *lanceolata* refer to the shape of the leaves.

Lance-leaved water-willow is an erect or sprawling perennial that grows from spreading rhizomes to form small colonies in wet ground. Stems reach twelve inches and are usually branched. Slender, opposite leaves are sessile or have very short stalks.

Flowers appear on long, slender, one-sided spikes from the leaf axils. About three-eighths inch long, they are pale lavender or purple with darker markings and are distinctly two-lipped. The narrow upper lip is two-lobed; the lower lip is broadly three-lobed. Lance-leaved water-willow blooms from March through June and may occasionally bloom again in the fall.

Justicia represents a large and taxonomically difficult group of about three hundred tropical and subtropical species found around the world. It has occasionally been divided into several genera on the basis of rather tenuous distinctions. Species identification can be difficult, but only American water-willow, *J. americana*, occurs in eastern Texas with the lance-leaved water-willow. We have not seen it in the immediate Houston area. *Americana* normally has paler whitish flowers borne in denser, more compact axillary clusters.

SMALL-FLOWERED RUELLIA

Ruellia caroliniensis

Hairy ruellia, Wild petunia

ACANTHACEAE Acanthus Family

SIZE
*Plant: 1–2 feet,
  sparsely branched,
  hairy.
Flower: 1–2 inches,
  funnel-shaped,
  5-lobed.*

LEAVES
*To 4 inches, opposite,
  crowded.*

BLOOMS
April – September

Named for early French physician and herbalist Jean de la Ruelle (1474–1537), the genus *Ruellia* contains some 250 species, most of them in tropical America, Africa, and Asia. Nearly two dozen can be found in the United States, including fifteen species and several named subspecies and varieties in Texas. The group is difficult to identify to the species level without reference to detailed manuals and keys. The various species are collectively called "wild petunias" by many, but they are unrelated to the cultivated petunias, which are members of the nightshade family, the Solanaceae.

Small-flowered ruellia is a wildflower of the southeastern states, and it ranges into eastern Texas. We found it in semishaded woodlands at such locations as Memorial Park, the Spring Branch Science Center arboretum, and the University of Houston at Clear Lake. Densely hairy stems reach one to two feet and are sparingly branched. The opposite leaves are usually short-stalked and crowded on the stem; the funnel-shaped, five-lobed flowers are stalkless and clustered in the leaf axils. The flowers vary in color from blue to purple. In the shade they appear visually bluish, but they photograph more in the lavender portion of the spectrum, a common photographic problem with blue and purple flowers.

A Mexican species, *Ruellia brittoniana*, has been widely planted in Houston and throughout Texas and has now naturalized in many areas of the state. A tall, wiry plant to three feet, it spreads quickly to form large clumps. A cultivar called "Kate's compact" has been developed more recently and is also proving popular with local gardeners. It remains as a low, spreading mound and blooms profusely throughout the summer.

VIOLET RUELLIA

Ruellia nudiflora

Wild petunia, Longneck ruel

ACANTHACEAE Acanthus Family

SIZE
*Plant: To 2 feet,
 densely hairy when
 young, becoming
 smooth with age.
Flower: To 2¼ inches,
 funnel-shaped,
 5-lobed.*

LEAVES
*2–5 inches, gray-green,
 opposite, stalked,
 with wavy-toothed
 margins.*

BLOOMS
March – November

Ruellia nudiflora is more common and widely distributed in Houston than the previous species, *R. caroliniensis*. It prefers open, sunny locations and occupies roadsides and vacant lots throughout the area. An upright or sprawling perennial to two feet tall, it branches in the upper portions of the stem and has stalked, oval or lancelike leaves that are grayish green with wavy-toothed margins.

Large, showy flowers are borne on short stalks in terminal clusters and measure two inches or more in length. Funnel-shaped, they have five nearly equal lobes at the rim, unlike many of the Acanthaceae that have distinctly two-lipped flowers. The blossoms open at sunrise and drop early in the afternoon. They fall almost immediately if picked.

Actually, violet ruellia has two different types of flowers. Smaller clusters of "cleistogamous" flowers appear in early spring in the leaf axils. They never open and are self-fertilizing. They are followed later in the spring and through the summer by the typical blossoms. Both types produce viable seed.

ANNUAL ASTER

Aster subulatus

Awl-leaf aster, Blackweed, Hierba del marrano

ASTERACEAE Sunflower Family

SIZE
*Plant: To 3 feet,
branching, erect or
sprawling.*
*Flower head: ½ inch.
Rays pale blue to
purplish, disk
yellow.*

LEAVES
*To 4 inches, upper
leaves small,
narrow,
sharp-pointed.*

BLOOMS
August – December

Annual aster is the most abundant of its genus in Texas and in the Houston area. Found throughout the state, it prefers damp, poorly drained habitats such as roadside ditches and stream banks. However, it also grows as an invasive weed in Houston lawns and vacant lots. Stems grow up to three feet tall, branching freely to give a bushy appearance. In mowed lawns the pruned stems creep along the ground, forming tough mats of slender, wiry branches.

Flower heads grow singly at the ends of the branches and average about one-half inch in diameter. Although not particularly showy, they attract attention when numerous. Ray flowers vary in color from pale blue to purplish, and some populations are almost white. The central disk is yellow. Annual aster attracts a variety of butterflies during its blooming season in late summer and fall.

The leaves are alternate and narrow, with those on the upper portions much smaller than the lower ones. Sharp-pointed, they account for the scientific name *subulatus*, which means "awl-shaped" in Latin. *Aster* is the Greek word for "star," and asters were called "starworts" in early herbals and flower books. With their yellow centers and slender rays, they do indeed seem starlike. We use the same root for such words as "astronomy" and "astronaut."

LEAFY ELEPHANT-FOOT

Elephantopus carolinianus

Carolina elephant's-foot

ASTERACEAE Sunflower Family

SIZE
*Plant: 1–3 feet,
   branching, hairy.
Flower head: To
   ½ inch, contains few
   5-lobed disk flowers.
   2–5 heads in
   terminal cluster
   above 3 leafy bracts.*

LEAVES
*Stem leaves 2–7
   inches, alternate,
   oval, short-stalked,
   toothed on margins.*

BLOOMS
August – October

Elephantopus is a genus of about twenty-five species found throughout the warmer regions of the world. Most books state that the scientific name comes from a resemblance of the basal leaves to the foot of an elephant. Rickett, however, asserts that the leaves of our species "in no way suggest the feet of a pachyderm," and Bare speculates the name may be a translation of some aboriginal word. Whatever the source of its unusual name, leafy elephant-foot occurs abundantly in woodlands and thickets throughout the Houston area.

Hairy stems arise from a basal rosette of leaves and branch freely to a height of one to three feet. The basal leaves normally wither before flowering, but other large leaves adorn the stems and branches. Alternate and oval, they taper at the base to short stalks and are toothed on the margins.

From two to five small flower heads cluster together at the tips of the branches, each cluster subtended by three leaflike bracts. Each head contains a few bluish to purple disk flowers. These tubular flowers have five elongated lobes all pointing in the same direction, so that the combined flowers fit together like sections of a pie.

Hairy elephant-foot, *E. tomentosus*, occurs less frequently in the Houston area. It differs in having only basal leaves, without the large stem leaves of *E. carolinianus*.

MIST-FLOWER

Eupatorium coelestinum

Blue boneset, Wild ageratum

ASTERACEAE Sunflower Family

SIZE
*Plant: To 3 feet,
   upright or
   sprawling.*
*Flower head: ¼ inch,
   rays absent, in
   flat-topped clusters.*

LEAVES
*2–3 inches, opposite,
   triangular, strongly
   veined, margins
   toothed.*

BLOOMS
*July – December,
   sometimes earlier in
   spring.*

A common perennial in moist fields and open woodlands throughout the Houston area, mist-flower has gained popularity in wildflower gardens. It resembles species of the genus *Ageratum*, which are widely cultivated but which are of tropical origin and differ in small details of flower structure. Mist-flower grows up to three feet tall, although the weak stems often sprawl, and forms dense clumps and colonies from the roots. Most references state that it blooms from July until December frosts; however, we have recorded it in bloom in Houston's Memorial Park as early as May.

The opposite leaves have a triangular shape and are strongly veined and wrinkled. Leaf margins are shallowly toothed and at times take on a purplish hue.

Quarter-inch flower heads lack ray flowers but contain as many as forty to fifty blue or purplish disk flowers. The heads combine in dense, flattened, terminal clusters that provide a solid mass of color in a mist-flower colony, attracting many of the late-summer and autumn butterflies.

Two dozen *Eupatorium* species occur in Texas, many with white flower heads. For centuries people have claimed medicinal properties for them, resulting in such alternate names as "boneset." The genus name, says Janet Bare in *Wildflowers and Weeds of Kansas*, comes from Mithradates Eupator, king of Pontus in the first century B.C. According to Pliny, he was the first to use a plant of this genus for liver ailments. *Coelestinum* means "sky-blue."

SLENDER GAY-FEATHER

Liatris acidota

Sharp gay-feather, Slender blazing-star

ASTERACEAE Sunflower Family

SIZE
*Plant: 20–30 inches,
    erect, slender.
Flower head: 3–5 small
    disk flowers,
    phyllaries few and
    flattened beneath
    flower head.*

LEAVES
*Basal leaves 8–16
    inches, slender;
    stem leaves shorter
    and grasslike.*

BLOOMS
July – December

A dozen species and several named varieties of *Liatris* occur in Texas, seven or eight of them in our area. Combined with their propensity for crossbreeding in nature, this diversity makes them extremely difficult to identify. It is usually necessary to resort to microscopic examination of the phyllaries (the small bracts beneath the flower heads) and the pappus (the tiny bristles at the base of individual flowers). The common names "gay-feather" and "blazing-star" serve for the collective members of the genus, which are readily recognized by their elongated, bright purple flower spikes containing only five-lobed disk flowers.

Slender gay-feather, as the name implies, has slender, stiffly erect stems up to thirty inches tall. Basal leaves are long and narrow, while the crowded stem leaves become progressively shorter and more slender as they approach the top. Only three to five disk flowers compose each flower head, the heads in turn forming a terminal spike four to eight inches long. The phyllaries around each flower head are few in number and smooth, and they lie flat rather than curving outward.

Slender gay-feather occurs in Louisiana and eastern Texas and is the most common *Liatris* species in Houston. Although it prefers moist, sandy soils, it can be found in open fields and vacant lots throughout our area.

BRACTED GAY-FEATHER

Liatris bracteata

Bracted blazing-star

ASTERACEAE Sunflower Family

SIZE
Plant: To 30 inches,
   erect.
Flower head: 1 inch,
   containing 8–10 disk
   flowers, occasionally
   more at tip.
   Phyllaries broadly
   ovate, with sharp
   points.

LEAVES
To 5 inches at base,
   grasslike, stiff.

BLOOMS
September –
   November

Liatris bracteata is endemic to the coastal prairies of eastern Texas. Correll and Johnston list it only for Harris, Galveston, and Matagorda counties; however, they consider it "frequent" within that limited range. We found it along Clay Road and in vacant lots in northwestern Houston. Other books give no common name, the generic "gay-feather" and "blazing-star" sufficing for most *Liatris* species. To distinguish it from the others, we have used a translation of the scientific name, bracted gay-feather.

This handsome perennial has erect stems to thirty inches tall and smooth, stiff basal leaves five inches long. These narrow, grasslike leaves decrease in size upward along the stem. Flower heads contain from eight to ten flowers, although those near the upper tip of the plant may have up to fourteen, a feature that distinguishes this species from similar ones. The large size of the clusters and the bright purple color make *L. bracteata* particularly striking. The phyllaries, the overlapping bracts below each flower head, are broadly ovate and end in sharp points.

The various *Liatris* species are bright, showy wildflowers that deserve a prominent place in wildflower gardens. They are particularly attractive to butterflies and other insects and are available from dealers specializing in native plants.

PRAIRIE GAY-FEATHER

Liatris pycnostachya

Kansas blazing-star, Kansas gay-feather,
Prairie blazing-star, Hairy button-snakeroot

ASTERACEAE Sunflower Family

SIZE
*Plant: 2–5 feet, stem
  finely ribbed.
Flower head: ⅜ inch,
  containing 5–12 disk
  flowers. Phyllaries
  reflexed.*

LEAVES
*4 inches at base,
  narrow, grasslike.*

BLOOMS
June – October

One of the most widely distributed of the many *Liatris* species, prairie gay-feather ranges from Minnesota and Wisconsin southward to the Texas coast. It is also one of the stateliest of plants, standing up to five feet tall and having numerous purple flower heads crowded into dense terminal spikes as much as twenty inches long. The imposing scientific name *pycnostachya* reflects that attribute; it comes from the Greek for "crowded spike."

Narrow, grasslike leaves are also densely crowded on the finely ribbed stem. The small, compact heads contain from five to twelve disk flowers and open from the tip of the plant downward. The phyllaries, or bracts, below each flower head have sharp, reflexed tips that curve outward and downward. They provide the best key to identification of the species.

Prairie gay-feather is less abundant in Houston than the smaller slender gay-feather. However, it does occur in fields and remnant prairies throughout the area. It is also widely sold by dealers who handle native plants and makes a lovely addition to a wildflower garden. Florists frequently dry the flower spikes for use in winter arrangements.

Teas brewed from the roots of most *Liatris* species have been used as folk remedies for a number of kidney and bladder ailments, gonorrhea, and colic. They were also gargled for a sore throat. A poultice of the root was used for snakebite, resulting in the name "button snakeroot."

Most books list the origin of *Liatris* as unknown. Bare, however, suggests that "Von Schreber, the German botanist who gave this euphonious name, apparently invented it."

DOWNY LOBELIA

Lobelia puberula

Purple dewdrop

CAMPANULACEAE Bluebell Family

SIZE
Plant: 1–4 feet, erect,
 densely hairy.
Flower: ½–1 inch;
 2 upper petals,
 3 broader lower
 petals; 5 stamens
 fused into tube;
 purple with white
 center; in tall, often
 1-sided spike.

LEAVES
To 4 inches, alternate,
 sessile, usually
 toothed.

BLOOMS
August – December

The tubular flowers of the lobelias have a characteristic and easily recognizable shape, with two slender petals forming a narrow upper lip and three larger petals forming a broad lower lip. Most of the lobelias are blue or purple, but one red species, *Lobelia cardinalis* or cardinal-flower, occurs in Texas and throughout much of the country. It is widely planted, as are several of the blue species. A few authors place the lobelias in the family Lobeliaceae with several tropical genera because of the unique shape of their flowers.

Downy lobelia is an erect perennial densely covered with short hairs, as the name *puberula* suggests. The stem is usually unbranched and may reach four feet or more. Leaves are alternate and sessile, or unstalked, decreasing in size to become bracts beneath the flowers on the upper stem. Highly variable in shape, the leaves may be lanceolate or ovate, pointed or rounded at the tip, usually with small teeth along the margins.

The bloom spike of downy lobelia may reach a length of twenty inches and contain up to seventy-five flowers. Individual flowers from one-half to one inch long often occupy only one side of the slender spike. They are purple with white centers and are subtended by leafy bracts.

The genus name *Lobelia* commemorates Matthias de l'Obel, sometimes written as "Lobel." A Flemish botanist and herbalist, l'Obel lived from 1538 to 1616 and served as physician to James I of England. The name was first applied by Charles Plumier, a French naturalist who collected plants in the West Indies in the 1600s. Later, when Linnaeus was reclassifying plants and applying to them his new scientific nomenclature, he retained the epithet.

Lobelias were used medicinally by American Indians for a range of ailments. One, the big blue lobelia, was used as a root tea to treat syphilis and was subsequently named *L. siphilitica*. Most species contain powerful alkaloids and are extremely toxic. Poisonings are rare, however, except when the plants are used in home remedies. The drug lobeline was once used in medicine as a central nervous system stimulant in the treatment of respiratory depression.

VENUS' LOOKING-GLASS

Triodanis perfoliata

CAMPANULACEAE Bluebell Family

SIZE
Plant: To 2 feet,
   usually shorter.
   Stems angled,
   usually unbranched.
Flower: To ¾ inch,
   5-lobed, in leaf axils.

LEAVES
To 1 inch, shallowly
   toothed, clasping or
   sessile.

BLOOMS
April – July

The erect, unbranched stems of Venus' looking-glass are angled and covered with short hairs. This pretty little species occurs abundantly in open fields and vacant lots and even springs up as an annual weed in lawns and gardens throughout the Houston area. Two different varieties, *perfoliata* and *biflora,* occur in our region and throughout most of the state. Previously considered distinct species, they are now combined by Hatch, Gandhi, and Brown under the specific name *Triodanis perfoliata.*

The nominate variety *perfoliata* has rounded leaves that clasp the stem, and its flowers span three-quarters of an inch. Variety *biflora* has leaves that are longer than they are wide, and they are merely sessile, or stalkless, rather than clasping. Flowers of the latter variety are also smaller. The leaves of both are small, usually with shallowly lobed or toothed margins.

Both varieties have two distinct types of flowers, the feature referred to in the name *biflora.* Those near the tip of the plant open normally, but those in the lower leaf axils have almost no corolla and never open. These "cleistogamous" flowers are self-pollinating and produce seeds; however, recent tests have shown that only a very small percentage of those seeds germinate.

Venus' looking-glass gets its unusual name from a European species *Specularia speculum-veneris*, a Latinization of "mirror of Venus." Most books attribute the name to the flat, black, shiny seeds that look like tiny mirrors. Bare, however, quotes Prior's *Popular Names of British Plants* in asserting that the name refers to the "resemblance of its flowers set upon their cylindrical ovary to an ancient round mirror at the end of a straight handle." As with many plant names, the origin may be lost in antiquity.

North American species have sometimes been placed in the genus *Specularia*, but most authorities now feel they are sufficiently distinct to merit their own genus, *Triodanis*. The name comes from Greek words meaning "three-toothed," referring to the calyx of the flowers. The common name, however, has been retained.

Some medicinal uses have been attributed to Venus' looking-glass, and Ajilvsgi notes that the Cherokee steeped the roots and other parts of the plant and drank the infusion for indigestion.

SPREADING DAYFLOWER

Commelina diffusa

Low dayflower, Widow's tears

COMMELINACEAE Spiderwort Family

SIZE
Plant: Creeping stems to 3 feet, rooting at nodes.
Flower: ⅜ inch, all 3 petals blue.

LEAVES
1–4 inches, lancelike, sheathing the stem.

BLOOMS
March – December

Spreading dayflower ranges from the southeastern United States to tropical America. It occurs in damp soils of fields and thickets throughout the Houston area and can be a troublesome weed in lawns and gardens. An annual, it sends out branching stems that creep across the ground and root at the nodes, quickly forming securely rooted mats up to three feet across.

Lancelike leaves sheath the succulent stem, and the tiny blue flowers appear from a pair of bracts fused along one side into a boatlike spathe. All three petals are blue, unlike several similar species in which the small lower petal is white.

About 170 *Commelina* species occur throughout the tropical and subtropical regions of the world. Five species and several varieties are found in Texas. The genus takes its name from the Commelin (also spelled Commelijn) brothers, who were Dutch botanists. *Diffusa* means spreading, reflecting the growth habit of this sprawling, trailing plant. The name "dayflower" comes from the short-lived blossoms, which wilt quickly in the heat of the day.

ERECT DAYFLOWER

Commelina erecta

Widow's tears, Hierba del pollo

COMMELINACEAE Spiderwort Family

SIZE
Plant: 2–3 feet, erect or sprawling.
Flower: 1 inch. Upper 2 petals blue; lower petal smaller and white.

LEAVES
To 6 inches, lancelike, alternate, sheathing stem.

BLOOMS
May – October

Erect dayflower is larger than the previously described spreading dayflower, *Commelina diffusa*, with broader leaves that clasp the upright or sprawling stems. The unusual flower is also larger, with two blue petals and a much smaller lower petal that is whitish and easily overlooked. Several buds arise within a single boat-shaped spathe. The blossoms close early in the day, particularly in direct sunlight.

Erect dayflower is either a pretty and unusual wildflower or a pernicious weed, depending on your point of view. Common throughout the eastern two-thirds of Texas, it occurs frequently in gardens and vacant lots across Houston. A perennial, it overwinters by means of tuberous roots and puts out vigorous growth in the spring.

Swedish botanist Linnaeus, who invented our system of scientific nomenclature, named this genus for three Dutch botanists, the Commelin (or Commelijn) brothers. Two of the brothers, Jan and Kaspar, published widely in their field; the third died before becoming well known. Linnaeus thought the unequal petals of the dayflower nicely represented the talents of the three brothers.

OHIO SPIDERWORT

Tradescantia ohioensis

COMMELINACEAE Spiderwort Family

SIZE
Plant: To 3 feet,
  usually shorter.
Flower: 1½ inch,
  3 petals.

LEAVES
To 18 inches, narrow,
  clasping stem.

BLOOMS
February – June

Spiderworts begin blooming along Houston roadways and bayous in late February and continue into summer in locations that receive enough moisture. They prefer damp ditches but thrive in yards and gardens, becoming an invasive weed at times. A single clump of Ohio spiderwort that was moved into our yard several years ago has generated plants around every tree and throughout the flower beds. The most common and widespread of the spiderwort species in the U.S., *ohioensis* occurs through the eastern two-thirds of Texas. Because of frequent cultivation and escapes, it continues to show up in new locations across the country.

More than a dozen spiderwort species occur in Texas, and several are known to hybridize. Identification requires careful examination. While many species have the stems and sepals covered thickly with hairs, the Ohio spiderwort has smooth stems and no more than a small tuft of hairs at the tips of the sepals. It appears to be the most abundant species in Houston.

Flowers are commonly deep blue, but rose or white forms also occur sparingly. Arising in terminal clusters, they have three identical petals and three green, leaflike sepals. Flowers open in early morning and last but a few hours, closing in the heat of the day. The six stamens are covered with long hairs, which are favorite subjects of study in botanical laboratories. The hairs consist of chains of single cells that can be easily observed while still alive.

The jointed stems reach three feet in height and sometimes sprawl when subjected to rain and wind. When broken, they exude a clear, sticky sap. The long, slender leaves clasp the stem and dangle like a cluster of spider legs, resulting in the name "spiderwort," according to several sources. Other authors, however, attribute the name to the gluey sap that strings out like strands of spider silk. "Wort" is a common suffix for plant names and comes from the Anglo-Saxon *wyrt,* a word for any plant or herb.

The spiderwort genus, *Tradescantia,* honors John Tradescant, gardener to Charles I of England. Sent seeds from America, he was the first to grow these plants that are still popular in English gardens. Tradescant published his botanical studies in 1658 and also founded a museum of natural history.

STEMLESS SPIDERWORT

Tradescantia subacaulis

Small spiderwort

COMMELINACEAE Spiderwort Family

SIZE
Plant: 1–6 inches,
   occasionally taller;
   branching; hairy.
Flower: 1 inch,
   3 petals.

LEAVES
To 6 inches, narrow,
   hairy.

BLOOMS
March – May

While many of the *Tradescantia* species are tall, rangy plants, stemless spider-wort seldom reaches a height of more than a few inches. Leaves are also much shorter than those of the previously described Ohio spiderwort, *T. ohioensis.* Both the branching stems and the narrow leaves are densely hairy. Three-petalled flowers average one inch in diameter. While most flowers are blue-violet, rose-colored and occasional white ones may also be found. Stemless spiderwort prefers deep, sandy soils of open fields and roadsides and occurs in scattered locations around Houston.

Root tea prepared from various spiderworts was used by American Indians for kidney and stomach ailments and as a laxative. They also made leaf poultices to apply to insect bites and stings and to cancers. Tull suggests using the edible flowers and tender greens in a variety of salads, soups, stews, and vegetable dishes; however, she also notes that the mucilaginous sap has a distinctly unpleasant texture and the plants "are known not so fondly as 'snotweeds.'"

Martin reports that recent research on spiderworts indicates they are particularly sensitive to pollution and undergo mutations that cause blossoms to change from blue to pink within two weeks of exposure. The number of mutant cells apparently correlated well with the severity of the pollution.

TEXAS BLUEBONNET

Lupinus texensis

FABACEAE Pea Family

SIZE
Plant: 12–24 inches.
Flower: Pealike, on
* 6-inch spikes.*

LEAVES
With 5 leaflets, all
* joined at a common*
* point.*

BLOOMS
March – May

Perhaps no Texas wildflower is better known or more popular than the blue-bonnet. J. Frank Dobie wrote of it, "No other flower—for me at least—brings such upsurging of the spirit and at the same time such restfulness."

This species, the Texas bluebonnet, is the most widespread of six related lupine species found within state borders. It is naturally most abundant on the limestone hillsides of central Texas, but it has been widely propagated and planted by the highway department in its beautification program. In spite of its wide distribution and scientific name, however, the Texas bluebonnet was not the first to be designated the state flower, nor does it currently hold that honor alone.

In 1901, the Texas Legislature voted the bluebonnet the floral symbol of the state over such contenders as the cotton boll ("the white rose of commerce") and the prickly-pear cactus. The latter was championed by John Nance "Cactus Jack" Garner, who later became vice-president of the United States. The resolution specified that "*Lupinus subcarnosus,* generally known as buffalo clover or blue bonnet," be adopted. It seems unlikely that the legislators knew there were other bluebonnets, or that the one they chose was less widely distributed than the one already designated scientifically as the Texas lupine. A controversy over the choice existed for seventy years, until 1971, when another resolution declared as state flowers all known bluebonnets and "any other variety of Bluebonnet not heretofore recorded." We currently have six.

Lupinus texensis is the species most frequently seen along Houston roadways and on the popular Texas bluebonnet trails. It differs from *L. subcarnosus,* the sandyland bluebonnet, in having showy white tips to the flower stalks and more pointed leaflets. The leaflets of the latter are usually rounded or truncated at the tips.

Not only do the bluebonnets serve as lovely harbingers of spring, but they rank among the most useful of all Texas legumes in returning nitrogen to the soil. Because the plants often grow in poor soils, however, people in ancient times seem to have confused the cause and effect. *Lupinus* was the old Latin name and stems from *lupus,* or "wolf," apparently from a belief that lupines destroyed the soil rather than enriched it.

DEER PEA VETCH

Vicia ludoviciana

Louisiana vetch

FABACEAE Pea Family

SIZE
Plant: Stems to 3 feet, sprawling and climbing.
Flower: ¼ inch, 2–13 in raceme, pealike.

LEAVES
To 3 inches, ending in forked tendril. 6–12 leaflets.

BLOOMS
March – May

The genus name *Vicia* and the Anglicized "vetch" owe their origins to the Latin *vincire*, meaning "to bind or twist." The various vetches sprawl and climb, sometimes forming dense mats. They prove useful for erosion control and have been planted along highway embankments in various parts of the country, further complicating the problem of identifying the many similar species. A dozen different species and several named varieties occur in Texas. They provide native browse for animals, while serving to enrich the soil.

Deer pea vetch is common throughout the Houston area, springing up as a "weed" in fields and fencerows and even in backyard gardens. Three different varieties range across the eastern half of Texas. *Ludoviciana* has leaves one to three inches long, terminating in forked tendrils that aid in climbing. Each leaf has six to twelve leaflets, and the small lavender-blue to deep purple flowers number from two to thirteen in an elongated cluster.

TALL PRAIRIE-GENTIAN

Eustoma exaltatum

Catchfly gentian, Bluebell gentian, Seaside gentian,
Lesser bluebell, Alkali chalice

GENTIANACEAE Gentian Family

SIZE
Plant: 20–30 inches,
  erect, smooth,
  sparsely branched.
Flower: 1–2 inches,
  5-petalled, on long
  stalks from leaf
  axils.

LEAVES
To 3 inches, clasping
  stem.

BLOOMS
May – October

Tall prairie-gentian and the next species, showy prairie-gentian, *Eustoma grandiflorum*, travel under a multitude of common names. One of the most frequently heard is "bluebell"; however, that name is also applied to several other unrelated wildflowers across the continent. The two species look much alike and differ primarily in the size of their flowers and in habitat. *E. exaltatum* has petal lobes less than an inch in length and prefers sandy saline or alkali soils; *E. grandiflorum* has petal lobes measuring more than one inch and grows in rich, moist fields and prairies.

The specific name *exaltatum* as applied to plants usually means "tall." Tall prairie-gentian is an erect, sparingly branched annual reaching twenty to thirty inches. The leaves are opposite and clasp the stem. They vary in shape from lancelike to oblong and may be either rounded at the tip or sharply pointed.

Flowers up to two inches across are deeply cupped and appear on long stalks from the upper leaf axils, forming showy terminal clusters. The typical color form is blue-violet with a darker purple blotch in the throat, but paler rose and even white flowers can be found.

Tall prairie-gentian ranges from Florida to Texas in sandy coastal areas and also occurs in alkaline soils across the southern and western parts of our state. In the Houston area it is most often found near beaches and coastal flats around Galveston Bay.

The genus name *Eustoma* comes from the Greek for "good opening" or "open mouth" and refers to the wide opening into the corolla tube.

SHOWY PRAIRIE-GENTIAN

Eustoma grandiflorum

Bluebells, Texas bluebell, Lira de San Pedro

GENTIANACEAE Gentian Family

SIZE
*Plant: To 28 inches,
    branching, smooth.
Flower: 2–4 inches,
    5-petalled, on stalks
    from leaf axils.*

LEAVES
*To 3 inches, clasping
    stem.*

BLOOMS
June – September

One of the most beautiful of all our wildflowers, showy prairie-gentian ranges across the prairies from Texas to Nebraska and occurs throughout most of our state. It prefers rich, damp soils in open fields and can be seen along Houston-area roadsides from June into September. A short-lived perennial, it may be abundant one year and difficult to find the next. Some populations are apparently declining, and Ajilvsgi noted that it is becoming rare in the Big Thicket.

The erect, branching stems have opposite, clasping leaves, and the foliage is often covered with a whitish coating that is easily rubbed off. The five-petalled, deeply cupped flowers span two to four inches and are much larger and brighter than those of tall prairie-gentian, *Eustoma exaltatum.* Most are blue-violet with a darker purple center; however, white flowers also occur.

Showy prairie-gentian does well in cultivation if given moist soil and plenty of sun. Cut flowers last for several days, but they should not be taken from the wild. Seeds are available commercially from several companies that handle wildflowers.

Flowers of *Eustoma* are adapted for cross-pollination by bees and other insects. In a strategy called proterandry, the anthers discharge their pollen before the stigma lobes have matured. When the anthers are empty, the style then elongates and the stigma lobes expand, ready to receive fresh pollen brought by an insect from another flower.

BLUE WATERLEAF

Hydrolea ovata

Hairy hydrolea, Ovate-leaved hydrolea, Water olive

HYDROPHYLLACEAE Waterleaf Family

SIZE
Plant: To 30 inches,
  spiny, covered with
  dense hairs.
Flower: 1–1½ inches,
  5-lobed.

LEAVES
1–2½ inches, alternate,
  egg-shaped, with
  sharp spine at base.

BLOOMS
August – October

A hairy, spiny perennial, blue waterleaf spreads from thick roots to form colonies around the edges of ponds and streams. It prefers muddy soils and can stand in water for weeks without apparent harm. In the Houston area it occurs most frequently in wet ditches and along the borders of marshes, but we also found it in low thickets within Memorial Park.

The sturdy stems reach thirty inches and branch in their upper portions. Leaves range from one to two and one-half inches long and are broadly "egg-shaped," as the name *ovata* implies. Each short leaf-stalk has a sharp, slender spine at its base.

Funnel-shaped flowers are deeply five-lobed and occur in terminal clusters and in long-stalked clusters from the leaf axils. Deep blue in color, the flowers measure an inch or more across. Caroline Dormon noted that the color "comes very near to being a true blue—a rare shade."

HERBERTIA

Herbertia lahue subsp. *caerulea*

Prairie nymph, Celestial

IRIDACEAE Iris Family

SIZE
Plant: 6–12 inches.
Flower: 2 inches.
   3 outer sepals large
   and petallike;
   3 inner petals small
   and triangular.

LEAVES
To 12 inches, grasslike,
   folded together.

BLOOMS
March – May

Although it is one of our most beautiful wildflowers, the delicate herbertia has suffered through a long-term identity crisis. Older Texas flower books called it *Herbertia caerulea* and then *H. drummondii*. It was later reclassified as *Alophia drummondii*, a name under which it appears in Correll and Johnston and most other books presently in use. A few authors, however, called it *Trifurcia lahue*. More recently, both Johnston and Hatch, Gandhi, and Brown have suggested the correct name should be *Herbertia lahue* subspecies *caerulea*.

These changes have apparently resulted from confusion between herbertia and another member of the iris family commonly called the purple pleat-leaf or pinewoods lily. This resident of the East Texas pine forests was formerly called *Eustylis purpurea* but now formally assumes herbertia's old name, *Alophia drummondii*.

Through all this, herbertia has had no widely accepted common name, perhaps accounting for the fact that it has received little praise or recognition. Occasional authors have coined such names as "prairie nymph" and "celestial," but most refer to it by the old and present genus name "herbertia."

Herbertia grows six to twelve inches high from a deep perennial bulb. Basal leaves are narrow and grasslike. Up to twelve inches long, the leaves fold together over most of their length. Blue-violet flowers span two inches and have two different types of "tepals," the combined sepals and petals characteristic of the iris family. Three outer segments are broad and spreading, their white bases heavily spotted with purple. The three tiny inner segments are darker and triangular in shape.

Endemic to southern and eastern Texas and western Louisiana, herbertia occurs in widely scattered colonies in open fields and vacant lots. Where it is established, however, it is often abundant. We found one small vacant lot on the western side of Houston that sported several hundred herbertias in full bloom. Combined with an equal number of wine-cups, they provided an astounding spring spectacle.

NARROW-LEAVED BLUE-EYED GRASS

Sisyrinchium angustifolium

Bermuda blue-eyed grass, Pointed blue-eyed grass

IRIDACEAE Iris Family

SIZE
Plant: To 20 inches,
*   forming clumps.*
Flower: ½–¾ inch, 6
*   combined petals and*
*   sepals, blue with*
*   yellow center.*

LEAVES
To 20 inches, narrow,
*   grasslike.*

BLOOMS
March – May

We use narrow-leaved blue-eyed grass in this book as the representative of a very large and confusing group of blue-flowered species in the genus *Sisyrinchium*. Authors list from 80 to 125 different species ranging through North America and into the tropics. Sixteen of those have been attributed to Texas. Many of the latter occur in the immediate Houston area and can be separated only by close examination and reference to detailed keys. To further complicate the issue, the species hybridize readily. Most wildflower enthusiasts will be satisfied to call our plants simply "blue-eyed grass."

S. angustifolium ranges throughout the eastern states, from Canada to Florida and Texas. It has long, slender, grasslike leaves and forms perennial clumps up to twenty inches high. The stems are broadly winged or flattened and frequently branched. Three petals and three sepals look much alike and are collectively called "tepals." Bright to pale blue, they have yellow bases.

This species and others occur in open fields and along roadsides throughout the Houston area. They bloom in spring and often carpet the countryside with sheets of blue.

Bare, in her *Wildflowers and Weeds of Kansas,* reminds us that while the name "blue-eyed grass" is attractive, it is inappropriate. The plants are not grasses but belong to the iris family. Moreover, the center or "eye" of the flower is yellow, contrasting with the blue tepals. "But one must admit the faults in vernacular usage will not be corrected by logic," Bare notes.

SELF-HEAL

Prunella vulgaris

Heal-all, Carpenter-weed

LAMIACEAE Mint Family

SIZE
Plant: To 2 feet,
usually shorter.
Flower: ¾ inch,
clustered in dense
spikes.

LEAVES
To 3 inches, opposite,
variable.

BLOOMS
April – June

The pretty self-heal can be confused with no other Houston wildflower. Individual blossoms form dense clusters on a squarish terminal spike, interspersed with green, leafy bracts. The upper flower lip is normally dark purple, upright, and cupped. The lower lip is lighter in color and three-lobed. It droops markedly and has a fringed margin. Only a few flowers on the head open at a time. Blooming from April into June, self-heal can be found in fields and along roadways throughout the Houston area.

Plants sometimes reach two feet in height but usually remain much shorter. Opposite leaves are long-stalked and taper at the base, but they vary greatly in shape. They have smooth or slightly toothed margins. Bees and butterflies find the flowers a highly attractive nectar source.

As its name implies, self-heal has been utilized in a number of medicinal applications. Ajilvsgi notes that the Cherokee used it on bruises, burns, and cuts and to flavor other medicines. Most members of the genus are Old World species, and they, too, have been applied medicinally for centuries. Authorities do not agree on the origin of the scientific name, as is often the case with archaic terms. Bare asserts *Prunella* is a diminutive form of the Latin *pruna*, meaning "glowing coal," implying a reduction of inflammations. Rickett, however, says the name was originally *brunella*, from the German word for quinsy, an acute inflammation of the tonsils, which the plants were supposed to cure. *Vulgaris* simply means "common."

LYRE-LEAF SAGE

Salvia lyrata

Cancer-weed, Lyre-leaf salvia

LAMIACEAE Mint Family

SIZE
Plant: 1–2 feet.
Flower: 1 inch, 2-
lipped. In whorls
around the stem.

LEAVES
To 8 inches, mostly
basal, lobed, often
purplish.

BLOOMS
February – May

This common perennial blooms throughout Houston in early spring, usually beginning in February and continuing into May. With abundant rainfall, the flowering period may extend even longer. The upright, hairy stem is square in cross section and rises from a basal rosette of leaves to a height of one to two feet. It is unbranched or branches in pairs only in the flowering portion. The delicate inch-long, two-lipped flowers are pale blue or bluish violet and are arranged in several whorls around the stem to form an interrupted spike. The stalked basal leaves are deeply lobed, with the largest lobe at the tip. They often have a purple tinge, especially during the cooler months.

The genus *Salvia* contains more than seven hundred species around the world, many of them in the American tropics. The name comes from the Latin *salvare*, "to heal," and refers to numerous medicinal uses through the centuries. Tull recommends using *Salvia* leaves for teas or seasonings, while Ajilvsgi notes that lyre-leaf sage was used by the Cherokee to brew a tea for colds and coughs and to use as a laxative. It was also mixed with honey to treat asthma.

Many of the salvias are prized in wildflower gardens. They attract humming-birds, butterflies, and bees with their nectar. Bees appear to be the chief pollinators of lyre-leaf sage, landing on the broad lower lip and tipping the two stamens to receive a liberal dousing with pollen.

DRUMMOND SKULLCAP

Scutellaria drummondii

LAMIACEAE Mint Family

SIZE
Plant: 8–12 inches, upright or sprawling, branching at the base.
Flower: ½ inch, 2-lipped.

LEAVES
¼–¾ inch, oval, hairy.

BLOOMS
February – November

Drummond skullcap will not stop traffic with its floral display along Houston's busy freeways, but this tiny wildflower is a charmer worthy of notice. It blooms from early spring into late autumn along the roadsides and bayous within the city. We found it abundant along the banks of Braes Bayou at Highway 288, within sight of Hermann Park and the Medical Center, from February through November.

The upright or sprawling stems reach eight to twelve inches and branch freely at the base. The small, opposite, oval leaves are densely covered with soft, spreading hairs. Lower leaves have slender stalks; upper ones nearly clasp the square stem. The half-inch flowers are borne in the axils of the upper leaves. Blue-violet or purple, the flower has a rounded, moundlike upper lip and an open, flat lower lip bearing a square white area dotted with purple.

Drummond skullcap ranges from Kansas to Texas and occurs throughout our state. Larger *Scutellaria* species occupy eastern Texas, but they do not appear as frequently within the city. The skullcaps take their name from the caplike calyx that remains on the plant after it has dropped its seeds.

Although tiny, this species would make an attractive border plant for wildflower gardens. While many of the mints are used for brewing herb teas, however, the skullcaps are reported to be toxic.

LANCE-LEAF LOOSESTRIFE

Lythrum alatum var. *lanceolatum*

LYTHRACEAE Loosestrife Family

SIZE
Plant: To 5 feet,
forming large
colonies. Stems
4-angled, stiff,
upright.
Flower: ½ inch, in leaf
axils, 4- to
6-petalled.

LEAVES
Lower leaves to
2 inches, alternate;
upper leaves smaller,
opposite, held
against stem.

BLOOMS
April – October

Lance-leaf loosestrife occurs in wet fields and ditches and along marshy borders throughout the Houston area. A tough, rangy plant, it spreads from the base to form large colonies and reaches a height of five feet. Our form was formerly given full species status as *Lythrum lanceolatum;* however, the most recent checklists consider it a variety of the widely distributed winged loosestrife, *L. alatum.* The typical form ranges from Canada through the eastern states and has slender wings on the stem, while the variety found in Texas merely has four-angled stems.

Lower leaves are alternate and up to two inches long; the smaller upper leaves are opposite and often fold flat against the stem. Half-inch flowers appear in the leaf axils and range in color from purple to lavender-blue. Most have six petals, but four- and five-petalled flowers also occur on the same plant.

The genus *Lythrum* takes its name from the Greek *lythron,* meaning "clotted blood." Most authors attribute the name to the flower color of the European purple loosestrife, *L. salicaria,* a species that has become a troublesome invader in North America. Other authors, however, suggest the name may also stem from the styptic qualities of the plants, and Ajilvsgi notes that lance-leaf loosestrife serves as a useful astringent in Mexico.

"Loosestrife" is a direct translation of the Greek *lysimachia*, an early name applied to *Lythrum* species during the time of Alexander the Great. According to Pliny, if sprigs of loosestrife were placed on the yokes of troublesome oxen, the balky animals became more peaceful and worked well together.

PURPLE PASSION-FLOWER

Passiflora incarnata

Maypop, Apricot-vine, Passion-vine, Pasionaria

PASSIFLORACEAE Passion-flower Family

SIZE
*Plant: Trailing,
    climbing vine to 25
    feet.*
*Flower: 2–3 inches,
    with fringed corona,
    on stalks from leaf
    axils.*

LEAVES
*3–5 inches, alternate,
    deeply 3-lobed.*

BLOOMS
April – September

A trailing, climbing perennial vine, purple passion-flower has stems up to twenty-five feet long that clamber over bushes and fences throughout the Houston area. It inhabits fields, fencerows, and woodland edges, and we have even found it springing up in parking lots and cracks in downtown sidewalks. The vines are supported by tendrils arising from the axils of the alternate, deeply three-lobed leaves.

The unique flowers are difficult to describe but easily recognized on any of the *Passiflora* species. Those of *P. incarnata* span up to three inches and appear on short stalks from the leaf axils. Five sepals and five petals look much alike and are covered by the fringed corona of crimped filaments. Five stamens unite in a tube at their bases and spread in the upper portion of the flower. The three-part pistil rises above the stamens.

The fruit is a two- to three-inch berry that turns orange-yellow when ripe. Edible pulp can be sucked from the husk or made into juice or jelly, and tropical species are raised commercially for their fruits. The name "maypop," according to Durant, is the Anglicization of the Indian *maracock*, a name that made its way from the Tupi Indians of South America up through the Arawaks and Caribs to North American tribes. In the original Tupi it was *maraca-cui-iba*, "rattle fruit," because the seeds rattled in the gourdlike fruits after drying.

American Indians used the passion-flower for a number of medicinal applications, and modern research has shown that extracts are mildly sedative, reduce blood pressure, increase respiratory rate, and decrease motor activity. Thus, the fruits are potentially harmful in large amounts.

The genus *Passiflora* contains more than four hundred species, with the population centered in the American tropics. They are the larval food plants of a family of butterflies called the heliconians, and toxic elements in the plant tissue serve to protect the butterflies as well. Both plant and insect have evolved a complex series of adaptations in the battle for survival. Houston passion-flowers feed the spiny caterpillars of the pretty gulf fritillary butterfly.

These fascinating plants were named by the early explorers, many of whom were priests. They saw in the unusual flowers the signs of the crucifixion. The five sepals and five petals taken together represented the ten faithful apostles (Judas betrayed Jesus, and Peter denied him). The fringed corona was the crown of thorns, the five stamens represented the five wounds, and the three styles of the pistil were the nails. When the Jesuits found the Indians eating the fruit, says Martin, they took it as a sign that the tribes were hungry for Christianity.

"This requires a pretty healthy imagination," the Loughmillers suggest in their book, *Texas Wildflowers*. "Such extraordinarily complex flowers can stand on their own merits." Indeed, few of our wildflowers are more worthy of closer study than the intricate purple passion-flower.

DOWNY PHLOX

Phlox pilosa

Prairie phlox

POLEMONIACEAE Phlox Family

SIZE
*Plant: 1–2 feet,
    slender, covered
    with fine hairs.
Flower: 1 inch,
    5-petalled, in
    terminal clusters.*

LEAVES
*To 5 inches, narrow,
    often with rolled
    margins.*

BLOOMS
April – May

Downy phlox ranges from New England and the northern tier of states southward to Florida and Texas. It is particularly common in open pine woodlands in East Texas but also occurs in fields and along fencerows throughout the Houston area. Flower color ranges from bluish lavender to pink or magenta, and occasional white blossoms are also found. We have chosen to put it with the blue/violet flowers, but some books place it with the reds and pinks.

A slender perennial standing one to two feet tall, downy phlox is covered with glandular hairs that render it sticky to the touch. *Pilosa* means "covered with soft hairs." Leaves up to five inches long are very narrow and often have rolled margins. They are opposite on the lower stem but may become alternate near the large terminal flower clusters.

Flowers have short, narrow tubes and flare into five broad petal lobes spanning one inch. Each petal often has a bilobed purple mark within a white patch at the base. The stamens are hidden within the corolla tube.

The name "phlox" comes from a Greek word for "flame" and was applied by Pliny to a red flower of unknown lineage. When Linnaeus subsequently named a new plant with reddish flowers from the southeastern states, he appropriated *Phlox* as the genus.

The genus is largely North American and contains approximately seventy species. Many were collected and sent to Europe in the eighteenth century, where they became popular garden plants. Only when they were brought back to America by European horticulturists were they widely cultivated here. The bright, sweet-scented flowers attract numerous butterflies, and our native phlox deserve more consideration for wildflower gardens.

WATER-HYACINTH

Eichhornia crassipes

River-raft, Water orchid, Wampee

PONTEDERIACEAE Pickerel-weed Family

SIZE
*Plant: Aquatic,
   floating or rooted in
   mud.*
*Flower: 2 inches, 6
   petals and sepals, in
   6- to 16-inch spikes.*

LEAVES
*Rounded blades on
   inflated stalks from
   the base.*

BLOOMS
*April – July, less
   commonly until
   frost.*

Despite its undeniable beauty, the alien water-hyacinth has become a noxious pest in the southeastern states, clogging waterways and crowding out native vegetation. The aquatic plant floats freely or roots in the mud, reproducing vegetatively from stolons at an incredible rate to form dense colonies. An inhabitant of bayous, canals, and freshwater marshes, it is not common in the immediate Houston area, but it is readily seen in waterways closer to the coast.

Tough, leathery leaves have rounded blades borne on stalks inflated with spongy tissue. Two-inch flowers are blue to bluish purple and have six combined petals and sepals. The upper petal is streaked with darker purple and centered with a bright yellow spot. The flowers form spikes six to sixteen inches tall and bloom from April into July. Under proper conditions some plants may flower through the fall until a heavy frost.

The genus *Eichhornia* takes its name from J.A.F. Eichhorn (1779–1856), a

Prussian statesman and court adviser. *Crassipes* means "thick-footed" or "thick-stalked," referring to the inflated bases of the leaves.

A native of Brazil, water-hyacinth was apparently introduced into the United States at the 1884 Cotton States Exposition in New Orleans. Aquatic gardeners were impressed with its beauty and carried home large quantities of the lush green plants. Within a decade they were choking waterways from Virginia to Louisiana. In one experiment quoted by Tull, two parent plants produced twelve hundred offspring in four months. Not only do they reproduce vegetatively, but they generate large numbers of seeds that sink to the bottom and remain viable for several years.

Experiments aimed at producing a food supplement for livestock and a flour additive for humans have been underway for several years. These additives are high in protein, minerals, and vitamins and may prove valuable in the future. Production of paper pulp and antibacterial drugs from the bountiful plants is also being studied. In addition, water-hyacinths have demonstrated a remarkable ability to purify polluted water and to remove heavy metals and other toxins.

Thus, this lovely, alien aquatic plant may someday be a valuable natural resource, but so far it has proved more of a curse than a blessing.

BLUE MUD-PLANTAIN

Heteranthera limosa

PONTEDERIACEAE Pickerel-weed Family

SIZE
*Plant: To 6 inches, in
shallow water or
mud.
Flower: 1 inch, 6
combined petals and
sepals.*

LEAVES
*1–4 inches, stalked,
oval or lanceolate
blade.*

BLOOMS
April – December

Although this relative of water-hyacinth and pickerel-weed occurs widely from Minnesota to Florida and Mexico, it is seldom noticed because of its small size and watery habitat. The specific name comes from the Latin *limosus*, which means "growing in muddy places," and mud-plantain does indeed grow on the muddy edges of ponds and ditches or in shallow water. We found it in flooded rice fields west of Houston and in water-filled ditches in northern Harris County.

The plants either form rosettes in the mud or send out elongated creeping stems that root at the nodes. Correll and Johnston note that what we now consider to be two forms of a single species might, with further study, prove to be two distinct entities.

Long-stalked leaves have oval or lance-shaped blades and range from one to four inches long. The one-inch flowers have six combined petals and sepals and vary in color from blue-violet to white. The genus *Heteranthera* takes its name from the Greek words *hetera*, "different," and *anthera*, "anther." Two of the three stamens have yellow, ovoid anthers, while the third has a longer, greenish anther.

PICKEREL-WEED

Pontederia cordata

PONTEDERIACEAE Pickerel-weed Family

SIZE
Plant: 1–3 feet,
  aquatic, with
  emergent leaves and
  flower spikes.
Flower: ⅓ inch,
  6 tepals forming
  2 lips, on crowded
  6-inch spikes.

LEAVES
Long-stalked, with
  heart-shaped or
  lancelike blades.

BLOOMS
June – September

The aquatic pickerel-weed inhabits sluggish bayous, freshwater marshes, and water-filled ditches throughout the Houston area. Sprouting from creeping rhizomes rooted in the mud, it forms large colonies, with the leaves and flower spikes held above the shallow water on stalks from one to three feet long. It blooms throughout the summer, from June until September.

A single leaf occupies the flower stalk just below the inflorescence, while others rise from the base. The leaf blades vary from heart-shaped (cordate) to lancelike. Plants with slender, lancelike leaves have often been accorded species status as *Pontederia lanceolata* or listed as a variety of *P. cordata*. Intergrades are common, however, and the two forms probably do not deserve consideration as separate taxa.

Funnel-shaped flowers are numerous on a slender, crowded spike six inches long. Each violet-blue, funnel-shaped flower spans one-third inch and has six combined petals and sepals. Two yellow spots ornament the central petal of the upper lip.

According to Tull, the seeds of pickerel-weed can be eaten like nuts, either raw or roasted, and the young leaf stalks can be cooked as greens. She warns that plants used for food should be taken only from clean, unpolluted water.

Most authors state that pickerel-weed takes its name from the fact that it shares its habitat with pickerel and other fish. Durant, however, suggests that the name came from England, where it was used for centuries for a similar type of pond weed linked with the ancient belief in "spontaneous generation." Certain plants and animals were believed to generate other animals. Barnacles, for example, were reputed to give rise to geese, and some trees blossomed with sheep. The 1558 *Historia Animalium* by Gesner suggested that certain water weeds spontaneously bred pike and pickerel.

Thus, Izaak Walton, in his 1653 *The Compleat Angler*, wrote: "The mighty Pike is taken to be the Tyrant (as the Salmon is the King) of the fresh waters. Tis not to be doubted, but that they are bred, some by generation, and some not: as namely, of a Weed called Pickerel-weed, unless learned Gesner be much mistaken, for he says, this weed and other glutinous matter, with the help of the Sun's heat in some particular Months, and some Ponds apted for it by nature, do become Pikes."

CURLY CLEMATIS

Clematis crispa

Blue jasmine, Curl-flower, Hyacinth-vine

RANUNCULACEAE Buttercup Family

SIZE
*Plant: Trailing,
   climbing stems to
   6 feet.
Flower: 1–2 inches,
   vaselike.*

LEAVES
*Compound, with 2–5
   pairs of leaflets.*

BLOOMS
March – October

Curly clematis seems to hide its beauty from would-be admirers. A perennial vine, it climbs freely over fences and shrubs or sprawls and trails across the ground, blooming while still quite small. However, the violet, vase-shaped flowers hang upside down on naked stems, often going unseen. Once discovered, their lovely color and unusual form make them one of our choicest wildflowers. There are no petals, and the thick, fleshy sepals unite to form the flower. They separate at the rim into four petallike lobes. Wavy and crimped, the thin edges curl backward and twist to the side, revealing the many stamens and pistils contained within the hanging vase.

The compound leaves of curly clematis divide into two to five pairs of leaflets, some of which may be further lobed. The tender vine climbs by twining of the leaf petioles around its support.

Clematis pitcheri, often called leather-flower, has shorter sepals and the leaves bear a conspicuous network of veins. Other species occur throughout the state. The genus name comes from the Greek *klematis,* a classical name for various climbing or trailing vines.

BLUE LARKSPUR

Delphinium carolinianum

Carolina larkspur

RANUNCULACEAE Buttercup Family

SIZE
Plant: 1–3 feet,
*   slender, perennial.*
Flower: 1 inch, in slim
*   spike, with long*
*   spur, dark to pale*
*   blue or whitish.*

LEAVES
Alternate, broad,
*   stalked, blade*
*   divided and lobed.*

BLOOMS
April – July

Most gardeners know the delphiniums, or larkspurs, as richly colored, showy cultivars; however, several species also grow wild across the country. Blue, or Carolina, larkspur ranges from the southeastern states through most of Texas except for the Panhandle. It occurs sporadically in dry, sandy fields and open woodlands throughout the Houston area.

The slender perennial grows one to three feet tall from tuberlike roots and has broad, long-stalked leaves divided and lobed into many narrow segments. Basal leaves sometimes form a rosette in winter, but they wither before the spring blooming season begins.

The unusual one-inch flowers appear on short stalks on a thin terminal spike. There are five colored, petallike sepals, the upper one projecting backward into a pronounced spur, and four smaller petals. The upper two petals have spurs that fit into the longer spur of the sepal.

Typical southeastern blue larkspurs have dark blue flowers, but most plants in the Houston area tend to be pale blue or almost white. Brown identifies them as *Delphinium carolinianum,* but he suggests there may be some intergradation with the paler prairie larkspur, *D. virescens.*

"Larkspur" is an old English name alluding to the fancied resemblance of the flower's spur to the long hind claw of the European crested lark. The Spanish name for the flower, *espuela del caballero,* emphasizes the likeness to a horseman's spur. The genus name *Delphinium* dates back to ancient times. It was used by first-century Greek physician Dioscorides, presumably stemming from the resemblance of the unopened flower to the head of a dolphin, *delphin* in Greek.

Larkspurs contain toxic alkaloids, and all parts of the plants should be considered deadly. Wild species in the western states have occasionally caused major losses of cattle and sheep. According to Tull, a lotion prepared from larkspur seeds was used until recent years to treat head lice. However, it was removed from the market because of human poisonings by ingestion and by absorption of the lotion through cuts in the skin.

SMALL BLUETS

Hedyotis crassifolia

Tiny bluets, Low bluets, Violet bluets, Star-violet

RUBIACEAE Madder Family

SIZE
Plant: To 5 inches,
  sprawling,
  branching, forming
  colonies.
Flower: To ¼ inch,
  tubular, 4-lobed.

LEAVES
To ½ inch, opposite,
  short-stalked, oval.

BLOOMS
February – April

With its delicate, branching stems that seldom exceed four or five inches and its tiny flowers, small bluets might easily go unnoticed. However, it forms large colonies in fields and along mowed roadsides, heralding spring with a blanket of blue before other wildflowers make their appearance. The low-growing winter annual blooms throughout the Houston area from February into April. If there has been no hard freeze, it may even put out its first flowers in January. The trumpet-shaped, four-lobed blossoms appear at the tips of the sprawling stems, surrounded by opposite, oval leaves on short stalks. Flowers are blue-violet to lilac, rarely white.

All of the flowers look alike at first glance, but Bare points out that there are really two different types. Some have long stamens and a short pistil; others have a longer pistil and short stamens. Bees seeking nectar from flowers of one type are daubed with pollen at just the right height to fertilize flowers of the other type, thereby facilitating cross-pollination.

Within this genus of nearly three hundred species, nineteen of which occur in Texas, species identification is often difficult. Small bluets appeared in older publications as *Houstonia minima* and then as both *Hedyotis minima* and *H. pusilla*. "The latest preference is for *Hedyotis crassifolia*," wrote Rickett, commenting on the vagaries of botanical nomenclature, "a name given by that eccentric genius Constantine Rafinesque-Schmalz. It means 'thick-leaved,' which the plants are not."

COASTAL WATER-HYSSOP

Bacopa monnieri

Smooth water-hyssop

SCROPHULARIACEAE Snapdragon Family

SIZE
Plant: To 6 inches;
aquatic, with
creeping or floating
stems, succulent,
smooth.
Flower: To ½ inch,
5-lobed, bell-shaped,
on stalks longer than
the leaves.

LEAVES
To 1 inch, elliptic or
spatulate, fleshy,
with only 1 major
vein.

BLOOMS
April – November

An aquatic perennial to six inches high, coastal water-hyssop has creeping or floating stems that form dense mats along the margins of streams and marshes and in water-filled ditches. It is fairly common throughout the Houston area. Plants are smooth and succulent, with fleshy leaves having only one major vein. Elliptic or spatulate in shape, the leaves measure no more than an inch long.

Flowers appear on stalks from the leaf axils. Those stalks, or pedicels, are longer than the leaves, a distinguishing feature of *Bacopa monnieri*. The bell-shaped flowers vary from blue-violet to whitish and have five lobes that are only slightly unequal in size and shape.

The genus contains approximately one hundred species. Most occur in tropical America, and only a few stray into the temperate North. *Bacopa* is a Latinized form of the aboriginal name for these plants used by the Indians of French Guiana.

CAROLINA WOLFBERRY

Lycium carolinianum

Matrimony-vine, Box-thorn, Christmas-berry

SOLANACEAE Nightshade Family

SIZE
Plant: 2–6 feet, spiny,
  semievergreen.
Flower: ½–1 inch,
  4- or 5-lobed.

LEAVES
1–2 inches, club-
  shaped, succulent,
  grayish green.

BLOOMS
April – October,
  occasionally later.

A spiny, semievergreen shrub, Carolina wolfberry grows abundantly in the brackish marshes around Galveston Bay and along the coastal beaches and salt flats. Normally two to three feet tall, it may reach a height of six feet. Club-shaped leaves from one to two inches long are thick, succulent, and grayish green. Blue-violet or lavender flowers appear in the leaf axils and measure one-half to one inch across. Most have four corolla lobes, but some flowers have five.

The fruits of Carolina wolfberry are fleshy red berries a half-inch in diameter. They resemble tiny tomatoes and were eaten raw or dried by the Indians. The leaves, however, contain poisonous alkaloids. No human poisonings have been recorded, according to Lampe and McCann, but there have been occasional fatalities in animals eating the foliage.

The genus *Lycium* contains eighty or ninety species, most from southern Africa and tropical America. The name comes from *lykion,* the ancient Greek name for a shrub from Lycia in southwestern Turkey. *L. carolinianum* occurs through the southeastern states, from the Carolinas to Florida and westward to coastal and southern Texas. Most botanists classify Texas specimens as variety *quadrifidum,* although Vines noted that "segregation of the variety does not appear justifiable."

WESTERN HORSE-NETTLE

Solanum dimidiatum

SOLANACEAE Nightshade Family

SIZE
*Plant: To 3 feet,
  sprawling, armed
  with spines.
Flower: 1–2 inches,
  5-lobed star, in
  clusters.*

LEAVES
*3–8 inches, broad,
  usually lobed, often
  spines on midrib,
  underside with
  stulked stellate hairs.*

BLOOMS
April – November

As its name implies, western horse-nettle ranges from Texas westward to California and northward into the Great Plains. It has not been common in the immediate Houston area, although it occurs west of the Brazos River. However, we found it on several occasions along the railroad tracks bordering Interstate 10 west of Loop 610. These are apparently some of the first specimens collected within the city. Given this start, the species will probably expand its range in Houston.

A sprawling perennial reaching two to three feet in height, western horse-nettle is armed with prickles along the stems and leaf veins, although it is not as spiny as the more common Carolina horse-nettle, *Solanum carolinense.* Leaves measure from three to eight inches long and are broadly oval, usually with conspicuous lobes or wavy margins. Flowers are blue-purple, more rarely white, and have five petals united in a broad, five-pointed star. The five pollen-laden anthers project from the flattened corolla.

S. dimidiatum has wider leaves and larger flowers than *S. carolinense,* and the flowers are normally purple. The latter species usually has white flowers, but bluish or purple shades do occur. Final identification rests on microscopic examination. The underside of the leaves of *dimidiatum* are densely covered with stellate (star-shaped) hairs having nine to twelve rays and a short stalk. Hairs on the leaves of *carolinense* are not elevated on stalks and have only four to eight rays.

As with many other members of the genus, the foliage and the yellow, one-inch berries are extremely toxic to both humans and livestock.

SILVER-LEAF NIGHTSHADE

Solanum elaeagnifolium

Trompillo, White horse-nettle, Bull-nettle

SOLANACEAE Nightshade Family

SIZE
Plant: To 3 feet.
Flower: 1 inch,
  star-shaped.

LEAVES
To 6 inches, narrow,
  wavy margins.

BLOOMS
March – October

A plant of the southwestern states, silver-leaf nightshade occurs across virtually all of Texas, blooming from March through October. It springs up in vacant lots and along roadways and bayous in Houston and is common throughout dry fields in the surrounding area. The perennial plants reach three feet in height and spread from deep-running roots to form large colonies. The entire plant is densely covered with branching stellate, or star-shaped, hairs that give it a silvery appearance. Stems and leaves may also bear sharp spines, although this species is not as spiny as Carolina horse-nettle and some other members of the genus.

The leaves range up to six inches in length and are usually no more than an inch wide. They have wavy margins but lack the pronounced lobes of related species. Their silvery color and similarity to Russian olive and other members of the genus *Elaeagnus* gives the species its name.

Purple flowers develop in sparse clusters from the leaf axils. The five petals unite at the base to form a star-shaped blossom with five points, setting off the large yellow anthers in the center. An occasional white-flowered form has been given the name *albiflorum*.

Ripening fruits of the silver-leaf nightshade hang on the stalks like small yellow tomatoes, slowly turning black with time. They are reported to be highly poisonous, and Tull cites deaths of both livestock and humans. In spite of their toxicity, many medicinal uses have been documented among Native Americans, and the Pimas used the berries as a substitute for rennet in making cheese.

BRAZILIAN VERVAIN

Verbena brasiliensis

Brazilian verbena

VERBENACEAE Vervain Family

SIZE
Plant: 6–8 feet, much-branched, 4-angled stems.
Flower: Tiny, 5-lobed, in short spikes forming larger flat-topped clusters.

LEAVES
To 4 inches, opposite, with stiff hairs and toothed margins.

BLOOMS
May – November

More than two hundred species of the genus *Verbena* occur throughout the world, most of them in the Americas. Thirty-six species and a host of named varieties have been identified in Texas. Many more horticultural varieties have found their way into cultivation. Identification to species often requires microscopic examination and reference to detailed keys, but several local species are easily recognized. Three of the most common in Houston are included in this book.

Brazilian vervain will win no award for floral beauty, but it is one of the most abundant and widely distributed of our local wildflowers. Originally native to South America, it has naturalized throughout the southeastern states and along the Texas coast. A tall, rank perennial, it reaches six to eight feet and blooms profusely in open fields and vacant lots and along the roadsides throughout the summer.

Square stems are much-branched and rough-hairy in the upper portions. Leaves are opposite, elliptic or lanceolate, and taper at the base. The upper sides of the leaves bear stiff hairs that make them rough to the touch, and the margins are sharply toothed.

Tiny trumpet-shaped, five-lobed, bluish purple flowers occur in short spikes that combine to form loose, flat-topped clusters. They are scarcely noticeable among the rangy plants but give a purple hue to midsummer fields.

Verbena was a classical Latin name for various sacred plants such as laurel, olive, and myrtle used for religious rites and in medicine. Linnaeus appropriated the name when he created the large genus. "Vervain" is the English equivalent of the Old French *verveine* and the Celtic *fervain,* according to Healey. It was a holy herb used in sacred ceremonies and to cure the bite of rabid animals. Considered a pledge of mutual good faith, it was worn as a badge by heralds and ambassadors. "Vervain" has now become a general term for the upright verbenas.

TUBER VERVAIN

Verbena rigida

Veiny vervain, Stiff verbena, Purple verbena

VERBENACEAE Vervain Family

SIZE
Plant: 1–2 feet,
  square-stemmed,
  forming colonies.
Flower: Tubular,
  5-lobed, in dense
  spikes forming
  spreading clusters.

LEAVES
1–4 inches, opposite,
  clasping stem,
  coarsely and sharply
  toothed.

BLOOMS
April – October

A native of Brazil and Paraguay, tuber vervain has been widely introduced into the United States and has naturalized throughout the Southeast. It occurs along the coast and into central Texas. A stiff-stemmed perennial, it spreads from rhizomes to form large colonies. The bright purple to magenta flowers can be seen on vacant lots and roadsides across Houston, particularly along I-10 through the city. A hardy, drought-resistant plant, tuber vervain begins blooming in April or May and continues more sparingly through the summer, reblooming profusely in early fall after heavy rains.

Leaves are opposite, lancelike, and covered with rough, stiff hairs on both upper and lower surfaces. They clasp the four-angled stem and have coarse, sharp teeth on the margins. Trumpet-shaped, five-lobed flowers up to one-half inch long and one-quarter inch across form short, densely crowded cylindrical spikes that are further grouped in showy, flat-topped clusters.

One of our most brightly colored wildflowers, tuber vervain provides brilliant accents along Houston roadways and deserves consideration for wildflower gardens and large plantings.

COARSE VERVAIN

Verbena xutha

Gulf vervain, Tall verbena

VERBENACEAE Vervain Family

SIZE
Plant: 2–3 feet, often in clumps, stem 4-angled, densely hairy.
Flower: ⅓ inch, 5-lobed, in slender spike.

LEAVES
1–3 inches, deeply incised or 3-lobed, segments further toothed, hairy.

BLOOMS
March – October

Unlike Brazilian and tuber vervains, *Verbena brasiliensis* and *V. rigida,* coarse vervain displays its blue-violet flowers in tall, slender spikes. Individual blossoms average one-third inch across and have the five flaring lobes typical of the verbenas. The square stems are densely hairy, as are the deeply incised or three-lobed leaves. Leaf segments are further coarsely toothed.

Most authors consider coarse vervain "uncommon" in our area, but we found it on dry, sandy soils and in disturbed areas throughout Houston. Its slender flower spikes ornament city roadsides from March until October.

Coarse vervain differs from the similar Texas vervain, *V. halei,* by having hairy stems. The latter species also occurs within our area, but it is smooth or only slightly adorned with appressed hairs that lie flat against the stem.

BAYOU VIOLET

Viola langloisii

Langlois violet

VIOLACEAE Violet Family

SIZE
Plant: 2–8 inches,
  smooth, stemless,
  spreading from
  rhizomes.
Flower: ½–¾ inch,
  long-stalked, side
  petals bearded.

LEAVES
Broad, pointed, deeply
  notched at base,
  toothed.

BLOOMS
March – May

In discussing the violets, Rickett points out that the species are numerous and some that are distinguished by only minor details hybridize freely in nature, "making identification almost impossible; this is particularly true of the 'stemless blue violets.' In fact it has been said that there are no true species in this group, or that they all form one vast and heterogeneous species."

Various authors describe between 350 and 500 *Viola* species, many of them ranging from North America to northern South America. Texas hosts at least seventeen species and several named varieties, almost all of which occur in the eastern parts of the state. A few have yellow or white flowers, but most are the traditional blue-violet color. They can be further separated into those with leafy stems and those without noticeable stems. Leaf shape may be diagnostic, but most species are subject to enormous variation. No one will be faulted for calling them simply "violets."

Bayou violet is a stemless perennial from two to eight inches tall that forms large colonies from spreading rhizomes. It occurs in moist woodlands and thickets and occasionally appears in Houston lawns and gardens. Long-stalked leaves have broadly triangular blades that are somewhat pointed at the tip and deeply notched at the base. Leaf margins are prominently toothed.

Violet flowers typically have a flat lower petal that serves as a landing platform for pollinating insects. It projects backward into a long spur. There are also two upper petals and two side petals, or "wings." Flowers of bayou violet top long stalks that exceed the foliage, and the side petals are densely bearded.

In addition to these showy blossoms, most violets have smaller "cleistogamous" flowers that never open and are self-pollinating. They usually appear after the normal blooming period. Experiments have shown that the cleistogamous flowers produce more seeds than do the showy, insect-pollinated ones.

Edwin Way Teale, in his delightful *North with the Spring*, describes his vernal journey northward across the eastern United States. He saw violets everywhere, on Florida's Kissimme Prairie and in the mountains, along the coast and in the northern forests. They were, Teale said, "like the multitudinous footprints of spring, scattered over the map before us."

LOVELL VIOLET

Viola lovelliana

VIOLACEAE Violet Family

SIZE
Plant: Low, clump-forming, spreading from rhizomes.
Flower: 1 inch, long-stalked, 3 lower petals bearded.

LEAVES
Long-stalked, blade 1–3 inches, broadly lobed at base.

BLOOMS
February – May

A large, brightly colored species of the southeastern states, Lovell violet occurs in moist, open woodlands and thickets in northern Houston and Harris County. The low perennial forms loose colonies by spreading from creeping rhizomes. Leaf blades have distinctive broad lobes at the base. The dark lavender or violet flowers are borne on stalks above the foliage; their three lower petals are bearded. Self-pollinating "cleistogamous" flowers that do not open have long stalks and normally lie on the ground, appearing after the showy flowers in late spring or summer.

Viola was the ancient Latin name for the flower and has no other known direct translation. Authors cite several Greek myths involving violets, including one version in which Zeus created the delicate flower for Io to honor her beauty. Later, during Napoleon's exile, French Bonapartists chose the violet as their symbol because Napoleon had promised to return with the violets in the spring. Popular in the New World as well, violets serve as the state flowers of Illinois, New Jersey, Rhode Island, and Wisconsin.

Tull lists the flowers and leaves of blue violets as tasty and nutritious additions to salads. Both are excellent sources of vitamin C, and the leaves contain large amounts of vitamin A. The leaves also serve as a cooked vegetable or as a thickener for soups. They can be dried for use in herbal teas. Tull suggests preparing candied flowers or using them in jellies and jams.

GREEN DRAGON

Arisaema dracontium

Dragon-root, Dragon arum

ARACEAE Arum Family

SIZE
*Plant: 2–3 feet, erect,
   succulent.
Flower: Tiny,
   numerous on
   slender spadix
   enclosed by green
   spathe.*

LEAVES
*Single, long-stalked,
   divided into 5–15
   long leaflets.*

BLOOMS
May – June

The unusual green dragon is not as well known as the closely related Jack-in-the-pulpit, *Arisaema triphyllum*. It occurs in the rich soil of woodlands and thickets across the eastern United States, but it is usually regarded as uncommon throughout its range. We found green dragon at Mercer Arboretum and in other wooded areas of northern Harris County, and Brown reports it from the woods near Armand Bayou Nature Center.

The single, long-stalked leaf divides into five to fifteen unequal leaflets up to eight inches long. Numerous minute flowers are crowded on a long, slender spadix (the dragon's tongue) enclosed by a green spathe (the dragon's head). The tip of the spadix is usually bent and extends well beyond the spathe. Pistillate (female) flowers cluster at the base of the spadix; staminate (male) flowers occupy the middle. These individual florets have no sepals or petals.

Although the root of green dragon is considered edible if it is dried, aged, and elaborately processed, the entire plant contains calcium oxalate crystals that cause severe burns in the mouth. American Indians used the dried roots to treat "female disorders," and the Chinese use a related *Arisaema* species to treat epilepsy and paralysis and as a local anesthetic.

GREEN MILKWEED

Asclepias viridis

Antelope-horn, Spider milkweed

ASCLEPIADACEAE Milkweed Family

SIZE
*Plant: 2–3 feet,
  sprawling or
  upright.
Flower: ¾ inch, in
  clusters 3–4 inches
  across.*

LEAVES
2–5 inches long, thick.

BLOOMS
March – September

About forty milkweed species and varieties occur across Texas, but the green milkweed is by far the most common in the Houston area. A perennial that sends out upright or sprawling stems from a stout, deep root, it begins to bloom in March and continues more sparingly throughout the summer in fields and vacant lots and along bayou banks and roadside ditches. The green flowers with purple centers grow in clusters at the tips of the stems. Ripened seed pods split to release the seeds on plumes of silk.

Named for Asklepios, the Greek god of medicine, members of the genus *Asclepias* contain a sticky, milky sap rich in toxic cardiac glycosides and alkaloids. The poisonous milkweeds are the chief food plants of monarch butterfly larvae, making the caterpillars and the resulting adults distasteful to predators. As the monarchs begin their migration northward from their winter home in Mexico, they lay eggs on early-blooming green milkweed in the Houston area. The next generation of butterflies develops quickly to continue the journey.

GIANT RAGWEED

Ambrosia trifida

Buffalo-weed

ASTERACEAE Sunflower Family

SIZE
Plant: Up to 10–15 feet.
Flower head: Tiny. Staminate heads in racemes.

LEAVES
To 8 inches. Usually 3- or 5-lobed, some entire.

BLOOMS
August – December

The ragweed genus may have taken its name from the Greek food for the gods, but allergy sufferers would doubtless refute claims that *Ambrosia* confers immortality. Ranging over most of the central United States, giant ragweed readily colonizes disturbed soils and forms huge, close-packed stands ten to fifteen feet tall. Hardly one of our more beautiful wildflowers, ragweed lacks the showy blossoms that attract pollinators to most plants and depends on the wind for its success. Consequently, it releases prodigious quantities of pollen on late summer and autumn breezes and is a major cause of fall hay fever. Tull calls ragweeds the "most despised weeds in America."

Texas populations of giant ragweed are assigned to the variety *texana*, which is abundant throughout the Houston area. The tall, angled stems and opposite leaves are particularly rough and coarse, with short, stiff hairs that impart a sandpaper texture. Some leaves are entire, especially along the upper portions of the stem, but most are deeply lobed into three or five segments. Three-lobed leaves usually predominate, giving the species the name *trifida*.

Clusters of staminate flower heads are borne at the tips of the stems and in the leaf axils. Tall and spirelike, they droop under the weight of heavy anthers loaded with pollen, especially on hot summer days when the plants become flaccid. There are no large or brightly colored flower parts, and the flowers grow in small greenish, saucer-shaped receptacles. Pistillate, or female, flowers are even less conspicuous in small clusters in the axils.

Although despised for its allergy-producing pollen and its unattractive, rank growth, giant ragweed was apparently cultivated by Native Americans for a number of uses. The seeds served as an important grain, while the stems supplied fibers for rope and thread. Among the medicinal uses was a treatment for poison ivy. Tull also notes that ragweed provides the best natural light green dye for wool.

SPANISH-MOSS

Tillandsia usneoides

BROMELIACEAE Bromeliad Family

SIZE
*Plant: Slender strands
  to 6 feet, covered
  with silvery scales.
Flower: ½ inch long,
  slender, 3-petalled.*

LEAVES
1–2 inches, threadlike.

BLOOMS
February – June

Although almost everyone recognizes Spanish-moss, it is the subject of many misconceptions. Even its name is misleading, for the plant is neither Spanish nor a moss. Early French settlers in Louisiana first called it, derisively, "Spanish beard," and the Spaniards in return called it "French wig." Indian names translate as "long hair" or "tree hair." Unrelated to the true mosses, which reproduce by spores, Spanish-moss is a flowering plant of the bromeliad, or pineapple, family.

Even the scientific name, *Tillandsia usneoides*, resulted from a misconception by Swedish botanist Linnaeus. Learning that the strange new plant hung from tree limbs in the swamps of America, he assumed it abhorred water. Consequently, he coined the genus name *Tillandsia* after one of his students, Elias Tillands, who was so afraid of the water that he once walked more than one thousand miles around the Gulf of Bothnia rather than endure the crossing by boat. The specific epithet recognizes the resemblance to *Usnea*, a lichen known commonly as "old-man's-beard."

Within the tangled mass of Spanish-moss are individual slender stems, each bearing threadlike leaves from one to two inches long. Tiny silvery scales cover the plant, absorbing moisture and trapping particles that serve as sources of nutrients. In spring each plant bears small green, three-petalled flowers that, in turn, produce seed pods opening to disperse parachuted seeds to the wind.

Spanish-moss is not parasitic and does no direct harm to the trees on which it grows. When wet, however, it becomes heavy, and moss-covered trees may lose limbs to wind and rain.

At one time "moss factories" existed throughout the South, and families made a meager living harvesting as much as a ton a day. Processors cured the moss by heaping it in piles or in pits and soaking it, sometimes with lye, until the soft outer coating decomposed. The tough, black inner fiber was then dried and baled for use in cushions, upholstered furniture, and horse collars.

Replaced by foam rubber and modern plastics, Spanish-moss now serves only the wild creatures that share the treetops. Birds use the fibers for nests, and several bat species seek shelter and raise their young almost exclusively in clumps of moss. Sensitive to air pollution, however, Spanish-moss is declining throughout much of its range in the southeastern states. In the drier areas of Texas, it is replaced by the related ball-moss, *T. recurvata*, that also occurs sparingly in Houston.

"Spanish-moss is the most influential plant in the Southeastern landscape—the most widespread, and by all odds the most distinctive," wrote naturalist Archie Carr in an *Audubon* article years ago. "A big old live oak tree without its moss looks like a bishop in his underwear."

WOOLLY CROTON

Croton capitatus

Doveweed, Goatweed, Hogwort

EUPHORBIACEAE Spurge Family

SIZE
Plant: Annual to
  5 feet, branched.
Flower: Small,
  inconspicuous, sexes
  in separate flowers
  on same plant.

LEAVES
1–5 inches, oval or
  lancelike, densely
  covered with star-
  shaped hairs,
  gray-green.

BLOOMS
May – December

The crotons are weedy annuals that inhabit fields and roadsides throughout the state, often becoming troublesome pasture weeds. The name comes from the Greek *kroton,* meaning "tick," because the seeds somewhat resemble ticks. Those seeds, however, provide a significant part of the summer and fall diet of doves and several other species of birds. The strong-scented plants appear grayish green because of a dense covering of white stellate, or star-shaped, hairs. The stalked leaves are alternate on the branching stems, while the flowers are small and inconspicuous.

At least twenty species and several more varieties of crotons occur in Texas, and they can be extremely difficult to distinguish. Detailed keys refer to minute flower characteristics and to whether or not male and female flowers are present on the same plant.

Woolly croton appears to be one of the most abundant croton species in the immediate Houston area. Its specific epithet, *capitatus,* comes from the Latin *caput,* or "head," referring to the closely packed clusters of both male and female flowers at the tips of the branches. Male flowers are located above their female counterparts.

Bare suggests that woolly croton may be poisonous to livestock and that even honey made from croton nectar might prove toxic to humans. Most of the manuals on poisonous plants, however, make no mention of the crotons.

CURLY DOCK

Rumex crispus

Curly-leaved dock, Yellow dock, Sour dock, Indian tobacco

POLYGONACEAE Buckwheat Family

SIZE
Plant: 2–4 feet, basal
  rosette is
  winter-hardy.
Flower: ⅙ inch, in
  slender spikes. With
  6 sepals, no petals.

LEAVES
6–12 inches; with
  wavy, curled
  margins.

BLOOMS
March – May

At least fifteen *Rumex* species inhabit Texas, and several range into the Houston area. While none has showy flowers, the docks are nevertheless conspicuous plants with interesting features. Curly dock, *R. crispus*, is the largest and most common of the local species. A native of Europe, this alien has become established in fields and disturbed ground throughout the United States. A stout perennial from a heavy taproot, it has a hardy rosette of leaves that remains green all winter, lining Houston roadsides even when other vegetation is withered and brown.

Curly dock is easily recognized by its long, slender leaves with crisped and wavy margins. The flowering stem reaches four feet, with tiny green flowers arranged on slender, branching spikes. There are six sepals in two ranks, but the flowers have no petals. Brown, heart-shaped, three-winged fruits fill the terminal spikes in late summer and fall.

While some authors regard curly dock as a "noxious weed," natural-foods enthusiasts praise it as a rich source of vitamins A and C. Tull suggests using the young leaves as a substitute for spinach in salads or as cooked greens. Large doses, however, may cause gastric distress. Native Americans ground dock seeds and used the meal in bread, but Tull points out that removing the papery husks entails a great deal of work for a small amount of flour. Dormon also notes that the Chitimacha Indians of southern Louisiana used curly dock, which they called "deer's-ears," for dyeing their cane baskets.

Herbalists consider tea from the dried roots of dock to be an excellent "blood purifier" and use it for a variety of skin diseases, rheumatism, liver ailments, and sore throats. It may either cause or relieve diarrhea, depending on the dosage, the season of the year, and the concentration of tannins and other chemicals in the plants.

COMMON CATTAIL

Typha latifolia

Tule espadilla

TYPHACEAE Cattail Family

SIZE
*Plant: To 7 feet or
more, spreading
from rhizomes in
fresh water.*
*Flower: Minute,
rudimentary. Sexes
separate on long
spike, male flowers
above but
contiguous with
female flowers.*

LEAVES
*Long, straplike, 1 inch
wide.*

BLOOMS
May – September

The cattail (sometimes written cat-tail) family contains only the single genus *Typha*. About fifteen species occur in freshwater ponds, marshes, and streams throughout the world. *Typhe* was the ancient Greek name for these plants, a word apparently related to *typhos*, meaning "swamp" or "marsh." Cattails provide a valuable wildlife habitat for such varied animals as muskrats, geese, rails, blackbirds, and marsh wrens.

Common cattail reaches seven feet or more in height and spreads from rhizomes to form dense stands in Houston-area marshes and water-filled ditches. The long, flat, straplike leaves resemble those of no other group of plants. Flowers appear in dense spikes, the male flowers in a slender spike above the thicker "cat's tail" of female flowers. Both sexes lack sepals and petals. Male flowers have only stamens; female flowers, only single pistils. Once they have shed their yellow pollen, the male flowers wither and drop, leaving a bare stalk above the swelling mass of fertilized pistils.

Narrow-leaved cattail, or tule cattail, *T. domingensis*, also occurs frequently in the Houston area, sharing the same habitat as *T. latifolia*. It has narrower leaves, and the male and female flowers are separated by a gap on the stalk rather than being crowded together. The ripening stalk is also slimmer, at about one-half inch in diameter, and remains light brown, rather than turning dark brown like the thicker spikes of common cattail.

Cattails have provided food and fiber to peoples around the world for thousands of years. Leaves were used for weaving, and the ripened spikes provided tinder and torches. Navahos and Apaches valued the pollen for religious ceremonies, and various tribes used poultices of cattails for burns and wounds.

Tull suggests ways for utilizing the pollen, roots, young stems, and young flower heads for food. Euell Gibbons, she notes, called the cattail the "supermarket of the swamps." In spite of these endorsements, Foster and Duke take a more cautious approach. "Warning:" they write in their field guide to medicinal plants, "though it is widely eaten by human foragers, cattail is suspected of being poisonous to grazing animals."

BIBLIOGRAPHY

Wildflower books number into the thousands and vary enormously in style and scope. During the writing of this one, we had at our disposal several hundred volumes including identification guides, botanical texts and references, monographs on specific families or groups of plants, and books on edible and poisonous plants and their uses. Those from which we drew information are included in this bibliography. Many of the older wildflower books covered what we call the "personality" of the flowers, discussing folklore, etymology of names, and history. We have tried to recapture some of that style in this book.

Ajilvsgi, Geyata. 1979. Wild flowers of the Big Thicket: East Texas, and western Louisiana. College Station: Texas A&M Univ. Press.

———. 1984. Wildflowers of Texas. Bryan, Texas: Shearer Publishing.

———. 1990. Butterfly gardening for the South. Dallas: Taylor Publishing.

Andrews, Jean. 1986. The Texas bluebonnet. Austin: Univ. of Texas Press.

Bailey, L. H. 1963. How plants get their names. New York: Dover Publications.

Bailey, Ralph. 1962. The self-pronouncing dictionary of plant names. Rev. ed. Garden City, New York: The American Garden Guild.

Bare, Janet E. 1979. Wildflowers and weeds of Kansas. Lawrence: The Regents Press of Kansas.

Bell, C. Ritchie, and Bryan J. Taylor. 1982. Florida wild flowers and roadside plants. Chapel Hill, North Carolina: Laurel Hill Press.

Brown, Clair A. 1972. Wildflowers of Louisiana and adjoining states. Baton Rouge: Louisiana State Univ. Press.

Brown, Larry E. 1985. An annotated checklist of the vascular plants of the Armand Bayou Nature Park and vicinity, southeastern Harris County, Texas. Duplicated.

———. 1990. Spring wildflower class of the Spring Branch Science Center. Duplicated.

Correll, Donovan S., and Marshall C. Johnston. 1979. Manual of the vascular plants of Texas. Richardson: Univ. of Texas at Dallas.

Crockett, Lawrence J. 1977. Wildly successful plants: A handbook of North American weeds. New York: Macmillan.

Dormon, Caroline. 1958. Flowers native to the deep South. Baton Rouge: Claitor's Book Store.

Duncan, Wilbur H., and Marion B. Duncan. 1987. The Smithsonian guide to seaside plants of the Gulf and Atlantic coasts. Washington: Smithsonian Institution Press.

Duncan, Wilbur H., and Leonard E. Foote. 1975. Wildflowers of the southeastern United States. Athens: Univ. of Georgia Press.

Durant, Mary. 1976. Who named the daisy? Who named the rose?: A roving dictionary of North American wild flowers. New York: Congdon & Weed.

Enquist, Marshall. 1987. Wildflowers of the Texas Hill Country. Austin: Lone Star Botanical.

Foster, Steven, and James A. Duke. 1990. A field guide to medicinal plants: Eastern and central North America. Boston: Houghton Mifflin.

Greene, Wilhelmina F., and Hugo L. Blomquist. 1953. Flowers of the South: Native and exotic. Chapel Hill: Univ. of North Carolina Press.

Hatch, Stephan L., Kancheepuram N. Gandhi, and Larry E. Brown. 1990. Checklist of the vascular plants of Texas. College Station: The Texas Agricultural Experiment Station.

Healey, B.J. 1972. A gardener's guide to plant names. New York: Scribner's.

Honychurch, Penelope N. 1986. Caribbean wild plants and their uses. London: Macmillan Caribbean.

Johnston, Marshall C. 1988. The vascular plants of Texas: A list, up-dating the manual of the vascular plants of Texas. Austin, Texas: Marshall C. Johnston.

Jones, Fred B. 1977. Flora of the Texas coastal bend. Sinton, Texas: Rob and Bessie Welder Wildlife Foundation.

Krochmal, Arnold and Connie. 1984. A field guide to medicinal plants. New York: Times Books.

Lampe, Kenneth F., and Mary Ann McCann. 1985. AMA handbook of poisonous and injurious plants. Chicago: American Medical Association.

Levy, Charles Kingsley, and Richard B. Primack. 1984. A field guide to poisonous plants and mushrooms of North America. Brattleboro, Vermont: Stephen Greene Press.

Liogier, Henri Alain, and Luis F. Martorell. 1982. Flora of Puerto Rico and adjacent islands: A systematic synopsis. Rio Piedras: Universidad de Puerto Rico.

Lommasson, Robert C. 1973. Nebraska wild flowers. Lincoln: Univ. of Nebraska Press.

Loughmiller, Campbell and Lynn. 1984. Texas wildflowers: A field guide. Austin: Univ. of Texas Press.

Martin, Franklin W., Carl W. Campbell, and Ruth M. Ruberte. 1987. Perennial edible fruits of the tropics: An inventory. Washington: U.S. Department of Agriculture.

Martin, Laura C. 1984. Wildflower folklore. Charlotte, North Carolina: East Woods Press.

Mohlenbrock, Robert H. 1983. Where have all the wildflowers gone?: A region-by-region guide to threatened or endangered U.S. wildflowers. New York: Macmillan.

Muenscher, Walter Conrad. 1975. Poisonous plants of the United States. Rev. ed. New York: Collier Books.

Newcomb, Lawrence. 1977. Newcomb's wildflower guide. Boston: Little, Brown.

Niehaus, Theodore F. 1984. A field guide to southwestern and Texas wildflowers. Boston: Houghton Mifflin.

Niering, William A., and Nancy C. Olmstead. 1979. The Audubon Society field guide to North American wildflowers: Eastern region. New York: Alfred A. Knopf.

Nokes, Jill. 1986. How to grow native plants of Texas and the Southwest. Austin: Texas Monthly Press.

Peterson, Charles D., and Larry E. Brown. 1983. Vascular flora of the Little Thicket Nature Sanctuary, San Jacinto County, Texas. Houston: Outdoor Nature Club.

Peterson, Lee. 1977. A field guide to edible wild plants of eastern and central North America. Boston: Houghton Mifflin.

Peterson, Roger Tory, and Margaret McKenny. 1968. A field guide to wildflowers of northeastern and north-central North America. Boston: Houghton Mifflin.

Rickett, Harold William. 1963. The new field book of American wild flowers. New York: Putnam.

———. 1967. Wild flowers of the United States: Vol. 2, the southeastern states. New York: McGraw-Hill.

———. 1969. Wild flowers of the United States: Vol. 3, Texas. New York: McGraw-Hill.

Rose, Francis L., and Russell W. Strandtmann. 1986. Wildflowers of the Llano Estacado. Dallas: Taylor Publishing.

Schmutz, Ervin M., and Lucretia Breazeale Hamilton. 1979. Plants that poison: An illustrated guide for the American Southwest. Flagstaff, Arizona: Northland Press.

Smith, Arlo I. 1979. A guide to wildflowers of the Mid-South. Memphis: Memphis State Univ. Press.

Sperry, O.E., J.W. Dollahite, G.O. Hoffman, and B.J. Camp. 1964. Texas plants poisonous to livestock. College Station: Texas A&M Univ.

Stubbendieck, James, Stephan L. Hatch, and Charles H. Butterfield. 1992. North American range plants. 4th ed. Lincoln: Univ. of Nebraska Press.

Tull, Delena. 1987. A practical guide to edible & useful plants: Including recipes, harmful plants, natural dyes & textile fibers. Austin: Texas Monthly Press.

Turner, B.L. 1959. The legumes of Texas. Austin: Univ. of Texas Press.

Venning, Frank D. 1984. Wildflowers of North America: A guide to field indentification. New York: Golden Press.

Vines, Robert A. 1960. Trees, shrubs and woody vines of the Southwest. Austin: Univ. of Texas Press.

Wagner, Warren L., Derral R. Herbst, and S. H. Sohmer. 1990. Manual of the flowering plants of Hawaii. 2 vols. Honolulu: Univ. of Hawaii Press and Bishop Museum Press.

Wasowski, Sally, and Julie Ryan. 1985. Landscaping with native Texas plants. Austin: Texas Monthly Press.

Welsh, Stanley L., N. Duane Atwood, Sherel Goodrich, and Larry C. Higgins, eds. 1987. A Utah flora. Provo: Brigham Young Univ.

Wherry, Edgar T. 1948. Wild flower guide: Northeastern and midland United States. Garden City, New York: Doubleday.

White, Alan. 1982. Herbs of Ecuador: Medicinal plants. Quito: Ediciones Libri Mundi.

Wills, Mary Motz, and Howard S. Irwin. 1961. Roadside flowers of Texas. Austin: Univ. of Texas Press.

Wilson, Jim. 1992. Landscaping with wildflowers: An environmental approach to gardening. Boston: Houghton Mifflin.

Xerces Society. 1990. Butterfly gardening: Creating summer magic in your garden. San Francisco: Sierra Club Books.

INDEX